Dedication

To NCR and AJR
To all women who have endured or are enduring

THESE ARE OUR STORIES

Women's Stories of Abuse and Survival

Edited by
Jan Rosenberg

Hamilton Books
A member of
The Rowman & Littlefield Publishing Group
Lanham · Boulder · New York · Toronto · Plymouth, UK

Library of Congress Control Number: 2006930855
ISBN-13: 978-0-7618-3584-4 (paperback : alk. paper)
ISBN-10: 0-7618-3584-9 (paperback : alk. paper)

Table of Contents

Introduction

In December 2003, Janet Lupher of a regional mental health center in northwest Florida asked me to play guitar instrumentals during a holiday party she was hosting for members of her support groups, many of whom are survivors of domestic violence. I came to the party on a cool afternoon, guitar in hand. Women were milling around the room, visiting with one another at long tables decorated with silver glitter snowflakes. A meal was being assembled in a kitchen next to the large room. Once the women were assembled, I nervously played guitar for them, playing instrumental improvisations made for the occasion. Three women spoke, each of their experiences with their abusers. There were moments of tears, there were strong statements of action and survival.

As I listened to these women tell their stories, my work as a folklorist, a student of traditional expression, was called forth. As a folklorist, I was particularly stunned by the stories, by the way they were being told as testimonies to survival. I believed that these women's stories should be documented. They would be a solid statement of survival; they would be an educational tool.

I discussed this with Janet soon after the party, and she agreed that the women had stories to tell that were worth recording. In the meantime I had renewed my meeting with Millie Jackson, a group member who was at the party, who said she could recruit women to be recorded. In February 2004, we started with a 64 year old woman from Graceville, Florida. Soon other women in the groups heard from Janet and Millie about the project as it developed: the creation of a book made up of their stories. Some volunteered to be recorded. They had a story to tell, and they were ready to record it on audio tape. Some wished that their names be used. Others wanted to be identified by their initials. A few didn't to be identified at all. For while the women wanted to tell their story, they did not want family members, including the abusers, to be involved. These were their stories, and their stories alone. Let the stories be told.

I began recording and recorded interviews through the summer of 2004. Each woman welcomed me into her home, from house to trailer. I was also able to secure space for recording one woman so her family would not hear her story. She did not want them to hear her experiences, although she wanted to record them for others to learn from. Another woman was recorded in the Life Management office in the presence of her counselor.

Learning. Each woman wanted to share her story so others could learn from her experiences. Each woman thought her story was special, although not unique. "I think others can learn from what happened to me," was a common sentiment.

When I recorded the women, I used an audio cassette recorder and an external microphone. Initially, I was worried that the tape recorder and microphone would be intimidating. They weren't. Once the tape started rolling and I said "Tell me a little bit about growing up," the women all seemed to forget there was a tape recorder there, recording each word, each emotion, each creak of the house, each moment of silence.

I was impacted by the content of the stories, and I was struck by the way the stories were told. There were rapes, violence with guns, incest, beatings, punched out walls, and controlling. There was chuckling, there were tears, there were rises and falls in vocal tone, there were segments of silence in a room whose quiet was crowded with ghosts and pasts.

Each interview ended with an embrace. I felt I had been allowed into a sacred world where few were allowed to venture. For some reason I had the trust of these women. Perhaps it was because I was genuinely interested in what they had to say, and I was willing to drive to their homes from my home in Tallahassee, some 70 miles away one way, with equipment that I worked hard to make unobtrusive. I was trusted, and this struck me deep.

When the interview was done I would hang around for a little bit, forming a decompression chamber for me and the woman who just bared her soul. We would talk about our families, about our experiences with the regional mental health center, and the project in general. When I left, I had a drive home to think about what I heard and how I heard it.

On my drive, I felt full and empty. I felt full of a story that I had just heard. I felt emptied out of my listening skills. I had just listened to stories that can make the hair rise on the back of your neck (and they will). The stories traveled with me every mile down Interstate 10. As I drove, I felt myself emptying out. I was drained, and getting some distance was very important.

I started a personal decompression ritual. I would leave the home of the woman I interviewed and would drive to a point where I could run an errand, anything that would expose me to other people, to a more peopled world. Once I got home I would put my equipment away and would get a drink out of the refrigerator. I would put the drink down on my table and would turn to my guitar. I would reach for the instrument and take it to the chair by the table. Take a sip, and then I would play. Play instrumentals, play improvisations, create my own quiet and sound. I would put aside the day by listening to the day inside me, accompanied by tunes. After 45 minutes or so, I put the guitar away, and worked toward the next steps of the day.

I would set up the tape recorder in order to begin transcribing tapes. I would then retire into the night in order to transcribe the tape directly into the computer the next day.

When transcribing, I used headphones to listen to the words and the emotions recorded clearly onto the tape. No outside sound; no glitches in recording. Pure tone of words, and tears. And some chuckling.

Since many of the women participate in support groups, they were accustomed to sharing and listening to experiences. As a result of this sharing and listening each had an internal outline that they could follow in bringing their stories to the table.

I was treated as one at the table, though I am not a member of a support group. My training and interest brought me there. I came as a folklorist interested in how women expressed their experiences of abuse and survival. As I listened, I became a vessel, filled with experience. I hardly asked any questions to urge or to clarify, My job, it seemed to me, was to listen, to be there for the testimony.

I came to the table as a folklorist who has had training as a hospital chaplain. The chaplain considers patients and others in need as "living human documents," individuals whose experiences and emotions tell a story. The chaplain listens, reading experience and emotion in such a way that a life story emerges. A chaplain utilizes listening and observation skills, along with questioning to encourage spiritual health care.

A folklorist is interested in cultural health care. He or she uses the same skills as the chaplain to support cultural health through the documentation of traditional expression. In the case of the women you will meet, that traditional expression is called "personal experience narrative." (Stahl, 1977)

As I thought about the interview experience, I wondered how I blended my skills as folklorist and as chaplain to share the environment of the session. The chaplain in me lets the story roll. The folklorist in me lets the story roll to my mind and on to audio tape. Both folklorist and chaplain let the story roll with the tides of emotion. One is concerned with spiritual culture and the other with human culture, of which spiritual culture is a part. Folklorist and chaplain blend into one another in such a way that you don't know where one starts and the other takes off.

In my interviews I dealt with the women's spiritual culture, not in the standard theological sense, but in the sense that I was listening to the experience of having one's spirit broken or attempted to be broken. With each woman's decision to leave the abusive situation a story within a story was told of a rebuilding of spirit. In listening to how they told their stories I was audience to rebuilding within the context of our social system and culture. As the voice told the 47 year-old woman as she left West Virginia to come to Florida, "It's over." It was time to rebuild.

As I thought about each occasion I came closer to the conclusion that it really didn't matter who was folklorist and who was chaplain. I felt called to do this project, to blend my skills, and include my heart in a way that I could show that I could be trusted. I could be witness and audience, I could be a friend.

Then I wondered what I would do with these stories. I knew I wanted to create an anthology, but what would I do with the feeling of being all filled up? Of being a vessel?

It was my sister who said that I should not be a vessel, but a conduit. A channel for these women to express themselves. I don't think one can be a conduit without being a vessel first. As I listened to the women tell their stories, I was a vessel, catching their words, catching their emotions. My decompression ritual helped me shift from vessel to conduit. As I transcribed the stories, I knew there was a purpose beyond listening. We were going to make a book, a tool for others to use to learn and deal with experience. In this context, I am at once a vessel and a conduit.

I've re-read the transcripts, and have listened again to the tapes. I continue to shake my head in wonder at how a person can do this to another. My breath catches when I listen to a scene revealed in tears, in exclamations. I feel strongly that these stories need to be shared, but shared in a constructive way. Hence this book, These Are Our Stories.

This book consists of many things, focusing on the women's stories. You will read of social services and the legal system and how they serve victims of domestic violence. You will hear about the cultural component of domestic violence, how the women constitute a cultural group with a dynamic bound by their stories.

Then you will be given the stories. Read the stories with a voice in mind. Someone is telling you an important story. Create a voice that you think sounds like the woman who tells the story. Use a voice that brings you into the experience of pain, of longing, of survival.

After the stories you will have access to two resource guides. One is a reprint from a group in Maine that has been adapted for use in north Florida. It has been included as a guide to the kinds of things an abused woman can do to identify and deal with her situation using these women's region as an example. The second is a brief bibliography of literature and resources for domestic violence that can be applied nationwide.

North Florida

Rural north Florida's landscape rolls deep in Southern soil. Primarily agricultural, the region stands in stark contrast to its southern counterpart. Rural north Florida is a part of the Deep South where conservative values fuel social and economic commerce.

Love of home, love of land, love of country, and love of God creates north Florida's rural landscape. The lay of the land is hand crafted and heart felt. It is a place where survivors live and work. People have survived many storms here, economic, social, and agricultural, and they thrive on faith and the desire to keep their world intact.

There are numerous kinds of survivors and this book is about a survivor previously unnamed. This kind of survivor deals with an intensely personal storm, that of domestic violence, that recurring emotional and physical harm that intimate inflicts upon intimate in the name of control. It is a storm in which many are involved: the legal system, the social services network, the religious community, and the family itself. The victim of the storm is usually a woman who, through a series of circumstances, became involved with a man who sought to control her by any means necessary. This is a victim of a storm who chooses to get out of the abusive situation by any means necessary. And the following are stories of journeys through the onslaught.

Rural north Florida consists of roughly 31 counties, extending from Escambia to Duval Counties. In 2002, the Florida Department of Law Enforcement reported approximately 23,000 cases of domestic abuse in this region. The women represented here come from an even smaller segment of the region, defined by Holmes, Jackson, and Washington Counties in the state's panhandle. In these counties, 452 cases were reported (FDLE).

The women who told their stories, by virtue of their participation in support groups, form a tight network of individuals who have experienced and survived abuse. Some of them come from north Florida, while others moved to the region. The women are lower to middle class, and White and African American. They range in age from the late 20s to mid 60s.

Looking at Domestic Violence

The Domestic Abuse Intervention Project (DAIP) published a diagram that well explains how domestic violence works. Called the Power Wheel, it is reprinted here. The wheel can be read from any direction. It must be remembered that these are a sample of tactics an abuser can employ. There are many methods at his disposal.

DOMESTIC ABUSE INTERVENTION PROJECT
202 East Superior Street
Duluth, Minnesota 55802
218-722-2781

A-7

The wheel identifies behaviors that an abuser uses to exert control and power over an intimate. Intimidation, threats, physical assault, economic oppression, verbal assault, guilt tactics, involvement of children: all of these are behaviors that an abuser engages in. He exerts his sense of power in a calculated way, one which may not seem to have any logic, but it does: in his mind. He has a sense of order and disorder that he chooses to impose on his partner, and he expects her to submit.

But does she submit? She may not fall into his trap and she asserts herself immediately upon the first instance of abuse. On the other hand, she may develop tactics to avoid a violent action: lying and bluffing are two examples of how she might do that. Instead of having a power wheel, she might have a survival triangle in which she progresses through stages leading to the ultimate goal, that of freedom.

Survivor's Triangle

Within a domestic violence situation, a culture is created that involves tension between the control of the abuser and the survival tactics of the abused. Each brings to the table behaviors, beliefs, and attitudes that were cultivated before they even met. In meeting, one tries to exert his culture over her culture. This exertion creates a tension that is engaged throughout the course of the relationship. A war-like environment is created whose battlefield is located under one roof and in other places where the victim may be, such as the workplace. The battlefield in this sense is portable, as it is taken wherever the abuser and the victim are in contact.

The Stories

The stories presented here are stories of empowerment within a culture in domestic violence. (Lawless, 2001) Through telling their experiences the women further recognize their strength and will to survive. Some credit God for their survival. Others credit individuals in the social services system. All feel that someone or something was looking out for them, and that they worked hard to be helped through the situation. They are at the apex of the triangle, and are now on a new journey, rebuilding their lives.

The stories are ordered according to the age of the teller, with the exception of a series of poems placed at the end. There are no specific themes that unify the stories, except for that of survival. Each woman is briefly described, and a key feature of her interview is pointed out.

In signing release forms for the project, each woman was asked how she wanted to be named in the book. While some women chose to use only their initials, and others chose to be named, other women chose not to be named at all. They are referred to in this book by their age.

While anthologies of domestic violence experiences exist, they are collections, not of transcripts from interviews, but of biographies reconstructed from interviews. *These Are Our Stories* is unique in that I have chosen not to edit the interviews and therefore provide the reader with experience in the voice of the experienced in a transcript format. The only thing lacking here is the sound of each woman's voice and a photograph of the tellers. However, the speech transcribed should be a key unto itself on the style and tone of the narration. As for the photographs, none were taken in interest of preserving some aspect of the women's privacy.

Each woman progresses through the survival triangle with tactics designed to get through days and hours. Their tactics aren't entirely clear, like those of the Power Wheel. Rather each woman chooses the ultimate tactic, that of leaving the abuser after a certain amount of time and abuse. They go through their days trying to survive, but each develops an ultimate plan for leaving, often through divorce and going through the legal system. They also choose to become involved in therapy and support groups to process their experience as they are experiencing it. They have chosen the means available to them to progress through the triangle. These means are conventional and useful, although certain means, like the legal system, can be frustrating.

Going through the triangle is painful. There is the frustration of going through the system, but more than anything else there is dealing with love lost. The women loved their intimate. They wanted to get out of their situation, but didn't want their situation to begin in the first place. They realized that they needed to get out. Often when they did get out they entered into another abusive situation. It wasn't that they were attracted to abusive situations. Rather, they were attracted to men with whom they felt love gained.

There are many reasons for why the women got into their situations, and this is what they explore in therapy. The stories here are not a recounting of the therapeutic process, although telling their stories was somewhat cathartic. As Dottie Smith wrote, "I guess that I would not have really gotten it [her situation], had I not spoken to you." The stories tell of complex problems without therapeutic reflection. Their stories are reports, a telling, albeit one more time, of experiences experienced and survived.

The women who have told their stories are survivors learning to rebuild and live their lives. They move from survival to daily life. They re-live their experience as they tell their experience, and they come out of it with weights lifted from their shoulders and hearts. Some choose not to get involved again, and maybe some day they will become involved. It is their choice, and now they know that they have the right to choose relationships where power is equitable and freeing. They know they don't ever have to go back to situations where the desire for approval and love is dependent upon one trying to control the other. By going through the triangle, they learn that they have strength within themselves to carry on productive lives, free from fear, free from submission. They learn freedom, they are encouraged to shape a life.

This project has benefited from the guidance and support of many people, especially of the women who have volunteered to share their stories. I single out individuals who have willingly given me chunks of their time so I can think through the following pages: Janet Lupher, Millie Jackson, Diane Sidener, and Penny Crandall. Janet has visited with me time and time again on the subject of domestic violence in rural north Florida, with which she is most experienced. She has supported my thinking, helped clarify my thoughts on the subject, and has given me warmth and humor when I was feeling the weight of what I was doing. Penny Crandall kept me on the straight and narrow when it comes to thinking about the role of domestic violence in today's society. Diane Sidener, a fellow folklorist and a survivor herself, has listened to me with a steady ear and heart. And finally, Millie Jackson, has provided me with support, and thought from an insider's perspective. This is everybody's book.

A note on the transcription orthography. A _____ indicates a space in words where the speaker skips in her speech. Brackets [ ] indicate a word that was unintelligible in the transcription process.

These Are Our Stories

NOTES

Pam Taylor

For all of her 25 years, Pam Taylor has experienced a lot. She grew up in Washington County, Florida where at the age of three or four she was placed in foster care. She lived in foster care and group homes until the age of 17. She has experienced street life, she has experienced the ravages of domestic violence. Today Pam lives with her mother in Chipley where she is active in the church.

PT: Pam Taylor
JR: Jan Rosenberg
JL: Janet Lupher

PT: I was born and raised in Chipley, I had a pretty bad childhood. I was taken away from my real mom, I was thrown in different foster homes, and included being abused.
JR: Uh huhm. Tell me a little bit more about that.
PT: Well (laughs) it was. I was in different places like foster homes that who strangers, that who abused me. Then my mom the way she treated me a little bit. You know, I always felt like I was left out. Felt like I was a nothing. And you know. And when I got grown enough, I stayed around Chipley till I got around 10. And then I left Chipley and they threw me in the foster home in Panama City. It was a good foster home. I stayed there till I was about 12, and I went to a place called Heidel House.
JR: Heidel House?
PT: Yeah, Heidel House. Like a Christian home.
JR: Heidel House
PT: Heidel House, something like that
JR: Can you spell it?
PT: (laughs) No.
JR: Heidel House
PT: Heidel House in Panama City, Used to be on 77.
JR: OK
PT: It was like a Christian center, you know, open home, people come to live there. And I left from there and they send me to Miami. And I went to a hell hole in Miami. They call that place Martenary.
JR: Martenary
PT: Yes, like group homes.
JR: Uh huh
PT: And they put me in a lock-up. The first time I got there that's what they do, you know where you've run so much. They call you a runaway. You know you run too much, get away.
   So I was thrown in Martenary, and I stayed in Martenary about five years. Till I turned 17.
JR: This is all pretty recent for you.
PT: Yeah, it was pretty bad, bad experience, where you in a place and see bad things, kids that been there longer than I ever have. When you see them take

things like bed rails and sticking it up in their arms, stabs. Take their arms and bend their arms back and their legs, put them back. You know, it was very bad experience. A staff she . . . choked me to death. Almost killed me. But it didn't happen. Thank God for that.

So I still felt real bad. I felt like I was still being abused everywhere I went. I felt rejected. I always felt like I was left out. I felt like, you know, my parents didn't care about me, just didn't give a darn about me, that's how I felt. And living a rough life, and then coming back here and I end up taking a man who's way older than I was . You know he was like a daddy to me. And I fell in love with him and I thought he was the best in the world, thought he was good, thought he was somebody special, and all that. You know, he treated me right at first beginning, he gave me this what I wanted and gave me money, you know, and then later on it turned out to be real bad. He got on drugs, he wanted me to mess around with other men. As I did, just to please him. But to find out I was messing my own life up. By doing something I shouldn't do. By putting myself out there like - - I call myself a whore at the time I was doing it, you know, like inviting somebody into your house. 'Cause your man want somebody to come there. He want to smoke dope, he want to use you to get the dope, and you just volunteer and you just do whatever he wants you to do.

And later on I woke up from that. You know I never know if you keep on doing this, you know, somebody's going to come by and they're going to take me from you. I just never know that. And when I told him that he slowed down from what he'd been doing.

But the hitting and everything begin when I was staying in Pitcher Hill on Old Bonifay Road. Apartments up there. . . . 1998 I think.
JR: Where is Pitcher Hill?
PT: Old Bonifay Road, that way (points).
JR: Oh, so it's in Bonifay?
PT: No, not Bonifay. That way (points). Here in Chipley.
JR: Here in Chipley
PT: But they call it the Old Bonifay Road 'cause you can go the back way from Bonifay.
JR: OK
PT: But that's where I was living at, I was staying there then he moved in. Now that's how quick it happened. I met him up there. When I was staying there. Telephone booth and like I say I thought he was the most [ ] man, you know. Lovely guy, attractive. Handsome, you know? But I find out the hard way how he really is. He start abusing me pretty bad. And I took the screwdriver, I remember, and stuck it to his neck. And told him if he hit me again, I'd kill you. You know, I didn't know. But it still didn't do no good 'cause he still beat me, you know. He start beating on me real bad when we moved from the apartments where I was staying and we stayed over here across the railroad track, apartments over here. Ones that got burned up. We stayed there and he kicked me out. He throwed my stuff outside. So I had to move in with my mama.
JR: Mmmm

PT: So. I was still messing with him though. I still want to be around him. Then later on I got my apartment back on Bonifay Road. And I start living back up there. And then this other man that I was calling myself just talking to he find out I was talking to another man, somebody told him that they saw me at the man's house. So one morning I got up and was walking going home. I was hoping he would not see me. But he saw me, just called my name. He was walking down the road at me, he was mad, he was upset. I could tell how way he was walking, he had his chest all puffed out. He was walking, coming up towards me, and I told him that I was going home. And we argued for a little bit outside and he grabbed me by my wrist, then dragged me to the apartment that I used to stay in with him. And we got up there fussing and everything and he popped me in my mouth. Hit me clean in my mouth. Bust my mouth open. And I was ready to fight him. You know, like I probably can't beat your tail but you're going to fight, you did the wrong thing by hitting me, you know. But it didn't do no good. He still beat me. More I kept taking him back the more he kept doing the same thing over drugs, abusing me over and over again.

JR: Hmmm

PT: He isolate me from other people, he starved me to death. There was hardly no food to eat. When I was pregnant with my second child it wasn't too much enough food to eat. 'Cause hardly there was no food. So.

After that, I start coming to group. And I met Janet and everybody else. And then I realized I wasn't the only one going through abuse.

JR: Right

PT: You know, I find out there was other people besides me. So. I've been here for a little while.

JR; How long have you been here?

PT: About three or two years. But I learned a lot from other people. People who have been here longer than I have.

JR: Yeah

PT: You know. And I thank God that I came out of from where I was being in abuse, you know, 'cause I felt like all the stuff I went through as a child and then went through with a man that I love. I could've came out being a murderer or somebody real bad. But I thank God that I did not come that way, you know. 'Cause I figure that [ ] I got treated wrong, you know I don't have to go out and treat somebody else wrong because of what happened to me.

JR: Right.

PT: So I thank God mostly for everything.

JR: Yeah. Talk to me more about what it was like to live in Miami. Did you live in Martenary the whole time? Or . . .

I lived in Martenary for five years. Like I say, it was a hell hole. When I first got there it seemed like it was okay. But later on, I start seeing how really staff do the clients. How they had them laying on the floor. They called it strangle something, whatever they call it, where they having their arms all pulled back and legs all pulled back. And then I started seeing some of the clients on medicine, taking medicine.

JR: But so you stayed there for five years and then you did you stay in Miami or did you come back here?

PT: Well, I finally left Miami and went back to Panama City. To the same place I was telling you about. I stayed there till I was about 17 and a half. And then I came back here to Chipley in 1996.

JR: And you've been here since.

PT: Uh huhm

JR: Pretty incredible. Tell me, when you talked about feeling left out, did you feel left out in the abusive situation? How'd that work?

PT: I felt left out all the time. [ ] when I was a child. You know 'cause it seemed like every time I look around I was always by myself.

JR: Yeah

PT: You know, my mom, she didn't have too much time for me, my daddy didn't have too much time for me. You know, and so I felt like I was just by myself.

JR: Yeah. Did you have brothers and sisters?

PT: Yeah, but it was taken. They were staying with my grandmamma.

JR: Hah. So you were pretty much left to your own devices.

PT: Uh huh

JR: It must've been incredible. It must've been frightening and aggravating at the same time.

PT: Yeah.

JR: But you came back up here in 1996, and you were in a relationship . . .

PT: It was later on up in the years where I got up in a relationship. . . .

JL: One year. Wasn't that one year after you got back here?

PT: No, it was later on. It was probably about '97, '98, something like that . . .

JL: Did you tell her about how you went back to the place in Miami after you'd been out on the streets?

PT: Oh, about the guy that picked me up?

JR: You didn't talk about being on the streets.

PT: (laughs) . . . I told her early on I would skip some things

JL: [ ]

PT: Oh yeah, well I was on the streets.

JL: Why.

PT: Selling drugs. Doing drugs

JL: But why were you on the streets?

PT: I ran away. From the program I was at Martenary. Teenager and wild.

JL: You wanted to go home.

PT: Yeah. I wanted to go home, I wanted to get away from that place bad it was like a hell hole. And so I ran away.

And this man came out from nowhere, I don't know where he came from, like a old man. He picked me up, he saw me walking on the side of the road, like I told Janet, and he picked me up and took me to a nice restaurant. And bought me something to eat, and he took me to his house, there was a little house behind his house, so that's where I slept at. And I had a little TV, little bed he laid out for me to sleep on.

JR: Hah

JL: He didn't bother you.

PT: No, he never touched me. He never asked me for sex or nothing.

JR: That's incredible.

JL: How long had you been on the streets when that happened?

PT: Until my birthday.

JL: So you had been on the streets for quite awhile, and you'd seen some pretty wild things. This is the streets of Miami and there was a lot of drugs and prostitution going on down there. And you really had to have your wits about you to be able to survive that.

PT: Yeah

JL: So you thought that this man was going to pick you up and ...

PT: Yeah, I thought he was going to pick me up, have sex with me and give me money, you know, but he didn't.

JL: So what happened as a result of that?

PT: He just showed his kindness. How he cared for people, you know.

JR: Hah

PT: How he want to reach out to help people living on the street.

JL: So did you go back out on the streets?

PT: No.

JL: What'd you do?

PT: Went back and stayed till I was released.

JL/JR: Went back to Martenary.

JR: Son of a gun.

PT: (laughs)

JR: Did they punish you for running away?

PT: Yeah. They locked me up

JR: They locked you up. Gosh it really sounds like a hell hole.

PT: (laughs)

JL: You told her all about the things you saw while you were there?

PT: Yeah, I told her about the clients sticking bed rails in their arm, staff's bending arms back and legs.

JL: It was a lock-down, wasn't it?

PT: Uh huhm. I mean they tried to kill me once they tried to kill me by choking me to death. I was telling her about that too.

JR: It's pretty incredible, that's just amazing. Talk about the will to survive. . . .
      Do you still have contact with your mother?

PT: Well, I stay with my mom now.

JR: You stay with your mother?

PT: But I'm getting ready to leave.

JR: You get along with her pretty okay?

PT: All right (laughs)

JR: What does she think about all your experiences?

PT: Well, my mom really don't know everything that happened to me while I was in Miami. She don't know. 'Cause I feel like my mom did me wrong too while I was a child.

JR: Yeah. How'd she do you wrong?

PT: Well, she leave me at home with her husband. You know, she goes down the street, she wants to party all night. You know, she have a child at home, responsibility.

JR: Yeah

PT: But she didn't see it that way. She seen the alcohol more important.

JR: What about your dad?

PT: My real dad, he wasn't around. He just known me when I was a child. But, hey, that's all right. [ ]

JL: The first time that they came to take you into foster care. Did you talk about that?

PT: No.

JL: How old were you?

PT: Between three or four.

JL: And how did they, how did they get you to go with them?

PT: Well, they asked me do I want some ice cream. And I say "Yeah."

JR: Oh my God.

JL: And then they took you away from your family and put you in a foster home? In Panama was it?

PT:I don't know where it was, all I know was a foster home filled up with kids.

JL: Uh huh. And they cut all your hair off.

PT: They cut my hair off and as I came back home, my grandma had adopted me then. When I came back home, I came home with a scar on my face from somebody just cchht.

JR: Hah.

PT: So.

JL: How old were you when your grandma got you?

PT: Oh boy, (laughs) gosh,

JL: 'Cause you were in foster care for a long time. Like before your grandma was able to get you. She was fighting for you, but she didn't actually get you till were you were about what, seven?

PT: I was probably between seven and eight. Something like that.

JL: So they took you with ice cream when you were three, and then her grandmother got her back at seven.

PT: So I've been in foster homes all my life, really.

JR: How old were you when you went to Miami?

PT: I was 12.

JR: You were 12 and you stayed until you were

PT: 17

JR: My word. And in between that time you lived on the streets.

PT: I was staying at Martenary until I got tired of it and then I just dipped. (laughs) I just got tired of staying there and I said well just forget it. I just hauled tail. You know. But I found how rough it is to be on the streets.

JR: Yeah, I bet.

PT: You start seeing things you never saw in life, women sitting on the corner selling their body, you know, I just seen the worst stuff.

JR: That's incredible.

PT: I almost got killed. I remember that.

JR: How so?

PT: Well, it was over some stupid, you know, this woman, two women was getting into it and I was in the middle. And it was over about a purse. But the woman took the woman's purse from her. And laid it on the ground and dared the woman to pick it up. And I was standing there, so, the woman that I was staying with asked me to pick the purse up and take it home, so I did. (laughs) I just picked it up and I said "Okay" and I just took it home, and the woman got mad she said "I'm going down here and get my daggone gun." And she went down there into her house and got the gun, and she came back.

JR: Oh my goodness.

PT: She was looking for me, I was in the other room, I was grabbing a mirror, about this long (a foot long and 8" wide) very sharp. So I said if I had a last breath, I'm going to take her life too; we both going to hell. (laughs)

(Sheriff's siren goes by.)

JR: They're after us.

PT: So she came at me with a gun, and point it to my face. And told me she would kill me. She was going to shoot me though, I know that.

JL: How'd you get out?

PT: It was a woman that came in the room. And told her to put the gun down.

JR: Shew

PT: So I know what it feels like to be [ ], you know with somebody there with a gun in your face? I know how it feels.

JR: Staring down the end of a barrel. That's really something.

 Talk to me more about survival?

PT: (laughs) It's wonderful. (laughs)

JR: It's wonderful.

PT: I mean it's wonderful, I mean survive from a lot of things in life. I mean, it's like a dream, you don't never give up on a dream. 'Cause you want for that dream to come true. That's just like survival.

JR: [ ] You say that you're a baby, but you have lived a lifetime. You ever think about that?

PT: About what?

JR: Living a lifetime

PT: Yeah. I think about my dream mostly. I think about just living my dream and hoping for my dream to come true.

JR: That makes sense.

JL: What is your dream?

PT: God, Janet. (laughs). Okay, what is my dream. My dream is mostly about everything. Except killing and stealing and all of that.

JL: That's good to hear. (laughs)

PT: I dream of being married. Hoping one day to have children. Finish school. Running my own business.

JR: What kind of business?

PT: I don't know, just something.

JR: Anything else?

PT: What? Oh yeah, and singing.

JR: Singing

PT: I forgot that, too (laughs)

JR: That's why we have Janet here.

PT: Why I asked her to sit here. No I had told Janet while I was 10 years old back in the days, I was 10, my first dream was to be a singer.

JR: Uh huh

PT: 'Cause I like to sing. You know all my life just being a little singer at home, you know. That was my first time dreaming something like that. So lately after New Years or something like that? I start singing at church.

JR: Oh. Okay.

PT: You know, so that was my first time singing at church. And I enjoyed it.

JR: Do you have a favorite gospel singer?

PT: YES. (laughs). Darlene Zschech

. . .

JL: She's from Australia.

JR: My goodness, that's great

JL: We have written to her to see if she can, she's going to be in Atlanta in November and we've written to see if and her and she's written back. Her helper has written back saying they're going to try and get Pam to go up there and meet her.

JR: Oh that's wonderful. That is wonderful.

PT: I'm praying to God I hope it work out. I really want to go. She's my favorite gospel singer.

JR: That's great. She sing like contemporary gospel?

PT: Yeah

JR: Okay, okay. You're the first person that has said contemporary gospel who hasn't said Kirk Franklin. So, I'm glad to know this.

PT: (laughs) I got his CDs, though at home. But most of the ones I listen to is Hillsongs, Hillsongs is the one I listen to all the time.

JR: Yeah

PT: Yeah

JR: Which church do you go to?

PT: Right now I'm going to none. (laughs). I go to a house. A woman's house.

JR: Why?

PT: Well, 'cause it shut down the church I was going to. So

JR: Why'd they do that?

PT: Long story.

JR: Well, we're here

PT: (laughs) Well, it's a long story, I don't want to be in the midst of it of it, but it's a long story.

JL: But they just shut it down? It's been a real trauma for you.

PT: Well I was at that church for eight years.

JR: Oh my word.

PT: So, you know, it's like my home. You know, I was very attached to it. I never wanted to let it go, but it was hard.

JR: Yeah

JL: The people from the church are still going from house to house now and carrying the church on, just not in the same building.

JR: Hah

PT: Well they... This is all my life, talking in a tape player.

JR: Keep telling more about your life.

PT: (laughs) Gosh.

JR: Tell me more, what you think about.

PT: Janet you got to help me out here.

JL: Well, when you got back to Chipley, and then how did you meet Albert?

PT: I just told her that.

JL: Oh, you already talked about Albert?

JR: Talked about Albert, yeah.

JL: Oh, okay. Did you talk about how you got out of it?

PT: Yeah, I said through here. (laughs). Coming to group.

JL: A little more than that. I mean, it took a lot of guts on your part. You got an injunction for protection against him; and that took a lot. You had him put in jail.

PT: Uh huhm

JL: And when he got out. And while he was in jail he wrote to you.

PT: Uh huhm. When he was in prison he wrote.

JL: What was he writing?

PT: All kinds of stuff. You know.

JL: Like?

PT: God, Janet, I can't remember all of it. I remember he asked me to marry him in one of the letters. Something about how he had changed, you know, he would go to church, he'd do this he'd do that.

JL: Start a business

PT: Start a business. Me and him having our own business and all this. And then he start making these little art pictures of me, him kissing (laughs). It was more like by Halloween.

JL: Each holiday he'd give you a card.

PT: Always something. On Mother's Day, 'cause he knew I lost both of my kids, he'd send me a Mother's Day card.

JR: Oh my God.

PT: I guess to bring back the memories of the children that I lost. And it was really painful because I lost them.

JR: Yeah

PT: But he'd do that all the time on Mother's Day, he'd send me a card. So it's like, what is he trying to prove? You know 'cause the second kid that I carried, I went through hell with him. Okay? I starved half to death for that baby.

JR: Right

PT: For there was hardly no food in the house for me to eat and to feed that child. You know I had to eat crackers or [ ] I cook a chicken or something. And the chicken was frozen. Who going to eat frozen chicken.
JL/JR/PT: (laughs)
PT: But, I mean.
JL: So did you fall for his. . .
PT: No. No.
JL: Did you ever write back to him?
PT: No.
JR: Good for you.
JL: Did you save the letters?
PT: Yeah, I saved the letters and gave it to the cops.
JR: All right!
JL: And what happened as a result of that?
PT:[ ]
JL: They put him back in jail!
PT: Yeah. 'Cause he violate the
JL: Injunction.
PT: Injunction and gave him another couple of months.
JL: 'Cause you gave them the letters and that was a violation of the injunction.
JR: Well, there you go.
JL: She did a great job.
PT: But it still didn't do no good 'cause he saw me one night, he came in my yard. But I had an injunction against him?
JR: Yeah.
PT: And he was never to step his foot in my yard. He was trying to beg me back.
JR: Jerk
PT: And he raped me the same night. He came to my house.
JL: He was quite a guy.
PT: Uh huhm. And now the jerk is in Bonifay, I don't have too much to worry about him. I hope not.
JL: Did you tell her about the change you made in your life? And how that came about?
PT: Well, say it took a long, long, long life. For everything I went through. But, first change I remember I took was accepting Jesus Christ in my life. That was the first one.
JL: What was happening around that period of time that you did that?
PT: Well, I was a sinner. (laughs)
JL: You were sinning; going around sinning. (laughs)
PT: I was living a very bad, dangerous life.
JR: What were you doing?
PT: Do like any other woman do. Getting drunk, having sex, get wild. (laughs) You just name it. But
JL: There was some violence during that that you were. . .
PT: I was real angry. All the time. I was just actually angry about everything, you know, 'cause HRS lied to me, told me that I was coming home. I never

came home. I was treated like I was a prisoner, 'cause every time I come home, that somebody was with me, you know. If I'm at Heidel House, going to bed at night, somebody's watching me 24 hours a day, seven days a week.

JR: Hah

PT: I felt like I was in chains.

JR: Why?

PT: Well it was a lie, you know, one of my auntie tell a story on me. Say that I tried to kill my grandmamma. Stab on her [ ] with a knife. That was lie. I never tried to kill my grandma. My grandma the one who raised me since I was a child. You know. But that was a lie.

JL: Describe your grandma.

PT: Describe her? (laughs) Well, she was short, chubby, she had long hair. Got about right to here (below shoulders). And she was nice.

JL: What was she like?

PT: She was very nice kind of person.

JL: You told me she was a lovely wise woman. I will never forget that.

PT: I did? (laughs)

JL: Was a lovely wise woman. And you loved your grandma. So that was the worst thing anybody could say that you did.

PT: Yeah

JR: Yeah

PT: But after all of that lies happened, that's when all that stuff happened, you know, 'cause they treat me like you know she's dangerous, you know, she's crazy (laughs).

JL: That's when they took you to Tallahassee.

PT: Yeah I stayed in Tallahassee, stayed in Tallahassee, that's something else I didn't tell you. (laughs) I stayed in Tallahassee, I stayed in Bonifay.

JL: Well tell her about Tallahassee. 'Cause that was a pretty traumatic time there. They took you from here because of that lie to Tallahassee.

PT: I was in a foster home in Tallahassee, it was all right. But

JL: What about the football, the girl you were walking with to take you to her house or something? You had crossed that field. You thought I forgot all this stuff didn't you?

PT: (laughs) Oh you got a very good memory than I got.

JL: (laughs)

PT: No, we were running away from school and it was like this big open field, and there was this very old man. He never messed with her, but he messed with me. 'Cause I guess I looked like I was older than she was.

JR: Yeah

PT: But he raped me.

JR: Huh

JL: In the field.

PT: Like there in an open wide field. Cars was passing by, you know, if anybody have seen it, they would have saw everything. You know. It was right in daylight.

JR: Oh my Lord. And what year was this?

PT: Oh God it was 1980 something. Like it was in the 80s

JL: Then what happened at that apartment?

PT: What apartment?

JL: In Tallahassee. Didn't you go and visit somebody in an apartment?

PT: Did I tell you that?

JL: Uh huhm.

PT: Oh God. I don't remember that one.

JL: Okay. Maybe that wasn't in Tallahassee.

PT: (laughs)

JL: Seems to me like you had been raped several times in Tallahassee.

PT: Oh, yeah, now I remember what she talking about. Thank you Janet. You're my lifesaver. But anyway, (laughs) I remember now, I had went to this apartment with this guy, and I thought it was just me and him, you know?

JL: You were 12

PT: Yeah. 12 and wild. (laughs). But anyway I was with this guy there and I was just with him, you know. I didn't know the apartments at all ... I guess he went out there and told his friends. And they came in there and had a little fun.

JL: One at a time.

PT: They run a train on me.

JL: 12 years old.

PT: I still remember that.

JR: And you survived that.

PT: Yeah. I survived my own death.

JR: How so?

PT: Well, because I saw my death. Albert tried to kill me with a car, he strangled me to death with his bare hands, a woman tried to shoot you in the head with a gun, so I know it had to be death.

JR: Like a cat.

JL: Uh huhm. Nine lives.

PT: Huhm

JL: When you decided to because as I remember you telling me that you know you were having some fights with Albert, and you put the screwdriver to his neck, you know because he was coming at you.

PT: Well he hit me and I just told him, I just stuck it to his neck, and said, if you hit me again, I'm going to kill you. (laughs) I let him know right then and there, you know, but it still didn't do no good. Well enough I did what I had to do , you know, it still he did what he wanted to do.

JL: Did you tell her about the cable cord?

PT: He take a cable cord, actually, he took the cable cord and wrap it around my neck.

JL: He did it in the yard.

PT: It was a wide open, in my own yard, day break, like this you know. And he took a cable cord that I had wrapped around my dog, to keep my dog tied up with. He took that cable cord and wrapped it around my neck, and took it did like that, real tight to my neck. And it was making a joke back in the days when they did people,

JL: The men that were walking by were joking about . . .
PT: There was a man who came and saw him with the cable cord around my neck, and they were joking about it. You know. What did I tell you , Janet?
JL: That's how they used to do it, that's how they used to keep women back in the days, something like that.
PT: That's how they used to do people. They say that's how they used to hang people back in the days. Like that. Take a rope and they hang them up.
JR: Right
PT: And so . . . that what they were making a joke about. But to me it was not a joke. 'Cause all he had to do was real tight real bad and it would've popped my neck.
JR: Sure
PT: You know. And he didn't care what he were doing. I mean everybody seen it. So when I told Janet about it and we talked to the police here, the police went and asked the same guy and he told them "Yeah." That that's what happened. That he saw had that cable cord around my neck, you know? But Albert make like he didn't do it, you know.
JR: Hah
JL: And he wasn't arrested.
PT: No they didn't put him in jail for it.
JL: And I felt really bad about that because you told me you didn't want to call the police because they wouldn't do anything, and I convinced her that you know, let's report it, he needs to be held accountable for that, and so we had the police come right here to the office, so they couldn't just discount her. And I'll be darned if she was right.
PT: They never put him in jail.
JL: They put him in jail later.
PT: Yeah. But on our own we got him in jail.
JR: How'd you do that?
PT: 'Cause he did something, what was that he did? I came here and told you about it. He did something.
JL: Trying to remember. . . .
PT: Well he treated me bad at the hotel. It wasn't at the hotel, it was over there at trailer court, I think. He did something . . .
JL: I can't remember what it was Pam.
PT: But he took me through hell, I mean, he tried to kill me more than one time,
JL: Well, he'd been in prison for murder in California. And he came out here, he had just gotten out of prison, a long prison stint for murder. So, he was perfectly capable of killing her.
JR: Yeah
JL: So for Pam to ask for help, to follow through on some of the things that were required to get that, that was just miraculous.
JR: Yeah
JL: Not a lot of reasons to trust anybody did you?
PT: Nope. And I still don't.
JL: Right

PT: (laughs). I just got to a point where I don't trust nobody. You know? And right now I'm in another relationship, kind of the same little way. Only he ain't kind of that bad yet, but.

JL: Emotional and verbal abuse, controlling.

PT: So I'm trying to get myself away from that too, before it get worse.

JR: Right. Keep that dream going.

PT: Oh yeah, the dream still rolling. It's just I've got to keep living. (laughs)

JR: Yeah, you have to do that.

JL: That's half of the problem, the deal is it?

PT: I mean, once your dreams keep going, you have to keep living to make it happen.

JR: Right.

PT: 'Cause if you die then your dream die too.

JR: Well, not necessarily.

PT: Well you dead you dead, your dream ain't coming alive. (laughs)

JR: Your dream can live on in other people.

PT: But mine won't. (laughs)

JR: Yeah, yeah

PT: So, I'm trying to survive, really enough it's hard to live a life. 'Cause every day you go through something.

JR: What kinds of things do you do to survive?

PT: Well, I go to school (laughs). Every Sunday I go to church. And sometimes in a room watching a Hillsongs video. (laughs)

JL: Reading

PT: Reading a book, Darlene . . .

JR: Yeah

PT: Another thing that keep me focused.

JR: So you have all sorts of things that you do. ...

JL: Sit in the park for hours.

PT: And hours and hours.

JL: Got a real active life internal life and she will sit in the park for hours and dream about singing and read Darlene Zcehech's books, and watch people, and hours every day.

JR: That's pretty cool.

PT: I'm busy. (laughs).

JR/JL: (laughs)

PT: Going to school and sitting in emotion. (laughs)

JL: Why do you go to the park so much?

PT: 'Cause it's quiet. I can think. You know, 'cause when you're around other people, you know and they nyare nyare nyrare, I'm like gone. (laughs) I cannot think. You know 'cause somebody just going going going. But when I'm by myself and everything then I can think.

JL: You can think.

PT: Then I can hear a little voice talking, you know. Ding ding. Read Darlene's book. (laughs)

JR: What kind of books does she write?

PT: Mostly it's about worship. And everything. Most of her books is about worship. Praise and worship. And she gives me a lot of ideas.

JL: Motivational kind of, motivates you to have kind of positive thoughts and live positive life.

PT: []. But you're trying to reach there. 'Cause you're going to go through the rough times and it seem like it get more easier and easier (laughs) [ ] You pass all this and then you get to the easy part.

JR: You got to get through a lot of hoops to get to a place. How did you hear about Darlene?

PT: (laughs) I heard about her at church. The church that they closed down, Braemer. Where I first start going there they start singing Darlene's songs, most of her songs.

JR: Uh huh

PT: And I had a woman there to make me some copies of the CDs she had. And I begin to start listening to them, like I could, I like this, 'cause there was something about the music, you know. It brings a lot of joy, peace, and all that to you. And I like the music. That was, that how I know about Darlene. (laughs)

JR: I'd like to listen to them sometime. It would be interesting.

PT: ... Janet heard some of them.

JL: I've heard you sing too.

PT: She heard me sing along with them.

JL: She got a beautiful voice.

PT: But I have to work on it. (laughs)

JL: Because you are. Shy.

PT: I'm shy in front of people.

JL: Well. Alone she's not shy at all.

JL/JR/PT: (laughs)

PT: Now by myself I'm not shy at all, but when I get up in front of people, and I just sing, then I am shy.

JL: But she's got a beautiful voice and she's working on that.

PT: But being abuse I thank God every day that I walked away from it. Now my story have finished.

These Are Our Stories

NOTES

Jessica B.

Jessica B. was born in 1975 and raised in Jackson County, Florida. She grew up in what she calls a "normal" family when she had her first child at age 15. Jessica's story is twofold. She speaks of a first marriage where her son became terminally ill and her husband was largely absent from the family. This is where she entered into what she calls a "co-abusive" relationship in which she was both the victim and aggressor. Her second marriage was also a violent one where her husband abused her emotionally and physically. She tells her story with animation and distance because these events are removed from her now. She lives with her third husband and their child in Jackson County.

JR: Jan Rosenberg
JB: Jessica B.
LB: Lucas, Jessica B's son.

JR: Why don't you tell me a little bit about growing up?
JB: About growing up? I was one of six, and there's five girls and one boy. (Talks to son) And we were poor, dirt poor, but we had a really good unit, very close. Dad worked, Mom stayed home. Normal family, just broke (laughs) with six kids, you know?
JR: Yeah. Where did you grow up?
JB: Here in Marianna.
LB: I grew up in Jackson Hospital.
JB: That's where you were born.
JR: You're still growing up, you're growing up here.
JB: He's grown, Miss Jan. He's grown. Okay? He's grown. (Sends Lucas away. (Laughs) A normal kind of life. I mean, no big whoop (laughs).
JR: How did you get into a relationship that wasn't quote unquote normal?
JB: I couldn't tell you. It happened. I should've seen it coming, but I didn't. He was, when we got married, he was a drug addict. He did crack cocaine. It really that whole walk can change the world theory. We had known each other off and on for four years. Like just casually. And then when we started dating we got married six days after we started dating. Yeah. But his sister was nurse . . . My first son? I got pregnant when I was 15. And I had him when I was 16. He had spinal meningitis when he was 10 months old and was severely brain damaged. He lived to be four, he was terminal the entire time. His... I've been married three times. My first husband was J.D. that's my child that died. That was his dad. My second husband, Tommy, was the one that was the worst incidence of domestic violence. My first husband, Jamie, was that way too. But he wasn't as cruel. If you can understand what I am saying. (Laughs) You gotta love him (referring to Lucas who has just come in with tape across his mouth)

But I contributed a lot of Jamie's anger and inability to deal with things with the fact that both of us were young. And I egged it on, towards the end I gave as good as I got. That was my first husband.

But this is my third marriage and this is the marriage that my parents have. Just it took me three tries, and I'm here now.

JR: Tell me more about the second marriage, Tommy.

JB: Tommy? Well, his sister was my son's nurse, he had to have hospice and respite care? I mean we couldn't just leave him with a babysitter unless it was one of us who was CPR trained and things like that. So like I said, I knew him off and on, knew his family, his family was all just stellar people. Millie is his aunt. That's his aunt. So you know the family, you know they're good people. I didn't think, really didn't think anything of it. I mean I just met him, and it was love at first sight. Kind of harbored a crush for a little while. And then when we decided we were going to go out, it was just (snaps fingers) boom. There it was. And, never, coming from that family, I really, maybe I'm blind, but I didn't see it.

JR: What kinds of things happened?

JB: Well, at first it was, okay I have to own my part in this. And this is why I stayed in it. I cheated on him. He was in the military and it was so easy just to go back in those old patterns of being single with him being gone. And not to make excuses, but my justification was he didn't pay attention, he didn't write, he didn't call. He wasn't really interested. So I said, "Well I'll just go over here where somebody is interested." And then I lied. Because when he came home, he was really angry. And have you met him? He's about 6-2, cut, very cut, very muscular. Formidable. (Lucas comes in again). But he got angry, and I got scared. And so I straight lied. No what? Who me? I didn't do it. You know. And then I finally told the truth, and that's the first time he hit me. He kept saying, "All you have to do is tell me the truth, all you have to do is tell me the truth." You know. "Nothing bad is going to happen, just tell me the truth." And so finally I told the truth, and things just went berserk. I mean like one minute he was fine, the next minute I was literally on the floor. And it just escalated from there.

It went on for probably about a year and a half maybe? We got married in February of '96. I divorced him November of '98. And we had been separated a year prior to that. But it just got. It got to where almost I was scared to tell the truth about anything. I guess the best thing I can liken it to is negative reinforcement? If you know that every time you tell the truth you going to be scrutinized and smacked and talked down to. If it's. Okay. Say I go to the store with my friend, my best friend Liz and see one of my old boyfriends. You know, or maybe my ex-husband. Stop to him, speak to him, hi how are you, da da da did a, I wouldn't "Where'd you go? With who?" "With Liz." "Who'd you see?" "Nobody." Because I knew it'd be misconstrued. Because I had laid the foundation for the infidelity. So that's how I kept at it for a year because, I said you know, this is all my fault. If I hadn't cheated on him, he wouldn't have been, he wouldn't have been that way. You know, pretty much lied to myself.

JR: Huhm. So it was kind of a knock down drag out life for awhile.

JB: Uh huhm (laughs). Yeah. And I had, I had issues myself. When I met him I was, I didn't have any addictions, nothing, and my life got to the point where I was running away. I was running away from my child's death, you know, just running away. And I had tried to run to Tommy, and that didn't work, and so I ended up running to methamphetamine, just trying to get away from all the craziness. Not realizing at the time that that was just going to make it crazier. I was young, I was stupid, I didn't know. Should've known, but didn't know.

And so at one point in time, you know, he was on crack cocaine, and I was on methamphetamines. The two do not mix at all. They don't mix. (Asks Luke to be quiet) It's been with age and wisdom that I own what I did. (laughs)

JR: Yeah

JB: It got to be where I was lying so much I couldn't tell you when I was telling the truth.

JR: Hah

JB: Just defensive. You know don't tell Tommy anything, anything that can be misconstrued. But that was also a carryover from Jamie. Jamie was the same way.

JR: Very possessive?

JB: Very possessive. I couldn't . . . And the weird part is . . . with Jamie, I didn't cheat on Jamie. Okay, that's my first husband. He hit me when I was pregnant. My left ear? I got 60% hearing loss in my left ear. Because he smacked me up against a wall. He threw me up against the wall when I was pregnant. And that continued on. But I think that laid the groundwork for Tommy. For it to be okay for those things to happen. I tried very hard to keep my marriage together. Because my parents have such a decent marriage. They've been married, I'm 29, so they've been married 30 years? You know, stable marriage, no infidelity, no domestic violence, just normal folks.

So by the time I got to Tommy I was already in the mind set that it was okay to be treated that way. And it escalated. You know, if it's okay to slap her, then it's okay to punch her. And if it's okay to punch her, it's okay to put out cigarettes on her. You know? It just further on, until I ended up with a brain bleed, hematoma, broke my nose, cracked my jaw, I had cracked ribs. Two black eyes, my ears were bruised. And that was the last time that he really laid it on me. I went to the hospital and he went to jail. Part of all that was that he go to rehab. And when he was in rehab, 'cause he always told me "If you leave me I'll kill you." And you know, as a domestic violence counselor now, I can say you know that's not true. We have this, we have that, we can keep you safe, da da da da da. (Laughs) But I believed him, I believed what he was saying. So I didn't leave. But when he got in rehab and I was so heavy into the drugs, it got to be, it truly got to be — and that's the one good thing that came out of my methamphetamine addiction, was the wisdom that came from it. Just the fact that I didn't care. I didn't care if I lived or died. He could kill me; I didn't give a crap. I didn't care. So, it was easy to leave him. You want to kill me, fine, put me out of my misery, you going to be doing me a favor. ... (phone rings)

JR: So, essentially, you didn't give a flying whatnot.

JB: I didn't care; he would have been doing me a favor. And so it was easy to say, "You know what? I don't think so." You know, we're not going there. And I wrote him a note, and didn't speak to him for almost a year after that. No contact. If he called, I hung up. If he sent me a letter I sent it back. Wouldn't have anything to do with him.

So it was shortly after that, that was in November, right before Thanksgiving. January 3 rd of that year I got sober of '96 when I . . . Lord have mercy, Jan, '98? 'Cause we were married January '97. Okay, January of '98 I was sober. Yeah, okay. Sorry. But I got sober January of '98 and then got scared. I was like oh no, what have I done? You know, just terrified when he got out of jail he would come kill me. And then I kind of got over myself and I was like pssht, you know you only give him as much power. That's how much power he has is how much power you give him, and I wasn't giving any I cut it out, I cut it completely out. No phone calls. His sister would call, don't want to talk to him. His niece would call, don't want to talk to him. You know, I wouldn't discuss anything personal about my life with them because I knew it would get back to him. So I just didn't say jack. Just completely shut myself off.

And then I was pregnant with Lu. It's kind of cool. I had wanted a baby since my son died. Tommy and I tried desperately to have a baby. God was watching out for me because I didn't. (laughs) You know. And I'm not a super religious person. I'm not. I believe in God, the rest of it's kind of conjecture. For me. But I was grateful. That I did not have a child with him. Even though I wanted one so badly. But then it was after that after I separated from him that I got pregnant. Three, almost four weeks 'cause the night I got sober I thought I was going to die. You know, I was praying, and I'm not a normal praying person. And I straight up, if you let me live, I will do everything you need me to do. You know, I'll be straight, I'll be sober, you know, I'll be ready for whatever you hand me. Let me live. And it's been rough but good since then. (laughs) It's been very good, I've been very blessed. It's just been kind of whoof!

JR: What other kinds of tactics did you use to survive?

JB: Besides lying, bluffing? Bluffing (laughs). Cowering. Just . . . When he burned me, the night he burned me he was... And you see his mama always said he had to be drunk or stoned to hit me? That's not true. I mean he did it more often when he was drunk or stoned, but he could be stone cold sober and was still cruel, still be physically violent. The night he burned me, I had a ten gallon fish tank that's in there? There was another one that he had knocked it over. The stained glass, not the stained glass, but the patio door? There used to be two sides, used to be a double set of doors. There's one now. Because he broke the one side with a beer bottle. And it was things like that, he would try to terrify me. My bed was just torn to pieces, just torn to pieces, I mean, holes punched in the wall. But that particular night, I'm an animal lover. I can't be cruel to an animal? He took my fish tank and pushed it over. And when he pushed it over, my fish were flopping around in glass and rocks without any air. So I had gone [ ] and I don't really even remember what we were arguing about at this point. It was just more of this random arguments that cropped up and escalates. But I had gone over to the thing and got a punch bowl and went and filled it up with water and just was ignoring him trying just to stay in the right and not to have him hurt me. And I went and got the punch bowl and filled it with water and when I came back I had three fish in there. And I got two of them and the third one he had stomped into the gravel. I just couldn't get to him in time. So I was bent over and I had the two fish and I had them kind of was hovering over them? And he started kicking me. And when he started kicking I put up into a little ball so he wouldn't hurt me that bad. And he had me up by my hair and he was smoking. And he had me up by the hair and put a cigarette out on me. Right there (points to top of chest). And said that's all I was good for, an ashtray.

JR: Was he sober then?

JB: No, he was drunk that night. He was drunk that night. Mostly when he was sober I got slapped.

JR: Oh

JB: (laughs) It was like a good night 'cause (laughs). Just knives held to my throat, just stupid, stupid shit. Stupid. And I mean looking back I'm like what were you thinking? You know? But I truly loved him. The fear was as great as the love. I mean they were equal parts. They were equal parts. I was as scared of him as much as I loved him. And you talk about not knowing where to go? Where to turn? I didn't know which way was up. And it's been. And it's ironic actually, because now, we get along. I can speak to him and we go out every now and again to dinner, kind of catch up, see how things are going and his baby is named after me. He went on and had a baby that's named after me. Part of the reason that I can do that now is because I can get in my little Acura and leave. There's not that romantic tie there. It doesn't matter what I'm doing. You know I don't have to watch him anymore because he has no part in my life other than that acquaintance. You know, I don't have to be scared or be nervous.

So I can go over to his mom's house and say hi to his mom, and say hi to him and things like that, that's not a big deal. It's not a big deal anymore. It's funny how it worked out that way. (laughs)

JR: When was the moment you decided you had to get out of the relationship?

JB: It was after he had gone to rehab. And I was high. I was as my mother called it "stunningly high." 'Cause with my addiction I was up to two grams a day. And I had done almost three that night. As well as snorted some cocaine. Stunningly high. It's a wonder I'm not dead. Truly is. Just it's God's grace that I'm not dead. But got that courage in a can. (laughs) I guess that's what you call it, courage in a can. Didn't care. At that point in time I didn't care whether I lived or died. And I was tired of living in fear. I was tired of being scared, I was tired of locking my doors. And trying to constantly think up a lie about something completely innocent. By nature I'm an honest person. It was just being married to him that made me into a liar. And that's something, I abhor liars, I can't. And I was one. And I stopped and looked and said that's not who you are, honey. That's not where you need to be. And I had enough dope in me to have some courage and a backbone and said I'm not doing this anymore. I don't care, let him kill me.

Do you listen to Janis Joplin?

JR: A long time ago I did.

JB: (laughs) Bobby McGhee? Do you remember that song? "Freedom's just another word for nothing left to lose." That's what it was. I had nothing left to lose. My life wasn't worth anything. For God's sake. I wasn't worth a penny. So what would he be taking away? Nothing. The fear was gone. You know. Screw you. I don't have to deal with this. Then there was sobriety (laughs). But it didn't come back enough to where I was where I went back. He asked me in June of '99, asked me to get back. He would come over and talk to me, I wouldn't allow him here if he was drinking or on drugs, and I told him I'll sic the cops on you, leave, you know, not a problem. You know because it's not a problem. But he would come over here and he'd be sober, and there were like two days a month, two or three days a month during our marriage that he was the White Knight, he was Prince Charming. Everything you ever wanted in a man was just incarnate in him. It was awesome. Because he had fronted out to everybody, he didn't have any money for drugs, didn't have any credit for drugs, didn't have anything left to sell for drugs. No money for beer. And he had to be nice to me in order to get these things. So, you know, those two or three days a month were awesome. They were great. Whenever he came back around it was the same deal, you know, he wanted something from me. If nothing else, then just to have that family back? And I wouldn't have him (laughs). Wouldn't have him. I did consider it, but I was like, oh, I have a child now, I have a child to consider. We're not on the off chance, on the off chance, we're not doing that again.

JR: So you had a hell of a time with Tommy. You were married from what year to what year?

JB: From '96 to '98. February of '96 till November of '98. From November of '97 ... till November of '98 we didn't speak. We were married, but we didn't talk to each other. As close to the furthest end of the county as we could get.(laughs)

JR: To me it's amazing that you get together now and you have a friendship.

JB: Yeah! When someone knows the absolute worst about you, knows just what you're capable of, and still loves you. To me that's worth something. At this point we don't have to lie to each other, there's no putting on a pretty face or anything like that. I know what he's capable of.

JR: Yeah

JB: He knows me, so we tried to salvage something. And what we decided was this, was a was an acquaintance. You know, not going out every night or anything like that (laughs). You know I might see him twice a year. But it's always very cordial, very cool, you know, very just smooth. . . .

JR: What about Jamie?

JB: I wouldn't piss on his gums if his teeth were on fire. That's the God's honest truth.

JR: (laughs) Wow

JB: (laughs) I would not. If he was laying on the side of the road I would run him over.

JR: What happened?

JB: I know there's a difference, okay? Because both of them were violent towards me, both of them were. Jamie wasn't violent towards my child. He ignored him. He wasn't good enough, my child wasn't good enough. And I think Jamie took a lot of his resentment and frustration towards that out on me. And what have you. And we were both in the same situation. We both had a child that was dying. We both had limited resources, both young, you know, why should I have to carry the mature responsible side of it. And I shut him out and he retaliated. You know, that was my child, until the day he died, it was my child.

JR: What's your child's name?

JB: J.D.

JR:J.D.?

JB: Jesse David. It was . . . I was resentful, why should I have to shoulder all that by myself? And so instead of putting it off on J.D. I put it off on Jamie. And put it solely on his shoulders. And I was extremely angry for quite a long time (laughs). For a long time.

But it got to be where I was the aggressor. When we first got together he would slap me, he shoved me into the wall, he would punch me and hit me and then I had had enough of it. And it was, we were married for four years, or three years, rather, our divorce took a year. Our divorce was a sight to be seen. People could have paid money and seen it (laughs). It was spectacular. We had to have a deputy everywhere we went. Even at my son's funeral, there was a deputy. I had had enough. I had, it was my breaking point. Breaking point truly.

It started two months before my son had died. He came in and was fussing about something, and just fussing. We had gone and bought groceries. And he was fussing because I bought a box of Cocoa Pebbles. At four dollars and something a box. Okay? Now mind you, he didn't have a job. Okay? I worked, and he was fussing about my Cocoa Pebbles. And I just, I flipped and I had had enough. And I ended up that night beating the tar out of him. I had him crying in the corner, begging for the phone to call 911. And I wouldn't let him have it. It was a train wreck. And it got progressively worse from there. Instead of him being the aggressor, him coming up pinching and slapping me and things like that. I was going to do it to him. And when the tables were turned; I could never turn the tables with Tommy. He was bigger than me and he was meaner than me. (laughs). So it was you know. But with Jamie it got to where every bit of anger that I had: if I didn't get a parking place close to the front; if the sun did not shine just the way I wanted it to, all that anger was directed at him. Whether he deserved it or not. And that's what ... See it's hard to judge at this point because I'm so far removed from it. But the tables, they just completely flipped. They did. And by the end of our marriage. He was, okay, he had a girlfriend. And had been seeing her for quite a few months. See, I'm trying to fill in the details. When my son got so sick, the hospital neglected to care for him. And so we sued. We sued the hospital and we sued the doctors. And came into quite a chunk of change. I mean that it was enough that my son could live out, if he lived, you know, for the rest of his life, normal seven year span. There was enough money that my son could live comfortably and not ever have to worry about medicine or anything like that, medicine, food, shelter anything. He was taken care of.

Well, from that we each got a portion just separate unto ourselves. Okay? And then the rest of it was put into trust for him. Well, so we had, we had money. We had enough money just from our portion of the settlement, I mean not touching anything of J.D.'s, just enough of ours, to buy this house, I bought my mom a house, you know, I kind of took care of things family-wise. But he had, as soon as there was a hint of money, he went and got a girlfriend. Well, whatever. Except she was 15. He was 22, she was 15. Yuh. (laughs) . . . And I didn't know anything about it for the longest time. Because he had cheated on me before. I was so focused on keeping the family together, it wasn't a priority. It was somewhere down here (points down toward the floor). You know, it wasn't a priority. But when that money came along and then he had always ignored J.D. I mean he didn't change diapers, he didn't you know, change catheters, anything. But when that . . . he ended up in April of that year, April of '95, he ended up leaving me for her. And I was devastated, you know, all I was trying to do was keep my family together. That's it. And so I moved, just pitiful teenage crap 'cause I was 20 at the time, I had just turned 20. And he kept coming around. He kept coming around and coming around. Well, it's like you know, I want to see my son. Okay, I would set up a time when he could see him, he never showed. "Well, I was coming, why didn't you wait on me?" Two days later. I mean he would make an appointment to see him on Monday and Wednesday he would show up. And I wouldn't be here. . . .

The two months previous to my son's death it was rough, it was very rough. And I'm a forgiving person, what I cannot forgive him for is my son laying here for four days, gasping for breath. I begged him to come. Told him let your mom come over here, I'll leave. I don't have to be here, I'll go to my mom's. Just come. That's all I wanted him to do is come. "I'll be there." Well, the first day he took his girlfriend to Tallahassee to buy makeup. The second day he had to take her to school. The third day she skipped school and went fishing with him. And the next day she had a doctor's appointment. Well, I called him, Wednesday, and I had just been begging him. I told him I'll leave, send who you want to over here, send your mother or your brother, they can come stay at the house, cause J.D. could not be, he couldn't tolerate being moved. I mean he was literally drowning in his own fluid. And wouldn't come, had slightly better things to do.

So on the fourth day I called and he answered the phone, he had Caller ID, he's like –it's going to get rough, my language – he said, "I told you I'm fucking coming over there: leave me alone. I said, "You know what? Don't bother: he's dead." And hung up the phone. Well 20 minutes later he came over here. My son's not even cold. Crying big huge crocodile tears. "I'm going to miss him so much" You know, "That was my son, that was my boy" duh duh duh duh duh. And that's when the anger really got the best of me. We were supposed to get divorced that Friday. Buried my son that Friday. Saturday he came over here, and I think he was looking for a fight? He had a lot of anger and didn't know where to put it. And I showed him where he could put it. He came back to the bedroom and called me a whore. Lots of nice little names. Lots of nasty little things. And I slapped him. And he slapped me back. And that was all she wrote. You know? I can tell it simply because my two best friends were out here and saw it. And then told me repeatedly. But I don't remember what happened. It's all like red. It was just like a red haze. But I had him – they said they don't know what happened in the bedroom, but I had him out here, I had wrapped my hands around his hair, he had kind of long hair, and was punching him in the face, trying to drag him out. And then I got him out here, and was just beating on wailing on him. And then he started to leave, and turned around and said, "Is that all you've got?" And I jumped over. Now Liz is a big girl, Liz is like 400 pounds, she's like 5-9, she's a big girl. And Denise is like your size, she's tiny, so I mean – but they tried to get them between us and I jumped over the two of them, because they had their arms out like that (outstretched). [ ] him again, knocked him into the china cabinet, and then he was trying to leave and I was steadily punching him. And he was facing . . . now I remember this part. . . he was facing that way and he was still calling me names? And I kicked him in the square of the back, and he landed face first out there by the pink part. I kicked him so hard, I mean he just landed face first. And it was just, it was bad. It was bad.

And when we got divorced, we got divorced that Monday. My child died Wednesday, we buried him Friday, got divorced the following Monday. They had to have the deputy, because we had to sit across the table from each other? And he was crying, saying all he wanted was pictures of my son. Now this man had ripped me for $50,000, ripped me. We had a CD, a joint CD that said Jessica or James. And he went and took it. Yeah. Okay. Just fought me tooth and nail for everything. Everything. And then he's going to get in front of the judge and say I just want ten pictures of my dead son, that's all I want she can have the rest of it. When he was late to his funeral? I think not still. And I got, it was Judge Roberts at the time. I had panty hose and a black dress on. And my lawyer was sitting, I was sitting on this side, and he was on this side, and Jamie was on the other side right across from me. Judge Roberts' table was fairly long, fairly wide. I came across and punched him then in front of Judge Roberts. We had to have literally, Judge Roberts sat in the middle and set us at either end with a deputy in between us. (laughs) It was spectacular. My lawyer said it was worth the price of admission. But I can't let go of that anger. What happened between Tommy and I happened between two adults. You know, I could have picked up and left any time. I chose not to leave. For whatever reason I was scared, but I chose not to go. I chose. There wasn't any young'n involved, there was nothing, it was us. Jamie had a responsibility, he not only had a responsibility to me, as his wife, he had a responsibility to his son. And I try very hard. Now, if I see him, I'll speak to him civilly, but I cannot speak over a minute to him. It's got to be, Hi, how are you, Well, I'm fine, how are you? I'm fine, thank you. Then I've got to leave. Because I just will violent, I feel extremely violent. And it's been eight years. It's been almost nine years. This August it will be nine years. And to this day if I stay with him over five minutes I'm going to slap him. It's just that ERRRR (laughs) Pitiful.

JR: What did it feel like being on the other side of the fence? JB: Scary. I've never been a violent person. Never been a violent person. And even when Tommy and I at the height of our fighting, the only thing I ever did to him, I bit him one time and I pushed him back. Out the same door as a matter of fact that I pushed Jamie (laughs). . . The night that I pushed and I bit him, I think it was defense of my [ ]. See that dent in the wall right there, below the clock? I used to have pictures, lots of pictures of J.D. on that wall, and ... when he didn't want to exert the effort of beating me, he would punch the side of my head to get his point across? Yeah. But he punched the side of my head and he hit one of the baby's pictures. And broke the glass and tore the picture. And I was, I was livid. And that's the only time I ever hit him back. I mean that's the only time I ever made a move to be the aggressor. Every other time I kind of rolled over and took it, you know.

It's easier to forgive him, because like I said, I could've left, I could've found somewhere to go where he couldn't have found me. I could've left. You know. With Jamie, it's all about my son. I can't, I can't forgive him. J.D. was defenseless. You know there was nothing he could do. Nothing. All he needed was his parents. And Jamie couldn't be bothered.

JR: Talk to me about life now.

JB: Life now: oh my goodness. I'm addicted to school now. I'm addicted to school. I've got an AA in International Affairs, I've got my EMT, a CPT, a certified practical therapist, I'm a dive master. I'm actually going for assistant instructor in diving over this summer, in August I'll start my graphic arts degree, and then knock wood in January of 2006 I'll start on my anthropology, my Masters in anthropology. So, I'm addicted to school (laughs). I've been to fire school. ... Got stuck in a tunnel. It was very embarrassing.

Okay. You tell me why they would put, the tunnel was 26 inches, okay, my left leg is 26 inches around. You put bunker gear and everything else on there and plus an SCBA. The tunnel was 26 inches or excuse me 36 inches. In the middle of it, 10 inches in there was a four inch pipe sticking out, so you couldn't go this way, you had to go around it. And it was 26 inches, 'cause I had to measure too, it was 26 inches from the end of the pipe to the end of the tunnel, to the side of the tunnel. That ain't about that big (laughs). There's no part of my body that's going to fit there normal. And it was 24 inches high. It was like sticking a marshmallow in a two by two space. (laughs). I got in there. I got in the tunnel, I got past the pipe, okay, I took my SCBA off, scooted it ahead of me, got up there, put my SCBA back on, and was just stuck. I was so stuck. Could not, I tried to wiggle backward, couldn't do it, my shoulders were too.. I couldn't squish myself up enough to go back. And I couldn't squeeze my hips forward. I was stuck right in the middle. It was horrible. My fire chief was yelling at me. "You bigger on top or bigger on bottom!?" I say, "None of your damn business chief!" (laughs) I was about to cry. . . I was embarrassed. And they finally. The guy came in this way (from one end) and grabbed the roof and put his boots on my clavicle. And pushed. And that's how I got out of the tunnel. ..... But I made it through the tower. I made it through the tower. I looked like I had been beaten half to death. Had bruises here (on legs). Somebody was ahead of me on the second turn. And the second turn was just masks, we didn't have on our SCBA, somebody was ahead of me with their boots on and kicked me right in the eye, I had a shiner. (laughs) I constantly came home, just like bruised up, cut up, pitiful, pitiful. But it was great (laughs)

JR: How do you think what you learned with Tommy and Jamie, how are you applying what you learned to life today?

JB: I actually learned, as bad as I make it out to be, I actually learned some really good stuff from Tommy. If I can survive that I can survive anything. There are fates worse than death. So everything else is gravy after that. You know. And being because J.D. died in August, okay, I married Tommy that following February. ... So you're looking at within a year, I left a co-abusive relationship or I got left in a co-abusive relationship. You know. My son died, I got divorced, I got re-married into another abusive relationship. I am a survivor. (laughs) You know there's not a whole lot past that that's going to kill me. Sort of makes it easier. You don't have that fear. There's nothing to be scared of, if you live through that, you can live through anything. And I also learned to talk up to myself. Tommy, Tommy was really good at talking down to me, really good. I mean he could cut to the bone. Things that just, horrible things. But he was also really good. He could talk down to me. But nobody else could talk down to me. If someone else said something negative about me, he was all over them like white on rye. But I could be his fat-assed whore, I could be no good for anything but an ashtray, you know, a liar.

JR: Well, survival...

JB: Hopefully I won't have to worry about it again.

NOTES

Dottie Smith

Dottie Smith was raised in Mesa, Arizona and Butler, Alabama. She experienced extreme poverty and family dysfunction, becoming pregnant with her step father's child at the age of 13. Dottie lived in a number of foster homes until she was old enough to live on her own. She held a string of jobs and at the age of 28 she enlisted in the US Army.

Dottie finds it difficult to be out of a relationship. She identifies herself as a sex addict, and is working to recover from the addiction.

JR: Jan Rosenberg
DS: Dottie Smith

JR: Where did you grow up?
DS: Mesa, Arizona
JR: How long ago was that?
DS: I was born in 1967. Is that what you're asking?
JR: Uh huhm
DS: My dad had been married before and I had an older sister. My mother was 19, she was one of 13 kids, and she desperately wanted to get out of her parents' home.
JR: Uh huhm
DS: At any cost. And I guess when she got pregnant with me that it was good enough excuse to leave her father and get out on her own.
JR: Now you were telling me that you didn't live in Mesa all the time, you had moved from Mesa didn't you? When did you leave Mesa?
DS: Well, I moved to California for two or three years when I was 21 or 22. My mother had moved our whole family to Alabama, is that what you're talking about?
JR: Right, yeah.
DS: When I was 12 my mom moved us out to Alabama and 'cause that was her home town, that's where she was from, and, I don't know why she wanted to go back there because it was horrible (laughs).
JR: How was it horrible?
DS: Backwards. We're from Mesa and Mesa's not by any stretch, was not then by any stretch a big town? But it was just more spread out and the people in Butler, Alabama, were familiar with each other for 100 years, they knew everybody's mistake and everybody's shortcomings, and good things too, but we were unfamiliar with all that, so they already had their little cliques and set ups and . . . Being from the west we weren't familiar with all this black rage that was going on at the time there was like a total thing about don't talk to the black people and we were like what's up with that? Not like that and a lot of being picked on.

But first, first when we moved to Alabama my step father had two businesses. So we were in a private school, and we were part of all the extracurricular activities, building floats and all that stuff. And then he went to jail and it was really bad.

JR: Oh

DS: He went to jail for embezzling the money out of his businesses and not replacing it or whatever.

So, my grandma and grandpa came out to Alabama and picked us up and took us back to Mesa, in a school bus (laughs), with a bed laying down on the floor and rescued my mom, took her back home and of course my mom had a very hard time, she never resolved any of her issues with her parents, so, she slept a lot. And then she decided she would go back to her husband. She left them, took our welfare check and bought us bus tickets and we had to drive all the way back out to Alabama with all four of us kids and it was weird.

JR: Huh.

DS: But then when we got there, he was still in jail for this embezzlement issue and we were all living in a hotel in Alabama, and it was just weird.

JR: Sounds it. Sounds kind of unreal.

DS: Yeah. Bizarre is how I would claim it.

And she started like cleaning the rooms so she could, you know, have us a place to stay. And he was a, I can't remember the name of it, but he was like allowed to leave the jail (laughs)

JR: Uh huh.

DS: He hadn't done a physical, violent crime, so he was allowed to leave jail, and he was the dispatcher for the police cars, I mean it was like very bizarre, 'cause like here's this prisoner whose more intelligent than anybody there in the city, you know, basically running things and hooked up real good with the sheriff. Very intelligent and everything. But he had his own agenda.

JR: What agenda was that?

DS: Well, to hear my mother tell it, she believes that he was always planning on molesting us, you know, that he had set this up, this disloyalty between me and my sister, and him not liking me and him treating me like a piece of crap the first five years they were married. So that when he did give me some attention, I would fall into that. And just love it and just need it and be so desperate I would do anything and that during the period of time I was being treated special, my sister would need it and want it and well, she'd be willing to do anything. You know? That's my mother's plot of how he did things, I don't know if it's true or not, that's what she thinks and that's what she's expressed a lot.

But he was, he was a very intelligent man. He was orderly, he was conscientious, he was the best thing that ever happened to my mom. And of course, so she felt like she had to do anything to make him happy. And she did.

I don't know, it was really weird because we were already out of the situation and she brought us back into it, so ...

JR: You were out of the situation where he first got put into jail?

DS: Yeah, no, he hadn't molested anybody up until then, as far as I know. He was just "Dad," "Joe," and you know he was part of the family. But then after we went back, you know, they'd have conjugal visits (laughs) which Butler, Alabama is the county seat, but they don't get conjugal visits for most prisoners, but because he was so wise, or manipulative, or whatever, he got conjugal visits. He'd take off out of the prison and go hang out at the hotel with my mom for a couple of hours, while they locked the door and left us outside. You know, it was whatever it was, you know, we knew that parents had to have time together or whatever, but . . .

Then I turned 13 and my mom had never had any issue about like little girls painting their fingernails, she didn't care. She didn't care about like earrings, she didn't care. But then when Joe came into the picture, I was about nine and, eight or nine. And he said no fingernail polish on little girls, no earrings, no pretend makeup, no lipstick, when you turn 13 then you can do all that. So we're like, okay. Well, I turned 13 and my mom's like no you're not doing all that. Joe of course was sitting in the jail and he was more powerful in jail than she was right there with us. He's like, yes she is, and went and bought me lipstick and shaving cream and razors and, you know, the whole thing, letting me have lipstick and fingernail polish and you know letting me get my ears pierced and of course my mom's going "No!" and I'm going "Look, I'm growing up, I want to do these things, you guys said, well not you guys, he said that when I got to this age I could do this, and now I want it, and I'll side with him if that's what it takes. Because you guys said that and I've waited and now I want it." You know, he kind of got me on his side there, you know,

And then he was teaching me and my sister how to French kiss, sitting in the jail lobby. It was just very surreal. I mean just peculiar beyond. Looking back I think why did any of these grown ups allow this bullshit to happen. Why did any of these people. The sheriff was sitting right there, the sheriff's wife was sitting right there, my mom was sitting there, Joe was doing this. We're all sitting on his lap and French kissing and why is this okay? You know? Nobody said anything and it just happened.

JR: Hah.

DS: Well then he got out of jail, and we moved into a shack, like a little ways out of town and he was very I guess he just wanted to be normal? Wanted everybody to think he was just normal. He like put pretty lattice in the front of this house and you know like planted roses there and we'd go and pick berries and stuff. The inside of the house was like you could see the ground from the floor, I mean it was just a shack, you know? Beds laying on the floor on top of the box springs. No electricity, no we did have electricity, but no running water. We all slept in one room when it turned cold we all slept in the living room in front of the fireplace because the house was totally uninsulated. That was peculiar, but once again no one said anything. My mom was doing whatever she wanted to, my grandparents even came out and visited us and made sure, you know that things were okay, and they weren't, but you know they visited us, and nobody said anything, nobody said " These kids don't need to be living in this shit hole", you know they just let it be. And I think that everybody kind of thought, and I have spoken to some of my relatives and they said "We didn't know what to do, we knew your mom wasn't right, but we figured if we took you guys away that she would even be more not right." (laughs) "At least she had a purpose when you guys were there." So a lot of things went on the wayside, a lot of inappropriate things.

JR: So your major issue is with your stepfather?

DS: I think my major issues are with my father. Because I loved him, I thought he was the coolest, and there was some stuff about his family, his parents like loved me and they named me, and they called me their Aunt Dot's namesake and there was a special connection there, and then Grandma Conn died, shortly after that Grandpa Conn was drinking, my dad was drinking a lot, and my mom was going to school to learn a trade, and I was like five, and I was watching me and my sister and my baby sister during the working hours or school hours that my mom had to keep, and you know, tending to them, feeding them and cooking for them, and hanging out, and making sure nobody got hurt. You know, a five year old doesn't have the discretion to figure out whether it's okay to, you know, go outside or, but that was my job and I did that, and

And then we had moved into a house because my dad had got us into HUD homes because we were so low income. And I don't know, somehow that got screwed up. Finally after five years of being with my dad, my mom finally married him, right after we moved into this brand new house

JR: Was this in California?

DS: Arizona

So we were living in this brand new house and my mom was scattered and dysfunctional, my father was raging and alcoholic, and (laughs) abusive. Absent as much as he could be, and apparently having sex with his ex-wife, you know, intermittently, and having relations with that family and having relations with our family and it was all just very not okay, you know my mom didn't have the gall to say, "You know this is breaking a lot of my boundaries, you're not allowed to have sex with your ex-wife if you're going to be married to me. (laughs) You know, and she'd pop out a kid, and he'd be like "No that's not my kid it doesn't look anything like me" and I guess that was pretty rampant during that period of time as far as men go, you know they'd go like, "No, this isn't my kid. You're screwing around on me, you're wrong, you're evil, you're a slut", you know. I don't know. I've never had anyone tell me that, but.

But anyways, that was what he'd always say, So she would pop out another one, and he'd be like, "No, this one's not even mine either. The only one I have is Dottie."

So I was special in that period of time, I was special and I was loved, I felt loved and you know, if my father hit me with the brush, then I must've deserved it or needed it, you know, it didn't affect my love because, you don't realize a five year old kid, people aren't supposed to do things like that to kids, you know. You just kind of go with the flow.

So I loved him, I just loved him to death. I would sit there and I would just be in awe, and maybe because I was afraid, I don't know, but, you know, I was just in awe of this person. And I would do anything. If he said, "Now you guys need to stay in the house and not go anywhere and not do anything, I was scared enough not to go anywhere or do anything. You know, if my mom said it, then

I'd be like well you don't know what you're talking about, and I'd go. I was five. You know? I

Anyway, so. Then, she got pregnant again, but they didn't either one know it. So this is like four kids in five years. And she would like hitchhike to Phoenix from [ ] Junction, which is like 40 miles, hitchhike everyday to go to school to learn how to be a nurse's assistant and stuff. And during that period of time supposedly, he would be there watching us and of course, if he was there, he was passed out drunk, and if he wasn't, if he didn't want to be there he'd be drinking somewhere. And he was really into western stuff, wanting to be a movie star, you know, said he was an extra in the movie Shane and you know, I don't know if any of that is true, but Mom told me he told her. You know, being famous and he played the guitar. When he did take us with him, we'd hang out at bars and me and Tracy would be dancing on the bar top for these stupid drunk people at the bar and.

So I learned I liked that kind of attention, that I could be outgoing, but I just never really did anything for me after that.

Anyway, so then they got in a fight and he threw her around and tossed her out the door and made me and my sister eat hot chili (laughs) you know. "Eat it! I don't care if it's too hot, eat it!" And so we were here eating this fiery hot, Tabasco sauce hot kind of chili at five and four. Just looking at each other going, you know, I'm going to throw up. "Don't throw up you'll get in trouble." You know, and my mom calls the police, and the police come and they take my dad, and I was more angry at her about that than I ever was at him. I mean, I didn't give a shit, I mean, she would let him beat her up all this other time, you know? But now she's finally going to take a stand and she took my father away, and it really pissed me off. I was hurt. And then we ended up going and living with my grandparents and my grandparents still had four of their kids at home, out of the 13. And my Aunt Joy was about four years older than me, but it seemed like, you know, eons, because she was more mature and she did whatever she pleased, you know, Grandma and Grandpa, by the time they had 13, they didn't care what she did, as long as she was still breathing and alive it was fine, you know.

And so here's my mom, who was like the second girl and the fourth or fifth child, and here's my Aunt Joy who's doing whatever she pleases, and my mother's 25 years old or whatever and here's my Aunt Joy doing better, you know, sneaking out and going out with boys and doing whatever she wants. Then here's my mother who's not even allowed to go out on a date 'cause she's got kids to watch and my grandma won't do it. Then my younger, my Aunt Donna who's younger than my mom would bring her kids over and my grandma would watch them, but she wouldn't watch my mom's kids. Just all jealous and stupid. Bizarre.

But anyways

So we stayed there for about three years. And then we moved out into this trailer that my Aunt Willie, who was the oldest daughter, let my mom pay for. And my mom only got like $250 on her welfare check for the whole month. But my Aunt Willie gladly took the $250 a month for you know four years or some crap to get this crappy piece of crap trailer my mom was living in. And my mom just wasn't tidy and she wasn't capable of functioning on her own or in her own world or something. She was like lost, you know? I find that I'm much more capable of functioning on my own than I am with a partner, 'cause I don't know where to stop. But my mom didn't know where to start, she couldn't do it by herself. If somebody tell her what to do then she could do it. But anyways.

We lived in that house and then she married Joe. And then from that point on, like he made grass in the desert? (laughs) Was incredibly difficult task. You don't make grass in East Mesa or nobody there in that point of time did, it was just too much water consumption, it was just a waste. So, you know, you just had dirt, throw some rocks out and make it look like it was landscaped. But he made grass and we had a car, which my mother never owned a car. If we had to go do laundry, we'd like walk the mile and a half, two miles to my grandmother's house. All four of us kids, just trotting along with bags full of laundry over my grandmother's house. Just recently I said to my mom, "Why didn't somebody come and get us? I mean if we had to do laundry over there, why didn't somebody drive over and pick us up instead of making us walk in this heat?" "They wouldn't because if they came and got me then they wanted gas money, and I wasn't going to give them no gas money." A lot of meanness, pathetic jealousy, and ignorance in my mother's family.

So then, my mom had just about paid off this trailer with her welfare checks and Joe decided to sell the trailer and that's when we moved to Alabama. Well, he basically told my mom that that was a good thing to do. We sold it to another one of her sisters and then we moved to Alabama. He apparently borrowed some money from my grandparents and then all the money was gone. Which if you're running two businesses it's really difficult to embezzle anything because I mean, businesses take money, you know, for copiers, computer, and typewriters, and he had a restaurant and pans and pots, and employees. I mean I don't know how he was embezzling money with no money to embezzle, it had all gone out on expenditures. But supposedly what he was in jail for.

And then my grandparents like I said came out and got us, and we went back to Arizona and spent the last six weeks or so of my sixth grade year there and then we came back out to Alabama, and I just always thought I was better than my mom. Always thought I could do it better than my mom. At five I thought I was better than my mom. I thought I was better at controlling and maintaining my sisters, you know, brothers and sisters. I thought I was more capable of you know, doing the grown up things I saw other people doing but not my mom. I just always thought I could do it better and if I did it better than her then that was good enough, I mean, I didn't have to be Rockefeller because as long as I could do it better than her that was my guideline that was all that I needed to do.

And so anyways, we were living in the shack, Joe started touching me. And my mom saw him, and my grandma even apparently saw him – later on I found out – she's like you know, "I told your mother when I saw his hand up your shirt. . . And I was like "You saw that?" (laughs) What is the deal here? Any ways, she's like "I told your mother that that should not be allowed." And I was like if that was not allowed and was not appropriate you saw it and you knew it was inappropriate, then why didn't you do something about it? But nobody wanted to destroy my mother, so destroy the children, they're stronger, they can handle it. (laughs)

So anyway, he was doing all this stuff, and I was like cool, I'm getting some attention now, and my mom got pregnant with my little brother Tony, and she would just, you know, be sick and not comfortable, and getting heavier, and not breathing and you know he just didn't like it. So he kicked her out of the bed and then he had like me and Tracy sleep in the bed with him, and he kicked Tracy out of the bed and me and Shane, and kicked Shane out of the bed, me and Nancy, Nancy pulled the covers so he kicked her out of the bed because he was working; he needed his sleep, you know. And so here it is. My three brothers and sisters and my mom sleeping in the living room, and me and Joe, her husband sleeping in this bedroom with a blanket covered, you know, between the two rooms. It was kind of like this. [DS's kitchen and family room space] you know, there was just a big opening and there was a blanket up there so that his, he and my mom supposedly could have privacy. Then he kicked her out and he kicked all the other kids out, so what was the blanket still there for? If I were the mother and I thought, "Hmmm, he's not with me in the bedroom, so there's no need for privacy. Maybe I should just rip this blanket down." You know, but that didn't happen either.

And then one night he touched me he said, I said, "No." Because I just barely found out I was a virgin. Before that you know, people had touched me before, and I was like, "I'm not a virgin." So I talked to this girl and she's like "What makes you think you're not a virgin?" And I was like, well, this and this and this happened, so I'm not a virgin." And she's like, "Was there any blood?" I'm like "No", and she's like, "Then you're a virgin." You know, "You're a virgin!" So here I am, 13 years old, just barely realizing that I'm not tainted, you know not a virgin, and he's like touching me, and I'm like "No, I'm a virgin. I don't want to do this." And he's like "Well you know what it does to me when you sit on my lap. You know what it does; it's all your fault." And I was like "Oh, okay, so if it's all my fault, go ahead. "(laughs) If you think that it's all me, if I'm so powerful, that no man can control himself, then sure, go ahead. And of course he did. And I got pregnant. Which was so so weird, because my mom and him had been trying to get pregnant for like five years, the whole time they were together. They were trying to get pregnant. Suddenly she got her pregnant, and now I'm pregnant. And so of course, the, you know we go to the Health Department 'cause I can't go to the bathroom. And they're like, "Well, she's pregnant." My mom's like, "No, that can't be." Because she knows I've never gone anywhere, I've never been over to a friend's house, I've never had a sleep over, never anywhere but at home. So she knows that this is just impossible unless. ... So she's like, "No, that can't be." And they're like, "Yeah it is." So she's like, "Who's is it?" And I'm like,"Um." Because Joe had known, I don't know if men can tell how a uterus feels or what, but Joe had known that I was pregnant. And he told me I was pregnant. And he said when they find out, you've got to lie because if you don't lie, then I'm going back to jail. Now, whatever else was going on in my little emotionally retarded brain about feeling like I was in love with this man, the fact is when my mom was by herself our life was more insane than anything else, so, even if he hadn't been abusing me or giving me attention or any of those other things that happened, the fact of losing him and losing any stability and any normalcy in our life was just not okay.

So I lied. I said, "No, it was some kid at school, we went behind the bushes during playtime." Or something (laughs). So they're like, "Oh, okay, Well tell us his name, we're going to make this child responsible." And I'm like "No, I'm not going to tell you the name.." Because there was no name.

Anyway, so kicked me out of school right away. You can't go to school in Alabama if you're pregnant. It's just not okay; they're not going to do it. If you're pregnant, you're a piece of shit, go to hell, we don't care but you're not going to school. We don't want anyone else to know what people do. Anyway . . .

So they kicked me out of school, so I was home all day with my mother and we're folding clothes and watching soap operas because that's what grown ups do, right? (laughs). Has nothing to do with what you want to do, it has to do with what grownups do. And grown ups all watch One Life to Live, All My Children, and General Hospital and fold clothes and cook food, and that's what grown ups do.

So here I am in this predicament, I'm pregnant, my sister's getting the crap kicked out of her everyday at school because people know that she's got a sister who's pregnant. And of course nobody would've known, but my cousins live there, so my cousins told everybody. So here's my sister poor taking the brunt of everything because I'm pregnant.

Joe's still working at this vegetable stand, you know, making minimal money, but he goes to work everyday and we're still hauling water over in oil containers because we don't have running water at our house and ...

So one day we're watching the soap operas and one of the girls' fathers did something and such and such. My mom's a great talker, you know, she "If she ever found out her husband did this "or this or "If her husband ever cheated on her..." she'd Superglue his dick to his belly and you know, she'd cut his balls off... you know, whatever, just a bunch of wind. And this particular day it was about incest, and she's like, "If I ever found out my husband," dad a da, I don't know have any clue, but it was something she was going to take an action about, and I said, "Really? You'd do that? You'd get out, you'd get away from him? You'd" you know. "What would you do?" And she's like, "Well, yeah. I'd kill him" I'd do this, take his whatever. I'd just do something.' Which she's not good at.

So I said "Yeah, you know who it is? It's Joe. Joe's the father of this baby." And she's like "Why didn't you tell me before!?" And I was like, "Isn't it obvious?" Well, and a couple of other things happened too, because like after he found out, after my mom found out that I was pregnant, he was telling her that he was going to send me to a teen baby place where they take the baby and you never see it. Before it was all about well you don't want to tell him 'cause then

I'll be gone. Now he's like YOU DON'T TELL ANYBODY ANYTHING and he's like physically violent with me and you know, things were changing with a quickness as far as what was going to happen with me and this baby. And at that point, 13 years old, I thought there was nothing better in this world than to have a child that no matter what you did would still love you. Which is bullshit (laughs), you know I don't love my mom and she did some pretty strange things, you know at that point in time, my brain was on like well then I'll have a family of my own, and I'll take care of my own kids, and I'll do better than my mom, and it won't matter if I don't do great, 'cause as long as I do better than her, everything will be okay.

But then, you know, he's like you know physically being obtrusive and he's like "Don't you tell anybody. If you tell anybody I'll kill you." And I was like, "No you won't (laughs) You're too busy, you know, trying to be the good guy and trying to make everybody like you and trying to make everybody think you're normal. You're not going to kill anybody." But I wasn't exactly sure, either, because things were changing, like I said.

So I told her, and I was like, okay, now what we need to do is we need to get the kids off the bus and we need to get the fuck out of here. We need to go. We need to get on the road, get away. She's like well, hold on, I don't know what to do. I'm like, hold on? You said that if you found out your husband did this, you would do this. And you're not doing it. Which really shouldn't have shocked me, but at 13 I thought that my mom had some sort of moral compass about her, but.

So she goes up and talks to our Bishop, we're Mormon. So she goes up and talks to our branch President. She says "Dottie says that Joe's the father." So the Bishop drives her back out there. He's like "Why should we believe you?" and I'm like bbbtt, I don't care if you believe me or not, I know the truth and my mom knows the truth, even if she doesn't want to admit it." And he was like "Well, we need to catch him in the act." And I'm like, "Catch him in the act? What we need to do is get these kids, get them clothes, and get the fuck out of here. That's what we need to do." He's like, "No, what we need to do is we need to, you need to go ahead and sleep with him again. And when you get done, your mom will be in the bathroom and take all your clothes so that we can get to a rape testing center tomorrow." I'm like, "Hello! Wait a minute. Not! I only told her because she said we'd get the fuck out of here. You don't need to know, I know. When the baby's born you'll know." No, they wouldn't let that be.

So they proceeded to do this whole set up, manipulative little underhanded scheming thing, where you know, if Joe came home, I'd go sleep with him, he'd have sex with me and then they could test the panties, and prove it so that he would have some kind of punishment or something. And I didn't think about it this way then? Now I think about it, if he had thought in some weird recess of his mind that I had told, if he had figured it out, or if he had known, in his heart that I had told, we could have all been in danger. He could have killed us all to keep his secret. So they not only put me in danger, they put all my family in danger by playing this stupid game that didn't amount to anything anyways. But you know, grown ups know best, they do what they're supposed to do, whatever.

So went and had sex, went in the bathroom, gave my mom the clothes, changed into something else, and then we went to sleep, me and my mom went to sleep in the other bedroom. She says "I know that it doesn't help, but for whatever it's worth, I was molested too." And dad a dad a dad a da. And I just fell asleep because I was just like this is just too freaking bizarre. I mean even a soap opera wouldn't do this. (laughs). This is just freaking weird.

So I went to sleep and the next morning we went to Mobile and had the test done, you know they shave you and do a gynecological exam and all this stupid shit, you know, I guess trying to prove that Joe was having sex with me. But and it did, I got to eat food out at the restaurant that day and so it was kind of cool.

So I went to my Bishop then took me to the I don't know, some kind of mental place, the Mormon mental place where they have psychiatrists and different people who are supposed to help people in crises. And I sat down with this lady, and she's like well you know since this was your stepfather's child you can have an abortion. Since you were raped you can have an abortion. And I'm sitting there thinking to myself our church, ever since I was eight years old or younger, I've always known that abortion is just absolutely unacceptable. There's just no purpose for it, no reason for it, it's wrong, it's evil. But you guys are telling me here that, you know, well, given this situation, you can go ahead and have an abortion. No, it's the farthest thing from my mind, because in my perception, I was going to do it better than my mom and I wanted my baby to love me no matter what, and you know, all those things that a 13 year old believes instead of, you know, like what's best for the child or what's best for you. You know, you're just believing your own little world. Your own reality. And so I said, no, I'm not going to get an abortion.

So we went back and they were supposed to pick him up in town, and put him in jail? But they waited until he got all the way to the house before the cops come and get him and take him to jail. Do this whole big stupid thing. You know my sisters and brother were just sitting there crying 'cause they're like devastated that Daddy's leaving and you know because they're not being involved in that particular cycle right now. They're just like what, why's he going to jail. Why is he leaving us? And we were all pretty devastated. I mean , he was the only normalcy we ever knew. So, you know . . .

So then we moved into a different trailer, or somewhere else where, you know, supposedly nobody would know our situation and it was like Gilbertown, which is just like 30 miles outside of Butler. And of course we had other cousins there, so they made sure that everybody in the school knew, you know. So my sister's getting teased and bothered, you know, beat up and who knows what, I'm sitting at home making hamburger gravy and hanging out with my mom and her new baby, and you know it was just as surreal is a pretty accurate statement, it was pretty bizarre. And painful. I mean for the first time in my life I felt like I had something in common with my mom. But this was obviously not the common thing I wanted with my mom. To have her husband's child. (laughs) You know, it was just really ugly and...

So then, we stayed there for awhile, I don't even know how long, but I was about eight months pregnant when mom decided to go back out to Arizona. And so we get on a bus again, and here I am , this 13 year old, imagine this little scrawny fat pregnant girl, you know, just, pathetic and here are these people on the bus and they're all trying to pick me up. Oh my God. I mean even as young as 13, 14 whatever I was at that point, I knew that these people had to be the biggest losers on the face of the earth to be trying to pick up a pregnant 13 year old. Something is wrong with these people to be trying to hook up with somebody who was so not okay at that point. You know?

Anyways, we finally got out to Arizona, and they had a school for pregnant teenagers, because they realized that even if you're, especially if you're pregnant you need to have an education. Be able to function in the adult world. You know they taught you how to write a check and you know, balance a check book, and taught me how to crochet and taught me how to bake a cake and you know, different things. It was an interesting experience.

And then I had the baby, and my dad, Bruce, Conn, his birthday was apparently January 10th . And about January 10th, 11th, timeframe I started going into labor, my mom was like, "You're going to have your baby on your daddy's birthday." And I was like no hell no I'm not, which was completely outrageous because number one I never known when my daddy's birthday was before that, ever. In my conscious memory I'd never known that January was important for any purpose. Number two he had left us, and he never had come back and he had created this situation where my mom was so bizarre, you know, left us there. You know, I wasn't happy about that. But I guess I just wanted to be on her side, it was like hell no I'm not, so I didn't. I don't know if I had anything to do with it, but I waited until the 11th and had this baby. It was really cold there, and my grandmother lived in a house that my grandfather, was originally like a three room house. Like a small kitchen, a living room, and a bedroom, and then they added a bathroom and they added a little bit more to the kitchen and they added more rooms and it turned into like an eight bedroom house. From my grandpa just building more and more crap. You know, it was crap, there was cement floors and roaches, roaches everywhere, and the paneling, it was that straight board, it was no paint, you know you could see the tape in the board in all of the rooms. You know, just half-assed. But at least it was eight bedrooms to keep the rain off the people.

My baby was born and we went back to that house and it was really cold and she got like some kind of fever jaundice, something, she had to go to the hospital. And that was the scariest thing I ever done, was you know to have this baby and I was so proud of it, and she was so pretty and perfect and had all of her fingers and toes, and you know, she was mine. And then she's in the hospital and she's really really sick and may not live, and I was just terrified. I was like, "I don't want to do this no more, I don't want to be as grownup, don't want to try and do better than my mom. Don't want nothing."

Well it wasn't long before my mom moved out and had to you know, find a different place to live because she couldn't stand living with her parents. I mean she couldn't stand living by herself either, she couldn't function, but she could not stand living with her parents. So we moved out and moved into this neighborhood, was really, really bad. With these two little babies under a year old. It was like, oh are they twins, no they're not twins. As a matter of fact, this one's from her and this one's from me and here's all these blonde-haired people laying around you know the house. And there's these two little Mexican babies, you know, and they're not twins? What's up with that? . . . You know you don't want to say I was molested by my step dad, but you know there's a story behind it, there's this whole thing. And I was like, now, so I said you know, "Mom, the best thing for this baby would be to give her up." And put her up for adoption. And my mom's like, "Well, I'll stand behind you whatever you want to do."

So I went into foster care. My baby was eight months old, I was there for like two weeks. And my mom called me every day, "I miss you and Mandy, I miss my baby, I miss my baby, I miss my baby." And eventually it just got so, I felt so guilty for taking my mother's BABY away from her, that I went back home.

So here I am, back home, with all these people in a two bedroom apartment in the middle of town, in this really really horrible neighborhood, you know. Once again my sister's going to school, she's being beat up by little Mexican people, you know, it was just outrageous, but you know, no one was concerned about them. There's always so much trauma

JR: So, what happened to your daughter?

DS: I gave her up

JR: You gave her up

DS: Well I spent that first three years really thinking that, you know, whatever I did was okay. And that you know, my child would still love me, no matter what, and you know as long as there's mother's love, that's what my mom kept saying, you know, as long as there's mother's love then that's all that takes no matter what you screw up your kids will still love you.

And then she had like some kind of nervous breakdown. And so she put us all into foster care. Which completely blew out of the water the whole prospect that I was to keep my child because there's always mother's love, but then when things get tough for her she can just kick us off the curb. You know.

And the first foster home I was in me and my child were both in foster care together. And the foster mother had gone to Idaho to take care of her mother who had had a heart attack. And during the course of that time while she was gone, her husband started molesting me. And I say molesting me but at that point I thought that I was so powerful that no man could ever control himself that, you know, I was just this little sexual energy emanating from me at all times, and you know, that it was my fault that nobody could keep their hands to themselves because you know, I was just this little nymph or something, you know?

And so we were having this sexual relationship and then we went back up to Idaho, we went to Idaho, and she's like I want to adopt you and we'll all move up here to Idaho, I want to adopt you and keep you and Amanda here with us. And I was like no, she's like well why not? Because I don't want to be here, I don't want to be in Idaho. And fact of the matter was I knew that it was wrong,

I mean it was wrong to be with somebody's husband anyways. But then when you're with that woman, you feel like you are betraying that woman, you know, you can kind of ignore it at first, but then when you're around them then you're like oh yeah, this is kind of shitty for me to be doing this. And of course it was all my fault because I was so powerful, so you know I had to get away so that he wouldn't want me anymore. Had nothing to do with the fact that this man was like a freak and that he had had affairs on her numerous times that she had chosen to ignore and forgive him for. Or that you know, here I am in their care and he's not acting like a father, he's acting like a man. But none of that played into it, all it was my power. I was just so completely un - - nobody was able to keep their hands off of me, you know, it was just my power.

At one point at this point I was 16. An my grandfather was going to teach me, my Grandpa Thompson who was always my father figure if there was nobody else around I'd give Father's Day gifts to my grandpa. And always my father figure, was going to teach me how to drive. So he had this job where he'd like drive down these, he was basically security for this big Arizona project where they were going through the entire state to make water available to all the cities. And so he was just making sure that no kids came and got on the machinery at night and messed with it or got hurt, fell off or died or something. That was basically his job, just to secure the area and make sure that nobody got hurt. And so during this period of time, he would teach me how to drive. He had this big like dirt hauling truck kind of, big stick shift and the whole deal, and he was going to teach me how to drive this big truck so that you know, no matter what I'd have a job that I could do, you know, I could be a truck driver and you know, and support my family.

And so I was out there learning how to drive, and all of the sudden one night he's; we'd have lunch out there, you know at his dinner break or whatever and he gives me this big old sloppy wet lip kiss, and I'm like WHAT! STOP! You know, it's bad enough that all these other people can't keep their hands off of me, but you're my actual family. And of course I went and told my mom, like Mom, I'm not going back driving with Grandpa. She says "Well, why not? You need to learn how to drive." Well I'm like because he kissed me on the lips." She's like "That son of a bitch." And so she goes and talks to my grandma about it. And my grandma says, "He wouldn't do that." My mom says, "Well I don't know whether he did it or not. But that's what Dottie said." You know? So here I am again, you know this person that nobody, not even my family can manage to keep themselves away from. I'm just this like whatever, this sexual energy.

And it just felt like everybody was, like there was no safe men. And there weren't, there was none. Because I was so powerful, you know, and the opposite of that would have been oh everybody's victimizing me, but no, I couldn't feel like everybody was victimizing me, I felt like I was so powerful that I had this ability to, you know, make the most sane man lose his mind, and you know, want to have sex with me. And later on when I talked to my grandpa about it, I was like "Grandpa why'd you do that?" You know because eventually I did have a relationship with him again. "Why'd you do that?" He's like "Well I just wanted to make sure you weren't having sex with any of those little boys that you were hanging around with. And I figured if I put it to you that you wouldn't be doing it with other people..." And I was like NO! I was out there having sex with all those little boys. "But I still wouldn't kiss you on the mouth. Freak."

So then I gave my baby up for adoption. And everybody in my family wanted me to give it to them. She was three years old at this point. But I realized that this was just screwed. I was screwing her up, I was screwing me up. Neither one of us was benefiting. And she definitely was not going to forgive me at some later date. For all the shit I was dragging her through.

So I decided to give my baby up for adoption and like my mom wanted her, and my aunts wanted her, and I'm sitting here looking at all these people, and I am 16 at this point, and I'm sitting there going, I know that you guys have already screwed up everything that you've touched. I'm not giving my precious child to you to screw up more. Number one, part of the purpose was to get her away from the fact that her and Tony were brother and sister. If she was still in my family, she would still be Tony's sister/niece, you know? No that's not going to happen.

So it took a long time for my family to forgive me for that because somewhere in the dim reaches of these people's minds, it's like embedded, ingrained, inbred, I don't know, but theirs a family's love, a mother's love, you know it doesn't matter what you do to your kids because they'll love you anyway. It's because, look what my mom did, and look what I've done to my kid, and they still love me, so you know, very pathetic and disturbing cycle.

Because my mom had taken me to the rape counselor, and because I had to go through a trial with Joe, which he only got 18 months anyways because I was in Alabama, I was a consenting adult (laughs). So it was considered statutory rape, even though I was sitting here months and months pregnant.

And I never forgave my mom for putting me through that too because she still to thirty years later, has never told me who molested her. But she put me out there in the spotlight. She made me tell, she made me go to court proceedings. She made me tell these men that were probably getting off, you know, putting me through the ringer. "So how many times did you have oral intercourse," You know, "What exactly did you do?" You know, and I'd be like well, "Six" I don't know.... I wasn't counting, you know and it just felt like they were more concerned about the details than they were about putting him in jail.

Anyway so she put me through all of this, so my whole family knew, anybody that my mother came in contact with, knew. Never go through the story without explaining how her daughter had sex with her husband, and had a baby, you know. There was just no safe place. So eventually I got away from her and I went into a foster family where I wasn't with my child, I gave her up for adoption. And didn't talk to my mom, you know, she was still under the impression that she could control things and make people do what she wanted them to do.

It was just weird, it was a weird experience.

So I get out into foster care and finally one group of people finally, one man, one family's husband actually acted like a father instead of a child molester. And I stayed there for a year. I really pissed the wife off because I was just this little know-it-all teenage don't have to follow your rules kind of thing going on. Because I had basically been the boss of everybody, in my household, and then I have to come here and act like I'm all subservient and babysitting for other people's kids. You know, washing dishes and doing chores. It was just a bizarre transformation that they expected me to become. You know, I didn't know how to become a teenager, you know, because I had always been a little grown up. By necessity.

So, so I stayed there for a year, and finally she got pissed off about enough and I had to move. I went over to some other foster home, and the lady died. Moved to another foster home and they were out of town, they decided to go on vacation, but they were going to let me stay in their home. So, here I was 17 years old, basically maintaining this household of somebody else's, basically house sitting for this family while they left on vacation. And then eventually I went into the last foster home I was in, the Weirs, and they were awesome, they were neat people. She was a very Christian lady, she was very loving, she'd tell you what was expected from the get-go, so that you couldn't, you know. I think everybody else was kind of floundering around, not knowing what to do with a teenage girl, but she had teenagers, so she said, this is expected, "I expect you to wash your clothes, I expect you" you know, "to make your bed. I expect you to be at breakfast at such and such, I expect" blah blah blah. And it made it easier for me to try to morph into this person that everybody was trying to help me become.

Really heavy into church, didn't screw around, didn't do anything with the boys. Finished high school, you know, did all the high school dances, I was just thinking about this the other day, too. This was my first car accident. I was driving her car, I had turned 18 and had finally gotten my license and I was driving her car, and I took the corner too fast and I crashed into the person in the left turn lane. And they never did anything to me. They never beat me up or you know made me feel bad or you know, they never did anything to me you know, they just let it go. Their insurance paid for it and it was done.

They gave me braces, which made me feel like I was more like other people my age.

Never quite got the part about how to be a family. Because you know there's always somebody in the family that you have to hate. At least in my family there is. You know, there's somebody that's got to be on the outs. And since I didn't want to be the one on the outs, I'd make somebody else the out one. I'd be the in one. I'd do anything that Mrs. Weir said, you know, if she said climb the top of the roof and stand on your head for four hours, I would've done it. You know, because I was just so impressed with her.

And they gave things like Scriptures for Christmas, you know. They'd put my name on Scriptures and gave me a set of Scriptures. They gave me like you know a gold bracelet and diamond earrings and stuff and I was like WOW, this is what a family's like? I thought, you know, family was like see who we can take advantage of and who we can use for our purposes at the moment. (laughs) You know, this was a completely different experience for me.

And I felt a part of it, you know, she didn't you know make me feel left out or I remember the first foster home I was in, they were like really into her family would do things and I always felt even when I was with them, at these like Easter parties, or Christmas parties or whatever. I always felt out of it, you know, like these people are looking at me going, "Who the hell are you and what are you doing here?" You know, you're taking away from our normal little family situation here, you know? But the Weirs, they didn't ever make me feel like that. They just cared about me, and they took care of me, and were kind, and she'd write me poems, and letters and you know when I did something wrong, she'd leave a little note tucked into my drawer where my clean clothes were put, I mean it was just was very different from anything I had experienced before. Because these people were all about giving and not taking. Not trying to manipulate people or you know, putting somebody out and leaving them out in the cold while somebody else is having a good time, you know, it was...

So that was a good experience for me. But then as soon as I graduated, I wanted to be out on my own, 'cause I was already 18 and I was ready to be out on my own. I had been dating this Mormon missionary, this missionary who had gone away and come back, he was 21 years old. And of course, you know, he was telling me that he was going to marry me, that we were going to be married. And of course I wanted to believe that, you know, I'd have sex with him. And eventually at some point his father found out that we were having sex, and he's like: "I'll tell you what, Darrell, I'll send you to school, you won't have to pay for anything, if you'll just get away from this girl." (laughs) I was like, so he did, he went to school and his father paid for everything, and he left me.

And I was like, but I wasn't having sex with anybody else, you told me you were going to marry me that's why I was having sex with you. And now you're not. Now you're gone and now you're and now I'm the bad guy, you know?

And then you know, right after that, that was just about all I really needed to let me know that nothing in my life was going to turn out right anyway? So I started smoking, and started drinking, started drinking coffee, everything the church said to do, not to do, don't do this, okay, I'm doing it, all right, screw you. I hate you. Get out of my face. Don't tell me what to do, nobody's going to tell me what to do, you know.

And so I went ahead and did my little promiscuous bit, and I was having an affair with three different guys at the same time, and I turned up pregnant. I was like okay, well. I just gave a baby up, because I knew I was screwing it up, and I didn't have a father for the child. So, I'm not going to do this, so I went and had an abortion. And the people that I was staying with at that time, the lady I was working for, didn't believe in abortion, she had had one, but she didn't believe in abortions anymore, she thought that that was a wrong idea, that I should have just had the baby and given it up. I was like no, umm umm, no, I've done that before, and that didn't work for me either. So we're no t doing that.

So I had an abortion, and of course they kicked me out. They couldn't stand that, they couldn't tolerate that. So I went and stayed with my grandparents. Here I am, bleeding like a stuck hog, miserable, in pain, my grandfather and his little moral issues, you know. And just sick, you know, just sick. I knew that a child was a child, I had a lot of guilt about it, you know, here I am, trying to deal with this emotional trauma and my family, and my own emotional trauma of my choices, anyways,

So, I got through it, and my aunt had been going out with this boy when she was in high school, and he was so in love with her that he like put his hand through, his fist through a windshield, and like he was some kind of jock football player when they had met. But because he had did that, he had ruined all the tendons in his hand so he couldn't play football anymore? But from that time on, for like the next six years, he'd hung around with my grandma's family, you know, just hung out there. Darwin was the bill boy, you know, you wanted to have somebody go buy you some booze, he would go do it, you know, he would just the good old boy, like an old she, you know, you didn't really like him, you didn't really not like him, but he'd let you use him, so go ahead. You know, and... No real feelings for him, just the fact that you know, he'd do things for you, anyway....

So I got a job, he got me a job up where he was working, and we started working there. And then he bought me this pair of shoes, really cool pair of running shoes. I'd never run, that was never my thing (laughs). But he bought me this really $45 pair of running shoes. And I'd never had a pair of shoes that expensive in my life.

And I just felt taken care of, I know that sounds stupid, but those shoes represented him taking care of me in a way I hadn't been before, so I married him. (laughs) And I was 19 and I'm married, and I'm thinking I can do this, shit, pffft, you know go to work, come home, have sex, drink a beer, you know, go to a bar, do whatever you want. Here, you're married. And that's weird thing because if you're married, you can go into a bar even though you're underage, because your husband's with you, did you know that?

JR: No

DS: Well, I didn't know that either. Nobody carded me when I was with Darwin. So about the time I turned 21, I wanted to go to the bars by myself. But of course I had no idea about boundaries, or what was appropriate or anything you know. So I'm going to bars and picking up guys and you know, hanging out and just doing whatever I wanted to and he's letting me because he basically just wants somebody to be there, you know, he doesn't really care who. Just kind of lonely and didn't want to be by himself so, he let me do whatever I wanted.

At one point I ended up having an affair with this guy that I was working with, he was my boss and of course you know, it was like '86 '87 '88 time frame. Just about the time when all the sexual harassment issues were coming out, you know, and you know, did he harass you? And what's sexual harassment? They're like well you know, if he told you that he would give you a job or a better job or more pay or la la la for sex then that's sexual harassment. And stupid me, I'm so pathetic, that I think that you know, I'm just so powerful woman that that's why nobody can keep their hands off of me, I'm like no, he didn't do nothing. He didn't do nothing. It was nothing, nothing happened, you know, protecting this jerk that had sexually harassed every person in the frigging building practically, you know? But I was protecting him. Any ways

So and it wasn't bad enough that I would like you know, take off from work. And like go home? And Joe would meet me at , you know, and we'd have sex, and then we'd go back to work. And my husband's there at work this whole time. It was weird.

But I didn't feel ashamed of it, I just felt like, you know, I was finally getting mine, I was doing everything I wanted to, you know?

And then my girlfriend moved in with us because we had a two bedroom apartment, my girlfriend moved in with us. And me and my girlfriend were out at the pool one day and this cute guy walked up. He started talking to me, I was look I'm married back off. And so then he went and started talking to her, and they started being boyfriend and girlfriend. And you know that was okay. He moved in with her and they were you know, together, whatever. Then they decided to move out, and ... Eventually he and I started to have a relationship. I was taking him away from her, you know, 'cause I'm so powerful. And my husband's stupid, because he's like sitting there knowing. And there's no way you can really not know when your spouse is having an affair. Unless you just don't want to . You know? I mean, aside from the fact that I was always very sexual, and that he would get it any time he wanted it. I mean, there had to have been telltale signs of me not paying as much attention to him or I don't know. Just it seemed like he would know. And of course he didn't act like he knew, and so I thought I was getting away with something. And it was all this illicit thing like Joe and me recreating my past and (laughs) disturbing.

So anyways finally I decided that I'd quit, quit my husband. So I left my husband, and me and Rick moved out together, and you know of course Ginger, who was my roommate before that. She was like coming to our house and popping balloons, and pulling shit out of our house into the yard and stuff and doing all this psychodrama and I was like WHATEVER.

And then we moved to Phoenix, and we were living in this little apartment that had the wall bed, you know, that you put up in the wall. And it was just this little studio and it was stupid, but we were in looove, so it was okaaay. And he was just too cute, I mean, he was kind of scary, actually, he kind of had these bulging Italian eyes, kind of like Sylvester Stallone, you know, and then he had this kind of heart-shaped face, but he was that dark skin, dark Mediterranean or Italian looking skin. And I always hated babies with blonde hair, I thought they were the ugliest things on the earth, you know (laughs) these babies with like no hair or towhead, or you know, all these scary white headed kids. And I liked the fact that, you know, Amanda had this beautiful brown skin and brown hair, because I had never had brown skin, I mean people used to say like "Let me connect the dots" because of my freckles, but I'd never been, even my tan is just like most people's white, you know, even if I lay out in the sun for 150 years, I am still not never going to get tanned, and I wanted that for my children. Wanted my children to have the ability to tan if they wanted to.

And he had a kid, and he had left his kid, abandoned his wife and you know, he was just a flake. There was no good reason, no intelligent reason to be with this man, but here I am. And, you know, I'm investigating co-dependency, 'cause during that period of time I was reading a magazine like there's a new thing, and it's called "co-dependency" and this is what they do, you know, and I was like "OH! That's me" And I was like this is what it says, it says you do this and this and this, and he's like "That's not you." And I'm like "Yes it is! It's me, it's me!"

So then him and I moved from Phoenix to Mississippi. (laughs) Which was right across the road from Alabama. It didn't make any sense, nothing we ever did, nothing to do with Rick ever made any sense. I was in love, and it wasn't something that I had ever done, I never even pretended to be in love with Darwin. I was just comfortable. You know? He was comfortable, I was comfortable, it was okay. And so suddenly here I am with this person and I'm in love and I'm willing to give up everything and willing to give up my furniture, my house, and my possessions, and my husband, and my friends for this man, so that must mean I'm in love. You know?

So we moved over to Mississippi, and I'm working at Pizza Hut as a waitress. Busting my tail. Having a really difficult time because in Mississippi they're real closed, cycles too that they're (imitates Southern drawl) You're not from around here, are you? You know, and I'd be like "No and I'm grateful for it" you know, or they're "Who you related to?" "What you doing in this part of the country?" "Why are you here?" You know, and I'd be like "Well I just landed here and now I'm here, and I'm not related to any of you crazy fricks.

So there was this one woman at the Pizza Hut, she was the boss, and my cousin, when we were first living in Waynesboro. And my cousin said, "She's a bitch. You don't need to go to work there. She's just a real bitch." And I was like, "A bitch? I can be friends with a bitch. I can understand a bitch." 'Cause I'm a bitch, you know. I like befriended her. And we ended up moving down to Hattiesburg with her and that's where people would be like "You're not from around here, are you?" You know, and I'd be like, "Nope." And like "Where are you from?" "Mesa." "What's a big city girl like you doing out in a small town like this?" And I'd be like, "You guys have a college, Mesa doesn't have a college." Why. Mesa isn't that big. It's out west, and it's more civilized, but it's not really a big city, you know, I mean, compared to New York, Mesa's a fly speck on the map, you know? But people were really somehow intimidated by that or questioned it, what was my purpose in being here, and I had no purpose in being there except for to be with Rick.

So Rick's telling me all about how he thinks that my friend Becky is so sexy, and I'm like "Well then just go sleep with her." So he did, and they moved in together (laughs). So here I am in the middle of Hattiesburg, Mississippi, this big phht. When my boyfriend just left was the only person that I had, you know, ever loved, had just left and went over to be with my girlfriend. You know, basically done me the way I had done Ginger, you know. So that was the first thing I did, I called Ginger up, I said, "Well," you know, "tables have been turned, you don't have to send no bad karma my way anymore. (laughs) He's with somebody else, he did it to me, it's okay. Don't hate me, don't try to send out an assassin for me," whatever freaky drama thing that you're going to do. And she's like "Well, I'm living with" so and so "and they really don't want to hear your name, so don't call here anymore." I'm like "Okay. You know, I just wanted to let you know." Which is actually bizarre, I don't know why I wanted her to know, I guess I thought it might make her feel better.

So I just did it, and I laid in bed for the next two weeks or something, I couldn't work, couldn't function. My back was killing me and I was in pain and I was alone, and, alone is the worst. For me. I mean I would be with a total piece of shit guy, but if I was alone, I couldn't do it, I couldn't function. I mean I could do everything in a relationship, but I couldn't function if I was just straight by myself alone. There was just no reason, no purpose to it. I didn't count that much. I wasn't important enough to do it for myself. You know.

So I went to the doctor, I'm like "My back hurts, my kidneys hurt, I have a kidney infection or something, something's wrong." Something's wrong, something's wrong. And he did all these tests and he's like "Nothing's wrong with you. All these tests came back clear; nothing's wrong with you." I'm like "No, no, something's really wrong." He's like "You're co-dependent, go to this group." (laughs) I knew it I knew I was co-dependent.

So I went to this group, and they're like damn girl, you know because you tell this sob story about how your boyfriend just left you and you're all alone, blubbadablubbadabla. And they're like you just need to stand up and get away from him. You need to get your income tax check and just go back home. I'm like, Yeah.

So once again, I gave him the option, I'm like "Oh Rick, I'm going to take my income tax check and go to, move to California, and live with my sister. But if you want me to, I'll stay here and spend the whole money on you. (laughs) He's like no, go to California, get the fuck out of my face. Like Okay, bye, are you sure? Bye are you sure? (laughs) We'll live together, me and Becky will live together, we'll share you. (laughs) Just don't leave me. Ah. And it was yucky. Anyways. So I went to California, and I started working two jobs. And I got out on my own, I was living with my sister at first, and got out on my own, was doing my own thing.

This guy, this little kid, little pimply faced kid, basically, started like taking me home, driving me home because I walked to work. Had two jobs where I could walk to work and back home. And I'd like get off of Denny's at like 3:00 in the morning, he'd drive me home, you know, he'd stay at Denny's till 3, take me home, well, he's taking care of me basically. And still wasn't doing anything with him, didn't want to have anything to do with him, kind of you know, okay, if you insist. I'll ride in your truck so I don't have to walk home, you know, after being at one job for eight hours and then going to Denny's and working for eight hours. I was pretty tired. So you know if you want to drive around and waste your gas on me that's you know okay with me. And it didn't last long eventually I had sex with him just out of guilt, you know, it's like okay, you've done so much for me. He took me to like Magic Mountain. You've done so much for me I'll go ahead and give you some sex. And that's when I found out that he was HUGE (laughs). It's like, okay, yeah we can do this, we could be in a relationship. And so we were. His mom was so freaked, they were like real Lutheran. But and her kid was 21, but it was just really freaky for her to think of her son, her little boy, having sex, you know? So we smoothed it over with them, we're not having sex. See there's a room and there's a room. Of course we did, we slept in the same room, but, you know, as long as she didn't know, it was fine.

We'd go to church with the parents on Sunday, and you know, basically playing house, basically. Not very good, you know, not in any well kept way. I was not a perfect wife, mother, or I didn't keep house well or any of those things that women are supposed to do. But we had sex and we lived together, and you know, shared the bills and stuff. Even then I told Chris, at that time I was like, "Dude, if Rick ever says that he's coming to California, ever? You're out of here. I don't care if we've been together for 15 years, you're out of here. If Rick ever looks me up and finds me, you're out of here." (laughs) And he's like, "Okay." Because I guess you know he knew that when somebody was done with me, they weren't going to come back for me again.

And so I had this relationship with him. Then I went up to Idaho and visited with my mom who had married some man and moved to Idaho. Had another kid. And my brother Shane had gone to Germany, he was eight at the time, and come back from Germany, and my mom decided she wanted to get him out of foster care because these people they were rich, and they were wealthy, and they were kind. They wanted to adopt my brother, but somewhere in the back of my mom's mind: mother's love is best. You know. Blah blah blah. These people were taking care of my brother for like three years. Had done nothing but good things for him. But my mother still wanted him back because it really wasn't about what was best for him. It was about what she wanted, you know. And so she had taken him back to Idaho.

Well, I go up there. He's like I guess he must have been like 16 or 17 by this time when I go up to Idaho. And he's like holding my mom down with an arm and having a pair of scissors in his hand. "Shit bitch, I'll kill you !" And I'm like WHOA (laughs) this is not okay. Because, you know, my mom just makes people react. (laughs) So you know I was like this is not okay, somebody's going to die, you know. Somebody's going to get hurt really bad, you know. He had been living up there for I don't know, two years or something, and he was just, he was done, he was done with her. He had been doing drugs, he had been drinking, he had been smoking pot, and whatever he wanted to, and my mom wasn't making any sense, and he wasn't going to listen to her, anyways, even if she did make sense because my mom's never commanded any respect.

And so and I guess by that point, you know, he was kind of like well, look I was with the Cardins and I was fine. You wanted me back, you've ruined my life, you're going to fucking pay for it. That's just where it's at. You're not going to get out of here free and clear. You know? You threw everybody else away, you've done this stupid stuff all this time, and now you know, you want to bring your family back and like be this happy little - - it's not going to work. You know? You're not the person that needs to be in control of us.

And so I took him to California with me. Which was totally stupid, he's not my job. He's my little brother, but he's not my responsibility. And if I had, you know, called DPS or HRS or you know Department of Children and Services

[Department of Children and Families] or whatever, if I had done any of those things, somebody would have come in and put that to a quick halt. But I didn't even think of those options. I thought well, you know, I'm not going to let somebody be killed. And know that that could've been stopped.

So I bring him down to California, and I'm like "Look Shane, you know, I know you're a little bad ass up in Blackfoot, Idaho, and I know you like to do your own thing, and you want to act like whatever you are, but the fact of the matter is, here in California, you cross over the wrong person, you piss somebody off, and they'll kill you. Gang members will en masse come upon you and kill you. You cannot be a little bad ass, you need to calm yourself down and act like a normal human being." Nah, not going to happen. Then, you know, I told him, "Well you need to go get a job." And not going to happen. And he and Chris started hanging out together, and smoking pot, and hanging out and you know, going to titty bars, or whatever they were doing, I don't know, but you know it was just not good.

So right about this time, I'm like, okay, this particular chapter's coming to an end. I cannot deal with either one of these immature people anymore. So, there was a guy at work, that I was working, at a taxi company. And he was a Navy SEAL, and he was a Tae Kwon Do triple black belt. He was this, and why he was working as a taxi driver, you know, it never came across me to think. (laughs) Why the hell have you fallen all the way down to being a taxi driver if you've got all these fabulous skills, you know. But he was all these things, exotic and wonderful things that I thought that I really liked. And we talked, and I told him you know basically about my life, because I always felt like if I didn't that somewhere along the line, somebody in my family would say, "Well did she tell you about Amanda?" you know, and if I hadn't then I'd be busted, which would make me feel like I had lied, you know, so I was always telling everybody this whole stupid long story about my child. And I guess at that point he felt like he was rescuing me and I felt like I was being rescued, and we took my brother, Shane, and Chris my boyfriend, and dumped them off at my sister's house in Arizona and came back to California and lived there for a couple of years together. (laughs) Which was so wrong. I mean I cannot tell you how guilty I have felt after that, that I had dumped this man, this bizarre man that wasn't related to our family on to my sister, but at the time, it didn't matter to me. All that mattered was get them out of my face.

And so, you know, here are these two freewheeling men and my little sister Nancy, who had been institutionalized at one point, who had gotten out of the institution, and married some guy that had been in the institution with her when she turned 18, and like three weeks later, a month later, he ends up, they found him in his bed, dead, with a big old imprint of a frigging cast iron frying pan on his chest. (laughs) And she disappears out of the state, you know we're all going okay, she killed her husband. No charges were ever made against her, she never had a warrant out for her arrest because they hadn't even talked to her about it, you know. She just disappeared. So she's kind of got this hanging over her.

So this woman and some man that she had met in California on a mattress under a bridge, (laughs) were procreating, my sister, my littlest sister, Nancy the one that had been institutionalized, the one that had supposedly killed her husband, they were living with my sister, Tracy, Shane was living with my sister, Chris was living with my sister, and my mom would dump my little brother Tony off at my sister's for the summer. So, you know, I real quick got out of being the parent in the family. Tracy took over that role, you know? Because obviously there's got to be a parent even if the parent isn't the parent, right? Your mom can't parent, somebody else will step up to the plate, because, everybody's got to have a home to come home to.

So me and Jeff, we were all smart, we were smart people, you know, we were all into Twelve-Step groups and getting our shit straight. He had apparently tried to commit suicide at one point, and his family had sent him money to come from Georgia to California. We'd go over to his family's house every week, and I hated his family, just like I hated Chris's family, just like I hated Darwin's family, because it didn't make sense to me, I saw these people and the way they acted and what they did, and I could see through it, I knew that it was just a sham, trying to make me feel bad about myself, you know. That they acted like they accepted me but they really didn't. That's been a continual string running through my whole relationships, all my relationships, I'd like the man or I wouldn't like the man, whatever my relationship to him was. But his family and I would never get along, you know, I was always the whore or bitch or the you know, some thing that they could point out that I wasn't good enough for their baby or their brother or, you know, whatever he was.

And did a lot of Twelve-Step groups, did a lot of working on myself, and reading, and up unto that point I knew that Amanda had been important, that whole process that had happened was important to me, I just didn't know exactly why it was important? What it was supposed to teach me, what I was supposed to have gotten from it? You know, except for that you don't bring children into the world without a mom and a dad. But other than that I couldn't figure out what the gist of my life was supposed to be. So I started reading about like Courage to Heal and The Dance of Anger, and you know, Bradshaw. And I was like oh okay, now I get it. The shame that binds me. Okay, yeah that's it. It's all because of shame. (laughs) Or, you know, whatever reading I would be doing, I'd be like , oh, okay, I get it, it's all because of the incest. Or it's all because my mother's a retard (laughs). You know, whatever my trauma my life crises at the time was all because of whatever I was reading about, you know, because I could gain things from things. Learn and understand things. It wasn't like I would just read it and go, huh what did that say? What did that mean? You know.

So I was trying to get better, but I still wasn't there, in this relationship with this man who I guess I made him dependent on me. I enabled him to become dependent on me? And once he was really good and dependent, couldn't do anything else, I'd like slam him for it. (laughs) Like "Yes, you stupid son of a bitch, I can't believe that you let some woman [you know] take care of you, and why can't you go get a job, and what's your problem." You know, and this whole thing, and I was horrible, I was horrible. But, you know, he'd basically keep the house clean when he was home and you know.

JR: Let' see. You JR: Let's see. You were living in California.

DS: I was with Jeff.

JR: If you want, we can move on. How is it you came to Florida?

DS: Well, I was with Jeff, and I was doing lots of work, I had a really great therapist named Jan. Was really weird when you called I was like Jan, Jan Rosenberg, did she find me, did she track me down? (laughs) Doing a lot of hard work on my mom, and my relationships, and had done enough, I guess just to be · dangerous, you know? (laughs) Just enough to be dangerous, not enough to be better, but just enough to be dangerous. Had realized that I was a sex addict, and that as long as I was being honest with my partner, and saying you know, look so and so is paying attention to me, and I just need to let you know that and not that anything happened or anything's going to happen, he was paying attention to me, I need to let you know that, because if I don't, it will get in my head and I'll be like oh what if this were to happen and I would get into this whole fantasy? About somebody else being better and then you know, get off into that tangent. And then have to start all over. And it's like.

So I wasn't being an active sex addict, was doing my therapy and I was doing lots of Bradshaw work, and meditation, and stuff like that. And one day I went into group, and I said, "Well, I decided that I needed to make a change." And they're like Oh yeah, well good great job what are you going to do, go to school? You know, and I was like, "No, I'm going to go in the Army." (laughs). And they're like "what?" "Yeah, I'm going to go to basic training starting next week," and blah blah blah, whatever I was saying. "Well, are you sure?" "Yeah, I'm sure."

So, I had to get divorced from my husband before I could go in the Army because, if you're a woman, you want to go in the Army, Navy, Marines, or the Air Force, you have to have a divorce, or you have to have your husband's permission. And even though I hadn't lived with this man for like ten years, was still married to him. (laughs)

JR: To Darwin.

DS: Yes, way back when. And so I sat down with him, we met at a restaurant to sign the papers and everything. And I sat down with him and he's like, "Well, you know, I've got this cabin up in Snowflake, and me and my mom got" this "and we did" that, and "we have "this and that and the other thing. You know, "we could try again." And I'm looking at him, going (laughs) "Are you insane? I mean you haven't seen me for eight years to be with me. Why would you want to be with me through all this nonsense..." Anyways, it was just incredible to me that somebody, anybody would be so pathetic whatever that they would prefer to be in a relationship that obviously didn't work than to sign the divorce papers and get on with it, you know.

And maybe that's love, I don't know, but that wasn't my perception of love, I was just like all weirded out.

So I took my little old divorce papers and I went in the Army, and I had cut off all my hair because I knew that you know, it doesn't really take a lot to make a guy interested in a woman. But if she's cute, and she attempts to be cute, then any man will pay attention to her, you know, and that's not what I wanted to do.

I went in there, I knew it was going to be hard, I knew I was going to have to work my butt off, I knew I was going to have to learn how to run, I knew I was going to have to learn how to shoot, and I didn't need to be distracted with some stupid boy. And stupid boy things. So I cut all my hair off and I went in the Army, and I went into this basic training with these kids that were like right out of high school, you know, like 17 18 year old kids. Here I am 28 years old. I mean I was right at the cut off before they wouldn't ever let me go in the Army, you know?

Of course I went in and I was like "Why can't you guys just follow the rules? The rules aren't that hard, just follow the rules!" (laughs) And of course they were all about trying to get away with something, you know, and "Well if I sleep with the drill sergeant, you know, maybe I won't have to do my two mile run," (laughs) You know? All this stuff and I'm like ehhhhh. Just go with the flow, follow the rules, do what you're supposed to do.

So I went into Basic, and I got through it, which was an amazing, an amazing amazing thing to me. I had no clue that I could physically or emotionally do it. Because before I'd been on lithium and stuff. And here I am straight faced, no smoking, no drinking, physically active, running through these things, and road marches and you know, shooting guns, you know, diving into holes and you know this whole thing, I had no concept that I was capable of functioning in that way.

And the other part of that was I had this big escape, you know, if I just couldn't handle it anymore, if I didn't want to do it anymore, I'd say well, I have a disease that you guys need to get me out of here. You know. So I had that open to me at any time if it ever got too hard I could just say, "Well, I've got this disease, so you might need to get me out."

And through my Twelve-Step working I had learned that I had to be very honest all the time. And through my basic Army training, I had turned that whole thing into - - the Army doesn't want you to follow the rules? They just don't want you to get caught not following the rules. And that's what the whole game is. The whole game in the Army, probably all the armed services. You just don't get caught doing the wrong thing. You know? Do what you want, we're not, you know, we're colonels and we're this, and we're telling you you have to salute and do this and that and the other thing, and if we walk up to you, we want you to do the things that we told you that we are supposed to do. But on your free time do whatever you want, as long as you don't get caught doing the wrong thing. So it was very anti-honest (laughs) very not real. You don't be real, you don't say who you really are, do what you really do or think how you really think. You have to keep your shoes, dress right dress, and you have to keep your hangers so and so such and such, and you wash your clothes on such a day. You know basically they tell you about how to do everything, you know. You don't have to do it that way, but your life would be easier if you do, you know, and ...

And I was fine, I got through basic training and didn't have and incidents, but some of the people who followed me out of basic training into my AIT thought I was queer. Well, there's nothing bad about being queer, except that I'm NOT. I'm a sex addict who's trying really hard not to work on sex addiction. They're like oh you're a dyke, and I'm like no. So I started like sleeping with all these guys, that I had no feeling for, no concern for, no care for. Because I wanted to prove that I wasn't a dyke. Because I already had these aggressive behaviors, and why can't you guys just follow the rules and telling everybody what to do and being a boss and being a bitch and whatever, so you know, so I had to prove that I was like THEM you know? So I'd sleep with these guys. And here's Jeff still in Arizona with my family, waiting for me to come out of basic training. And I'm sleeping with black guys, and I'm sleeping with -- Well, the first time it kind of an accident. I had gone to the bar to meet my girlfriend at this bar, and this guy started buying me drinks. And, I drank them. And she still hadn't shown up. I should've left at that point, but I didn't. He's like "No, she'll be here any minute, she'll be here any minute." And I like was "Okay." I continued to drink way more than I needed to drink. Falling all over myself out of the bar trying to get home. Our barracks was just up the hill a little bit. So he's going to walk me home, being a gentleman. And on the side of the road he starts touching me and so I'm like "No, you're doing this all wrong." And so I just jumped on him and gave him some sex and got off and left him you know. Basically it was probably rape? But because I couldn't stand the thought of somebody making me do something that I didn't want to do, I made it so I wanted it? You know? Anyways.

So after that I was like, okay, I'm a horrible person, I am just a sex addict, I'm just sick and I can't make any big choices and I never do anything right, and just spiraling into I'm a horrible person, I knew I couldn't do this, and so I am sleeping with all these guys, and basically I was lonely, just wanted somebody to be on my side. And there was nobody was on my side. I mean maybe somebody liked me, maybe those people liked me, but I didn't feel like anybody cared about me or liked me or had anything to do with me. And sex gave me that avenue to feel a part of something, even if wasn't something I wanted, even if it was nobody I cared about. It was that, well now we're a couple and now people won't mess with me so much. People won't think of me so bad, something.

So then I came across this little boy, and it was stupid. And I was still going to go back with Jeff, because I had joined the Reserves, so I was planning on being in Arizona with Jeff after this whole mess was done. And I still hadn't told him I had been unfaithful. And up to that point he was the only person I had ever been faithful to at all, you know, so this was a big thing that I had lied to him or not told him about this.

And this young man and I started hanging out. He reminded me a little bit of Chris, well see I remember something good about Chris. (laughs) And he took me to see Braveheart, and isn't that sweet, and he was so romantic, he was going to be the big protector guy. I slept in his dorm a couple of times, and he didn't touch me. I was like WHOA, you know, well after a couple of times I was like "WHOA, you know, well what's wrong with me, why don't you want to touch me? What the hell. (laughs) So I like basically raped this poor boy, and I was like yeah I can do this. And in the back of my mind, Jeff had had a vasectomy, so he wasn't ever going to have kids. And my goal in my whole world had been to have kids at some point when I was sane, you know, to do it right. And I'm thinking okay I'll never have kids, this is my punishment because God's punishing me, you know, for giving my baby up or having the abortion, a little bit of both, you know, and not really being clued into the fact that , you know, if you want to have children, it's probably not a good thing to be with a guy who has a vasectomy, you know. Has nothing to do with my choices, it has to do with God's punishment (laughs)

So I started being with this guy, and I was like okay, not somebody I would want to be with forever, not somebody I want to be married to, but you know, but if I could get pregnant, I could handle children with this guy's genes. You know.

So, I basically tried to get pregnant for a long time, for that last six weeks or whatever before I left. Well, by then, you know you start getting into this pretend emotional connection place? Where you don't really know who you are or who you're with? But you want to, you want to be together, you want to be with somebody so you're there, even though you're you really have nothing in common, and there's ... I don't know. He was really into dragons, he had tattoos all over his body, he wore his hair long when he was in school, he was from a pretty well-off family, who had just happened to get divorced when he was about eight. His mother had always been there for him ... He was real dark and gothic, and I was real less dark (laughs). I kind of I guess it was kind of the opposite, like he was dark and I was white, pure, had some intelligence about me.

So I had this relationship with him and then it was time for me to go. And I should have known, had I had an ounce of intelligence at that point in my life. I would've known when I went to get on the airplane to go back to Arizona. He was going to walk me into the airport, and at that time it was a lot easier to walk into an airport than it is today. And instead he just stayed in his car and waved me goodbye. And I was like, okay, well I guess this isn't love, you know. And I was okay with that because I was going home to Jeff, you know? But I got home and Jeff's like this big, fat creature, and I'm just sitting there looking at him going, you were in the SEALs, you were a Tae Kwon Do expert, you did all these things, and here you are, just this blob, you know, you haven't taken anything that you have learned and integrated it into your life. I don't respect you, I don't think that you're a good person. Which should've been my first clue, I could've just, you know, left and went and moved into my own house and been fine, and done that. But instead I joined the Army full time and I moved out to Kentucky to be with my boyfriend, Mike.

And we got married, and he moved, first he was going to school up in Kentucky in Louisville, and he had just really gotten himself motivated, and he was the same age as my little brother Shane, and you know there was a lot of strangeness about it. He was like the opposite of everything that I was, or at least that is what I thought. He was young and immature, and I was older and more mature, and he was flaky and liked to be on his computer all the time, and I was in the Army and I had to be at work at 6:30 in the morning to do PT, you know. So like he had no structure in his life and I had all the structure and we were going to come together and meet and become some better something, but instead it turned out that he hated me because I was always working and wanting him to be involved in my Army stuff and I wanted him to be kind of my window to the younger generation or something? 'Cause here I was , 28 years old, in typical Army people, privates and stuff, if you're 28 years old and you're a private, the reason is usually because you were a sergeant or something, and did something really screwed up and got all your rank taken away. You know? Being 28 years old and a private just wasn't a nice thing to do.

And so, I guess I was looking for him to be my window to the people his age. That I was affiliating myself with now in this... Anyways, it was very weird and very bizarre, and he was dark and didn't want to involve himself with anything I was involved in. He liked going in at night, you know, he'd sleep all day and he'd get up at night and play these Dungeons and Dragons games, fantasy games with these people. And if I were smart at that point, I could've said, okay, I made another mistake. I got married to you and that was really stupid. But I didn't. I wanted to be pregnant and I got pregnant, and I had Jessica.

Here comes this beautiful baby, and everybody's proud of her, except for now my attention isn't focused on Mike all the time. And he starts getting really pissed off about this, you know, before where I'd be cooking for him, at least attempting to be a wife, now I'm focused on this baby, and making sure she's bathed and fed and clothed, you know, and taken care of. At one point when she was about six weeks old, I said, "Look I need to go drop this film off at the Wal-Mart, I'll be back in half an hour. And when I came back, my baby's sitting in her bassinet on the bed, by his computer and he's screaming at her "Shut the fuck up!" You know, because he was playing his game and he couldn't be bothered with this child. And I was like shit. No it was younger than that, she must have been three months then.

And right after that I found I was pregnant again. He's like, "Well, you're just going to go get an abortion, I don't even think it's mine." I'm like "You're full of shit, you know it's yours, I've never been with anybody since we've been together. You know that; you're so full of crap." He's like, "Okay, I know, but" you know "I just don't want to be a dad anymore." And I'm like "Oh, okay, well then don't. You don't want to be a dad, don't be a dad. Just go live your life, enjoy." You know. (laughs) He's like, "Okay."

And so I was like, "So what's the real deal here. What's really going on? 'Cause I don't believe you just don't want to be a dad." He's like, "There's nothing, there's nothing, I just want to be on my own for awhile. " And I'm like "Okay" So he moved out and moved into his own little house and...

He told me that he would baby-sit Jessica while I went and did some charity work so that we could get cheaper food. And I drove up and I knocked on the door, and I could see there were people there, or at least a person there, but nobody answered the door, nobody answered the door. And it clued into me that he was with somebody. He had somebody in the house with him. Whoa, no. I mean I had thought this before, but you know, I didn't want to believe it so, now here's the proof, and I'm like banging on the door, and I'm like, Mike just come and get her, I need you to take care of her so I can do this thing, because if I don't I won't have food for the week, na nanna na. And he won't, he won't answer the door, won't answer the door.

Finally I go and I take his parts out of his car, and I'm like okay, you don't want to be a father, you don't want to act right, then I'll just take your car apart. And I did, I took the distributor cap off, threw it across the frigging yard.

Any way, so I found out later that she was like 17 and that he was afraid I'd like call the cops on him. Which I probably would have done. But.

I guess there's still part of me that didn't want to hurt him. I should've (laughs) but at the point when I stopped caring that I realized that he wasn't coming back, he wasn't going to be a father, that I was just much better to him after that. Because, you know, when somebody's lied to you and deceived you and stuff, you can kind of go into a rage, but, once you've realized that nothing you do is going to change that, then you can just get on with your life.

During that time when Mike had gone, and everybody was really concerned for me. You know, here I am pregnant, I have a little teeny tiny baby, and you know, my husband's just left me, got all these stupid bills and the Army doesn't like you to have bills. You can do anything, you can practically murder a person, and that would be better than having bills. Because if you're in the Army they don't want you to have bills. So like I got some help getting some of my bills taken care of and John started calling me. "So I heard that you had your baby. How are you, how is everything? "And I'm like "Who is this?" (laughs) Like "This is John Smith" And I'm like, who's John Smith? Oh! Sergeant Smith? And he's like "Yeah." Like "What are you calling me for?" He's like, "Well somebody told me you had your baby and I just wanted to see how you were doing." And I was like, "Doing fine." You know, "I'm surviving, like always, I will survive." He was like "Oh, okay."

Well, during the course of that period, he was like getting separated from his wife, his wife had left him, and moved into some other man's house. But had told him to just hang out and wait to see if it would work out with him before she would make a commitment to either one of them. Now just hang out here until I can really decide if this is what I really want to do. And he tells me this, and I'm like, "What! What does she do, spend the night with you, spend the night with him? What are you talking about? Why are you doing this?" Like, "I just don't want to lose another wife, I've already lost one, and I don't want to get divorced again, and I'll do anything I can to have my family kept together." And I was like family? Together? Oh, this man cares about a family. (laughs)

And then he came over one day. My sister and brother in law were there at my house, and he saw this picture on my wall, he's like "What religion are you?" And I'm like "I'm Mormon." He's like, "Me too!" "Really?" And had he not said that had we not had that particular connection, I probably wouldn't have spoken to him again. But at that moment in time, I was really trying hard to do the Mormon thing, go to church and be a Mormon. You know all of this life that I had led before this, I was you know, trying to raise my children right and whatever.

And so him and I started talking, and the more we started talking, the more similar our stories were. But just because somebody's story is similar to yours, doesn't mean that they are going to make a good mate for you. (laughs) But I wasn't thinking that way, I was thinking, oh, okay, we can rescue each other. And so I finally talked to him "Well, you're really stupid if you if you're going to let this woman tell you that she's going to leave her, you know, go and stay with her boyfriend and wait until, see whether she likes it or not before she comes back to you. You're really stupid to put up with that, that's dumb." And he's like, "You're right. Will you be my girlfriend?" "Yeah, I'll be your girlfriend. Is that what it's going to take to get away from your wife?" (laughs) Was stupid.

At anyways, she called the Army, and told them "My husband's still married to me and he's living an adulterous life with another woman, and I want to have him thrown in jail." And see, in the Army, that's a bad thing too. I mean the fact that she had left him to be with some other man and she was still married to him, didn't matter a flying fuck. All that mattered was he was currently in the Army, and he was doing something against the articles of their laws. So, we got together and of course we sat in there, and they said, "Have you guys ever had sexual intercourse?" And I was like "No." "Okay." Well, in my mind I was justifying it going , "No, we make love." You know (laughs). No, I'm not lying, we only make love.

And she did several things, she sent HRS to our house to have them check my house, 'cause she's just trying to cause problems . She'd tell her four year old son, he didn't have to listen to me because I wasn't his mother. So, here's this four year old child standing in my face, going, "I don't have to listen to you 'cause you're not my mother." I'm like, "You're right, I'm not your mother, I don't want to be your mother. But this is my house and you are going to listen to me in my house. Your dad isn't here, your mother isn't here, I'm the one here. I'm the boss. Get over it!" Yeah. That was real fun.

So when John finally got out of the Army, we were going to move. Obviously we didn't have to live there anymore, 'cause we weren't stationed there anymore. So we're going to move. He's like "I want my children to go to school in the same schools I went to. Now see, I didn't have any of that. When I was a kid, we went to 15 different schools in the same school district, you know. Every couple of months my mom was moving us somewhere else, you know, so we went to Jefferson, and we went to Salk, we went to, you know, Franklin Elementary, we went to you know, Butler, Alabama Elementary, and we went to the private school, so I didn't have any one place where I wanted my children to go to. There was no conflict there, you know. "I want my children to go to the school that I went to and I want my children to be raised in my hometown. " And I was like "Well, that makes sense, you know, there's less crime, I don't have to worry about people coming and stealing my babies out of my window." You know. And there's less stuff that can go wrong. They can be a big fish in a small pond. Okay, I'm willing to go along with that. I said, "But we're not going to live on your parents' land. (laughs). He had $35,000 to get out of the Army.

Well, we get out here, and we're spending it on this and we're spending it on that, we spent this much on the house, spent this much on this bullshit and that bullshit. Suddenly we have no money to buy any land anywhere else. We have a house, but no land to put it on. So we're like, okay, I guess we can live on your family's land. And there's been nothing but crap since. And I guess that's my story.

JR: So how do you survive?

DS: I hug my children a lot. I let them do whatever they want to as long as it doesn't hurt them. And I don't work or do anything outside of my house, so I can have control (laughs). If I stay here then nobody knows, those people are going to come over and get in my house or in my space. Talk to my kids. It's how I see life.

NOTES

YB

YB is 41 years old. She grew up in California and Colorado. In 1983 her mother committed suicide and YB continues to deal with that tragedy. She has been in and out of relationships, many of which have been associated with drug use. She finds it hard to be out of a relationship, is working on this issue through her story and through counseling. She lives in Jackson County.

YB
JR: Jan Rosenberg

YB: Okay, I grew up in California. For the first 19 years I started experiencing depression, oh I want to say in sixth or seventh grade. At which time I caught myself trying to hurt myself taking a bunch of Midol that didn't do anything just made me very sick. At that time in my life I felt like I didn't fit in anywhere. My mother being Italian and my father being Black. There was no area for mixed children back in my day.
JR: How old are you?
YB: I'm 41
JR: Okay
YB: So that's when all the chaos started as far as. . . trying to commit suicide, and dropping out of school and smoking marijuana and drinking and you know, just everything you're not supposed to do, I had done for one reason or another.

We moved into another house in California, this is Huntington Beach, California. It was a bigger house, and I always felt moving into that house did something to the family, it's like we all spread out. And it got a little more serious, the running away, running away and leaving town, dropping completely out of school.

So anyway I got past that. My mom and dad and grandmother at that time, sold the house in Huntington Beach, and moved to Colorado where they bought some land and a couple of businesses, and since then it has really been a downhill battle. We moved in '80 to Colorado, and my mother committed suicide in '83. At the time I was, I don't know, I guess I do pretty well under pressure, but then I fell apart later. After, you know, helping everybody with grief. Oh about six or seven months after my mother killed herself, I moved back to California, I felt like the Colorado mountains were closing in on me. So I went back to familiar grounds in California.

I lived there probably three or four years. Came back to Colorado Springs, my dad and my brother were there. My dad is my stepfather, he raised me, and he's the one I call "Daddy."

Anyway, after going through a bunch of changes in California, being alone and first time any of that, things just started to get worse as far as the chaos, well just the bad experiences. And learning, I guess that's what made me what I am today, but it was a hard time at the time.

Anyway, going back to Colorado and living with my dad, I got married when I was 26 or 27, I don't remember now. That was an abusive relationship before I married him, and then we lost a baby, it was too premature. In them days they weren't saving them at that age. Now they are.

Anyway, after we lost the baby, we got married. He never again put his hands on me but he started the drug abuse. And I had been there done that as far as that's concerned, both sides of the fence.

Anyway, we moved to his hometown, which is St. Louis, Missouri, and it just got worse. I had never lived in anybody's ghetto, I was always like the only Black person in a crowd. Here I am only light-skinned in the crowd, and everybody's looking at me like I'm the monster. I don't know what you call that, but that's my experience.

Anyway, I moved back to California, divorced my first husband. Then within a year I met my second husband and divorced and married him. I met him in the booking room in the Colorado Springs jail house. (laughs)

Okay, when I was in St. Louis, we were going through domestic violence. Before me and my husband moved to St. Louis, we were going through domestic violence and counseling and all of that. And then things got okay between us, and we moved and got married. Well, when I left my first husband, I went back to Colorado Springs – I always seemed to run back to Colorado. And I had a warrant for my arrest, I wasn't aware of. My tail light had busted on the car, and so they pulled me for that and they had a warrant for my arrest. And what it was, was not complying with the counseling that they had ordered me to do a few years earlier.

So I had got arrested and I was sitting there getting processed and all that, and my second husband was coming from Minnesota, getting ready to be, getting ready to get out and they checked the main computer system or whatever to see if any other states was wanting him, and he had a warrant from Colorado Springs, Colorado, that dated back to 1988. Okay. I married him in 1993. Moved from Colorado Springs, quit my job, moved, sold stuff out of the house, got in my little car, and whatever I was able to fit in the car is what I took with me.

He was incarcerated. I went to go set up the home, whatever, you know get everything settled up in Minnesota. Went through a lot of changes there, being by myself, didn't know anybody, or anything. Was kind of lost. But I managed to survive.

Six months after I went to Minnesota, my husband then was released to a private prison in Minnesota with a Colorado Springs sentence.

Anyway, I got settled in the Twin Cities at first, and then I moved to a small town closer to the private prison he was in. And I guess that was really a big downfall for me. I followed this man all over the place and starting over and starting over, only for him to come out and with two days I look like Rocky as far as my eyes being blackened, and my chest being blackened, and he really just beat the hell out of me. Kicked me with steel-toed shoes. Anyway, needless to say, I'd fallen apart, I'd done a lot of preparing for our life for when he was released, and it was all down the drain. Come to find out, the little girl, and I call her that because that's just what she was at the time, I think 15 or 16 years old. Who she had been following him wherever he went. At least in the state of Minnesota. When he was released, he ran straight to her. I already had a job waiting on him, and I was renting from the Mayor a little house. Life was supposed to be good; life could've been good.

But he had this little girl. I paved the way for her. And so he knew where to tell her to go get a job, you know, where to live, 'cause I'd already done it.

Okay! So that got crazy. It took me nine months to break from him. I was literally afraid for my life. Probably for the first time in that sense. As far as a man beating on me.

Anyway, I managed to escape, come back to Colorado Springs (laughs), divorced my second husband and I haven't been married since. A couple of serious relationships, one particular relationship was kind of the downfall in my life at the time I had went backwards as far as the drug scene was concerned. I don't know what I'm supposed to say.

The relationship that got me into that was a different relationship. It was me and another woman. And I just assumed, hey, you know, it can't hurt, let's see what's going to happen. ...I ended up falling in love with the lady, and that was just as abusive, she was acting just like the boyfriends in my life, the husbands in my life. So that was exed. (laughs) I couldn't win, I couldn't win.

So, to get away from her, because I went backwards in the drug scene, you know, and she was stealing my checks and stealing stuff, and using my ID, it just got stupid. And she had introduced me to a man who was an older man, who I thought was going to take care of me while I was going through these changes with her, come to find out, he was just using me and I was a pretty trophy for him. And he made sure I kept a pipe in my hand. And threatened to kill me and my dog, so I was finally able to get my dog from my trailer to come with me. He threatened to kill my dog and me or whatever if we tried to go, that he would shoot me, I've had guns to my head, I've had knives to my throat, I've had bottles and what have you thrown at They came, they had a warrant for his arrest because of the traffic in and out of the house. I called him like "the Godfather" type. You know, it wasn't a little rooty poot drug boys, this was a big guy in that life. . . .

Anyway, they came in and took him to jail, and that was the start of my beginning here in Florida. I came on vacation with a male friend who I just started dating before I left Colorado, in fact, he was in the same crowd I was trying to get out of. Anyway, we came down here to Fort Myers, Florida, and he started to put his hands on me also, and by this time I was fighting back like I don't know what, physically, and I left him. Our plan was to try and stay in Florida, once I got here I loved the beach being from California. The beach scene was a different scene that I hadn't had in a long time.

So I left him, I was working at FedEx, and I was doing good, came here and within a few weeks I was working, you know, meeting some people, and ended up just staying, the Lord just looked out for me, you know, steering me toward the right people so that I was able to stay here in Florida.

Anyway, I was in a car accident here in Florida. Trying to leave my man at that time. I guess I was a damsel in disgrace, you know that need, needing help, needing love, needing that and I guess like projecting from me. So I met this man, and he was really good to me, and but a couple of weeks after we started dating, he put his hands on me. Knocked me on the side of my head enough to drop me down, make me fall.

So, anyway, I had gone back to California to take care of my business there, with my trailer and all that, selling stuff and whatever, since I decided, well I decided I would stay in Florida. Got here on Mother's Day and by September I was going back to Colorado to finalize life there.

Came back from my trip to Colorado, moved in with this man, I was staying at a rooming house before.

JR: Was this in Fort Myers?

YB: Yeah

I was staying in a rooming house when I met him anyway, he was so jealous, and I'm thinking oh well, he just loves me. Because there were a lot more men living there than women did, and so he didn't agree with that. And I thought it was okay at the time. Although I had been in domestic violence situations for some reason, it didn't trigger. And when it did it wasn't enough to steer me away.

So anyway, he got me out of the boarding house and I had moved in with him and his mother and his sister and her husband, and four kids and all oh it was just a mess. Then I was leaving him and was in a car accident. While I was moving my stuff from one place to another. I was moving in with his niece who me and her got along pretty good. Anyway, got in a car accident and so I wasn't able to work at FedEx anymore, or any job at the time. And I haven't worked since, with the different back surgeries and stuff I've been through.

Anyway, before . . . his mother died. [2000 or 1999]. And so he had come into a little piece of money at that time. Well, we were in love, his mother knew me and loved me, I was considered his wife and everything. We were going to get married and life was just wonderful. Well, I ended up having to leave to his niece's house.

Anyway, ended up in the hospital because of the accident, severe back injury. They sent me home. Told me to stay off my feet for a few days, anyway them few days passed, I wasn't able to go back to work; I did try.

Okay, so, not being able to do that and needing assistance I stayed with my partner instead of moving out from away from him. And it just one thing after another. Six or seven months, maybe eight or nine months after his mother died, it just got crazy again, and I had already moved back and out and back and forth, back and forth. His grandmother died the year to the day after his mother died. And her house was empty, so Nathaniel's auntie asked us to move up here and live in his grandmother's house. So that's what we did, we moved up to Campbellton, Florida. Oh we got a big settlement from my back, we got that before we left Fort Myers. So when we moved to Campbellton, you know, we had the money to do what we wanted to do. And I need to backslide a little bit.

In one of our breaking up times and getting back together he admitted to using again after this time we had fought and everything you know, he was just a typical drug addict and I didn't know this type of a person. His drug of choice was heroin, which I didn't know anything about.

So, anyway, we were going to move to the country, Campbellton, Florida, and well was going to be well. Well, that didn't happen. We moved here on December 15· 2001, I believe, with $37,000 and by March 14th we were broke. This is my settlement for my back. When I received the settlement at the beginning, I paid off all his street debts, dope boys, whatever, everybody in the family got big money, and his family ended up getting more out of that than my own family. So that was a big mess.

Anyway, I called the police on him, March, we moved in December, I called the police on him, first time he put his hands on me, and actually he didn't hurt me as much as these times when I called the police like he did in the past. The worst beatings, I was too scared and didn't call the police for fear.

Anyway, I managed to call the police, or at least dial the number and have a hang up call, 911 calls it and automatically calls back. Lucky for that. He heard me talking to the police and he left. I knew where he was going, so I sent the police to him. He went to jail. I had a restraining order on him, I was to come back to court and extend the restraining order or lift it. I chose to lift it, we were going to try again and this and that, and anyway two months after that to the day, I called the police again. And this time he got out of my life for sure. ...

I stayed in his grandmother's house a year after we broke up. He only got two months for the second time, same amount of time he got the first time. No probation, no nothing. I packed up the grandmother's car which I had paid off and packed up his stuff and sent it to his aunt's house and I was through with him. I never, I haven't seen him to this day. He went back to Fort Myers.

Right before we had left Fort Myers, I got into the drugs with him. I didn't get into heroin, I wasn't into that, needles or anything, but I was into crack, whatever, cocaine, whatever, and so that's where the money went. I say seven to eight thousand dollars is spent on drugs. You know the problem with that, knowing that it's not good anyway, he was buying double of what we had agreed on, and he was losing his mind. Frying his brain. And I'm thinking, what the hell's going on, he's not supposed to feel like that with that amount. Come to find out, I think he's going to buy one or two hundred, he was buying three and four hundred. So it didn't take long for the money to go. I had extended his grandmother's house, the bathroom, all new that. He wrecked two cars, sold everything out of my house, as far as electronics were concerned. So it took me quite awhile to get settled again on my feet.

So up to now I've been away from him and his family completely. Since June of last year when I moved to my own apartment which is my home. I've been here a little over a year, with no man living with me and that's a record for me.(laughs) And I'm finally starting to be okay with not having a man, of needing a man in my life.

But I'm going through a lot of changes. A lot of suicide attempts, in Fort Myers the last one was the big one, the doctors didn't know why I didn't die.

Anyway, I got over that. Then we moved up here, so I hadn't done that again. Well, when he put his hands on me when he socked me to make me fall, I realized I had fall right back into the same mess with Crystal who was the female, and she played the man role as far as putting hands on me, so.

Anyway, the first time he went to jail was when I met Janet. Through a domestic violence hotline, got in with her and was really trying to heal and doing pretty good until he came out which was only two months before, two months after I had already started with Janet, and of course, he was there when he came home from jail the first time, he didn't allow me to go see Janet. So I didn't see Janet for two months. Then I put him in jail again for domestic violence. His second time up here in Jackson County. I loaded up the car and everything and sent him on his way when he got out of jail, and I haven't seen him since. And I've been back with Janet ever since.

I got in a relationship with a married man, I guess two years now. First of all let me talk about him, I call him my "guardian angel". My ex-aunt, the one we were staying at her mother's house, knew a gentleman who had been really kind to different women in Campbellton, and she knew that he would help me out. And so and he did. And he's really been taking care of me ever since. He paid for everything, from my cat food to work on my car, and he's been just an angel, my guardian angel.

Anyway, six, seven months into the friendship I felt a little obligated, so I went ahead and did what women do when they feel obligated. (laughs) But it blew up. He was 20 something years older than me and it was not lust or love or anything, it was just obligation. So when that blew up, we stopped. There was no more of that. And we're going on two years now where it was just a godfather relationship.

I've had a major surgery on my back, since I met my guardian angel, and if I knew now, if I knew then what I know now, I wouldn't let them cut on my back again. But I did. And he took care of me during that period too. A married man, he wasn't able to do too much, being married and whatever. So

Okay. So I've moved into my own apartment. Mind you I'm not dating the guardian angel anymore, we're just very good friends. And my relationship with the married man got more intense and more intense. He's never put his hands on me, but there was a drug abuse problem. His side only, thank the Lord. I've been clean for almost three years. After, when I got with the woman, I had been sober for 13 years. So that kind of broke down a lot, a lot of me, you know after being clean all them years and I'm following someone who doesn't mean me any good, but I'm following them, I moved into their world instead of them moving into mine. Now my main thing is the men will come to my world. If they can't come to my world, I don't want none of them. And I can thank Janet for that. Janet has really been my backbone. I get lost, I can't stand it when she goes on vacation because if I don't have, if I don't see her within a couple of days, my world seems like it's just falling apart. So I really thank God for Janet.

I've had that support team two, three years now. And truly that's been my backbone.

I've gotten out of this need for a man, and then going with the married man kind of made that easy. Although me, I devote my whole life to my partner, you know, and all of that. I've had a couple of suicide attempts. Taking pills, and in fact I just took had an episode last week over the Fourth of July. And I don't know, I just, I'm just alone and I get lonely in my mind. I live by myself, I don't have any friends, you know like anybody I'm friends with. I try to be friends with the neighbors and they just abuse. Seems like no matter what kind of relationship I get into, I'm being abused. Male, female, friend, lover, whatever. I end up giving my all and getting nothing back.

So, I don't know, I thought I was doing pretty good. And here I go with July 4th. I'm at it again. You know, I just realized. July 4th was the last weekend I spent with Nathaniel. The one I sent back to Fort Myers. I hadn't thought of that. Hmmm. So I don't know, maybe … I just thought about that. Hmmm.

Anyway, I survived. And it's a hard road again, but I'm working on it.

NOTES

Faye

Faye is 44 years old. She grew up in Kentucky and south Florida. She experienced emotional and physical abuse at the hands of her parents, uncle, brother, and husbands. She survived by becoming a "tough kid," and used her wits to deal with the abuse. She lives in Holmes County, Florida where she is learning her right to be safe and secure.

Faye's Story
    A toddler at 2 years of age. . .
    She starts screaming and rocking all the time, she remembers her aunt coming in the room where she was kept; saying to the toddler's father, "Cecil, that child is crazy!" The two year old is 44 now and she still sees the toddler's aunt telling her father, that she's crazy!
    The toddler is three now: she starts wetting the bed every night. The toddler's older sister had to stay out of her senior year of school to watch her because the mother had to work, the father was disabled the year she was born.
    The father didn't want to watch her until she re-learned to be potty trained and stop screaming!
    The sister, thank God, knew what had happened and figured out that she would have to take me in public and teach her to interact with people and to learn it's okay, not everyone is here to hurt you.
    The toddler had several brothers and uncles around her, but no one could figure out what was going on. At 27-30 years old the young woman has flashbacks so violent that she ended up on the psych floor in Dothan and then into therapy at Spectra Care.
    That's the beginning of the attempt for this two year old toddler, me, to learn how to survive in a family of physical and sexual abuse.
    At kindergarten age I was to go to school; well that didn't work, so the middle sister had to sit with me everyday for a week and was unable to go to her class. Others my sister's age made fun of her because of her crazy younger sister. Well my sister took a lot just to protect her baby sister.
    When I was around 5 years old, I saw my father bang my mother's head on the hearth at the fireplace, and then she was lifted in the air by siblings and literally thrown over the couch to hide and be protected from the drunk, abusive father...
    By the age of six, my father says: we're moving to Florida the sunshine state! He didn't want his boys to work in the Kentucky coal mines. You see in Kentucky the boys were gods and the women were nothing - other than slaves and idiots to him.
    We moved from Kentucky to Hollywood, Florida. By this time I answered to crazy, stupid and retard along with my given name. At age 6 I'm in school at Driftwood Elementary. I become quiet, yet excited at school but had no social

skills that would allow me to make friends with my class mates, not knowing why my class mates always picked on me and made fun of me. ...

By the time I turned nine years old I experienced and saw the many beatings my father gave my mother, sisters, and me. I thought getting beat was just part of life and didn't really know any different except by eight or nine I knew not to tell anyone what happens in the house of abuse! At this time my brothers (5) and sisters (2) were teenagers or older trying to date and find a mate to live with the rest of their lives. At this time the drunk uncle moves in, move out. He decided he liked Fla. Well at the age of nine my uncle had me smoking cigarettes to be cool I guess, but the reality was it was so she wouldn't tell on him for slipping in booze.

By the age of nine I was smoking and drinking. Vodka – I smell vodka now and become sick on my stomach and thrown into flashbacks now. One day, me, my brother, who was ten and a half, and my uncle went to the dump. On the way my brother and I waited in the parking lot of every bar on the way as my uncle got drunk; we were told not to get out of the car, so that's really all we or I knew what was happening. Then he stops at the liquor store and got a bottle of vodka and cigarettes. My brother, and I had to smoke and drink at the dump with him or he would tell Dad we were smoking!

Now think for a minute don't you think you would have known if your 10 year old son and nine year old girl were drunk?

Here comes the hard part and the determination of how I was going to survive in the house of abuse. It's so clear to this day. We got home and my uncle kind of kept us away from everyone especially Dad until supper. I loved green beans and Mom fixed some that day or evening, I remember getting seconds after Dad was done and my uncle kept tryin' to tell me not to eat anymore I thought, hey, it's not everyday I'm allowed to have seconds; I'm eating them.

My uncle told Dad that he'd stay up with us so we could watch TV. About 30 minutes later and he made my brother go to bed. Without the preliminaries, my uncle was messing with me sexually. I didn't know what to do. He was telling me how I couldn't tell on him because of the cigarettes and drinking: Dad would kill me and my brother. He took me to the laundry room, made me have oral sex with him, and I remember it like yesterday. I got sick -- I threw up all over him: he got mad and made me clean up him, me, and the laundry room. I was so scared and sick he started again making me do more to him and I remember he was on top of me in the floor I looked up and the shelf and I saw another little girl looking at me. She was telling me it would be okay: "I'll take the pain just look at me. "

When my uncle was done he told me to go to bed so I did after I went to the bathroom. I didn't know what to do. I couldn't tell and I couldn't wake Dad up because he would beat the hell out of me. So I cleaned up as much as a nine year old knew how to and went to bed freaking out.

The next morning we had to get up and clean house and Mom was home. I went to the bathroom and I was bleeding pretty bad. So I come out and asked Mom if she had a Band-Aid she said for what? I froze, I didn't know what to say or how to tell and scared as hell. Mom said for what and I pointed "down there", she took me to the bathroom and pulled my pants out some and she saw all the blood on my panties. She was mad; I thought I was fixing to get my ass beat. Guess what she was mad about? A daughter nine years old starting her period! Mom got a pad and showed me how to put it on, the belt thing before the sticky type now. Cussing, raising hell had Dad mad 'cause she told him, I was in so much trouble and didn't know why or what was going on! Yeah, I bled for a week. And that was that, I couldn't say or do anything else. I just knew I was in trouble and went to my room and climbed on the dresser and got in top of the closet and shut the doors.

Then after supper guess who comes to see about me, yeah my Uncle. . . . After a few more times of my uncle, my brother the ten year old starts the same thing and I wasn't allowed to tell. This went on till I was 16-17 years old. With the beatings for nothing and the beating for still wetting the bed and for every other reason my dad could think of to beat the hell of out me and my brother. So after awhile you learn what you have to do and keep your mouth shut.

When I was 13 my dad started calling me "slut" "whore" "bitch" to add to "crazy" and "retard" and "stupid." By this time I am smoking pot in the morning and during and after school to maintain or numb out. ... I was tough by then. I would basically do what I wanted to 'cause I was being beaten for everything so I didn't care.

I got a work permit at 13 and got an after school and summer job at the rec center. The janitor Jim he was so good looking and he had the best reefer so we became good friends in fact he was the one who taught me how to shoot pool. His girlfriend was a nurse and between the both of them they taught me how to be a hooker. I was five foot one and a half inches, 95 pounds. Most of the johns were pedophiles!

A couple years on down I couldn't get out of it. All the reefer I wanted and all the cocaine which was pure in the 70s it was just beginning to be flown over on the east coast. I was making money – getting high and numb before I got home to get drunk with my uncle, my brother, and by then there were some others in the neighborhood whom my uncle invited. ... All I did for myself is buy albums and clothes and saved back so when I had to run away I wouldn't be broke. I also had more jobs plus working for Jim and Diane.

My dad started telling me "When you're 17 I'm putting you in the state hospital" so he could draw a check off me every month. Needless to say I got married at 17 'cause nobody would rent an apartment to a 17 year old. Big mistake. I was 17 he was 27. Six months into the marriage he comes home with one of his coke buddies. This wasn't unusual, except I'd never seen this guy before. What does my husband do? He passes out. There I am at 17 not knowing what was going to happen. But I she knew something was up. I was in trouble and I couldn't wake my husband up! The man told me he didn't have the money to pay for his stuff but that's okay he'd get it out of me. I was raped so badly. I did something and then finally had to call Diane and Jim 'cause of what happened and I couldn't stop the bleeding. I sat in the shower just watching the blood go down the drain. The water was ice cold before I realized I needed help.

Diane came to the apartment and picked me up, saying that she wouldn't ever let anything like that happen to me. Get rid of the husband and stay with her and Jim. She called one of the doctors to meet her at the hospital. The doctor sewed me up as quick as he could without them getting caught and no paperwork. I still carry the scars to this days.

And it was a miracle that I never got pregnant with husband #2. This takes me up to two kids later and 27-30 years old with flashbacks so bad I ended up on the psych floor in Dothan I can't drink now 'cause I was an alcoholic by the time she was 30 years old. So I realized it and with two girls I knew I had to stop. I wouldn't have started drinking again (I quit to have kids) but husband #2 was a beater and never was home screwing he always did that with someone else all the time when he turned thirty years. I divorced #2, raised the girls myself, went to parenting classes and the PACE Center in Dothan.

The girls couldn't handle Dothan anymore because of where we had to live due to lack of income. I knew I had to get them out of there, so I returned with them to Graceville-Esto area. I knew I had to make a stable environment for them and hooked up with #3. Big mistake, another beater.

Now I am back in therapy learning coping skills and going to empowerment groups and individual therapy to get help and try to live instead of surviving.

So it's 2004 and now my girls finished school, they're married and I have one grandson and two granddaughters. I tried to hard to drive it into them to not to hook up with an abusive man, emotionally or physically. Don't take any kind of abuse from anybody. Guess what? They didn't listen. Women take care of yourself 'cause nobody else will. And Mothers please watch the environment your children are raised in because . . .

Children are a product of their environment.

A 47 year old woman

A 47 year old woman described her experiences of incest at the hands of her brothers in rural West Virginia. Her tone is steady, punctuated with tears. One of 18 children, a 47 year old woman tells a story of extreme emotional and physical abuse from her parents who chose not to acknowledge the incest. A 47 year old woman moved to Florida 25 years ago with a man who became her husband, only after meeting him once. She lives in Jackson County, Florida.

JR: Jan Rosenberg

I: A 47 year old woman

JR: So let's just say that you've experienced abuse ever since you were a kid.
I: Uh hmm. Day after day after day
JR: Day after day after day. All physical abuse? Emotional abuse?
I: Yeah, with the beatings from my mom. Course I said my mom hated me.
JR: Uh hmmm
I: And she beat me with everything she could get a hold of.
JR: Uh hmmm
I: I was locked in rooms, couldn't get out. And she always beat me. (crying) She accused me of being a wife to my dad. And I don't know . . . can't remember.
JR: You can't remember.
I: But she always told me I was never a daughter to my dad. Was his wife. I can't
JR: Remember it
I: Remember it. All I know he wanted of everybody else at the house, all them kids, he always wanted . . . to go with him here, . . . go there. Do this. Would never ask for nobody else.
JR: Uh hmmm
I: So, and she then would just get much madder at me. Because I stayed with Dad. I don't know. I can't remember. But till the day she died she always accused me of that.
JR: Hmmm
I: There's parts of it I can't bring back. And I can remember some days that my dad would get mad at me and come after me, saying he was going to take care of me and then it just like the day ended. There's just a black spot there.
JR: Uh hmmm
I: That day just vanished. But she always accused me. But I know with my brothers it was nightly.
JR: How many were in your family?
I: There was 18 of us. My mom had 18.
JR: And you grew up in West Virginia?
I: Way back up in the hills of West Virginia, yeah. And I couldn't wait till the day come till I got old enough to get out of that.
JR: Uh hmmm
I: 'Cause I couldn't. You'd go to bed hungry every night, you slept in the woods at night, and all. Which is a complete nightmare.

At 16 my mom threw me out. ... I ran. I ran. Remember running up the road, she got a rifle and start shooting at me. And she started shooting at me and I ran that much faster.[notes why she thought microphone stand was a rifle]

JR: Where'd you run to?

I: I just ran up to the neighbor's, 'cause we only have one decent neighbor. Rest of them are just alcoholics and everything like that. One decent neighbor, I ran up there and I finally got a ride to Ohio. I just got my way to Ohio.

Got a job out there babysitting. Just had it for room and board. Until the guy out there too, he was a _____ too. But I had to survive.

JR: Uh hmmm

I: And I was I was there a year with them till I got, I said there's got to be a better life than this, got to be. So.

I didn't have nowheres to go, no money, no nothing, so I went back home to my mom's. Things were pretty good for maybe a week or so. Then the abuse started again.

One night, (crying) my brother got drunk, drunk as could be, and usually when they come in like that, that's what they went for. Then when he come in drunk and he come after me. And I made up my mind that, hey, it not going to happen again. He started beating on me. I don't remember the rape, but I remember him beating on me. The more I fought, the stronger he got. He started tearing my clothes off. I started to scream and he just hold over my mouth and I don't know how long it was or nothing. I just seem like he would. And the room black and it was way up in the morning hours. When I came [to] I can't really remember anything. I was up, you know, under like a dresser ... like a desk. I was back curled up in there. No clothes on and everything. And I don't know how long I was up in there, I know nothing. But I just want to die.

I heard my mom holler. I wanted to go to her, and tell her what happened. She didn't want to hear it. She didn't want to hear it, she just accused me of sleeping around. She didn't want to hear it.

I was 17 at the time. I just absolutely died inside. I wanted to die. Didn't want to live.

So, I just went, completely shut down inside. Until, just hoping every day, every day, and I prayed, I want to die. (crying) I prayed to God, take me home. And as the days went on, and everything, I began to get lightheaded, like that, and the worst nightmare come true. I got pregnant that night. I was pregnant with my (crying) brother's baby. I didn't want it. I even hated myself more. I didn't want that baby. There wasn't no way.

But I couldn't tell nobody. I couldn't tell nobody. So I just wished and prayed more and more, just let me die. You know. So, I finally took some, I said, I took a bottle of aspirins, I took the whole bottle of aspirins. Was sick. . . . I was just hoping to die. Wanted to go ahead and die. But.

I felt like I was dying, but somehow, God saw me through for some reason. The next day I was so sick, I couldn't get up, do anything, but my mom, I had to. I had to take care of the animals outside. I went out and was trying to slop the pigs, and I just basically fell over. I started to, I was so sick. I begin to hemorrhaging real bad. I went inside and told my mom I couldn't do it, I was sick, and she just started beating on me. Called me all kind of names. And if I wasn't out whoring all night all night I wouldn't be like that.

And she started beating me with her fists, started kicking me in the stomach, I started hemorrhaging that much more. And I begged her, go ahead and kill me, I begged her, I pleaded with her, I said "In God's name, please kill me." And on she beat me. And then I mean I begin to hemorrhage real bad, and she seen it and it kind of scared her. And she called the ambulance. I was 17 years old that was the first time I was ever to a doctor.

She called the ambulance and they carried me on to the hospital. And I miscarried, had to have an emergency DC[D&C].

I begged them and begged them, I said "Please don't tell nobody." To the doctor. I was underage, so they had to tell. So when I got back home, the beatings got worse, the beatings got worse. Worse and worse and worse.

And that didn't stop my brothers from coming in, going to bed with me. Drunk. (crying) They would do their thing, and they'd use the bathroom inside of me. Then pass out. I only weighed 118 pounds. And they would pass out on me. And I couldn't get them off of me, just laid there. . . . They was just too heavy. So I'd have to lay there. Finally, they would waken up and just get off of me. And there wasn't a day that went by that I just wanted to die. Said, "Please God, just take me, I don't want to live no more." But He just. It seem like it got worse and worse and worse. Until finally when I, I turned 18, I took off again. I said I'd rather die on the street than go through this anymore.

So I ended up in Kentucky for awhile. Just where I could get a place and have a roof over my head. Sometimes I had to sleep on the street. But I didn't care. I honestly didn't care. Was out there for awhile, maybe 8, 9 months. Things didn't work out and like a fool I said "Maybe I can try it again, maybe things'll get better at home." So I went back home because my mom got a hold of me, she told me to come back home. I wanted to respect my mom. So I went back.

And I said, "Gosh, what kind of mistake did I do?" It just went on and it went on and went on. And she accused me of worse, of sleeping with my dad, see, I just can't bring parts of it back, I mean, there's days I know he was coming after me, he'd grab me. I can't remember what happened afterwards. I just can't remember what happened. And it's just like the day ended. I can't bring nothing back.

And then we had this uncle. Stinky, nasty person. He drank all the time, never bathed or nothing. I was afraid of him. I was always afraid of him. My mom knew that. He would always . . . come to the house when my dad wasn't there, he would come in and I would run outside. My mom would purposely call me in the house. 'Cause I wouldn't go in the house at all when he was there. I would walk in the house, she would grab me. Get me and he would grab a hold of me, and he would just start grabbing. And my mom would sit there and watch. (crying) He would just grab. And grab you all over. Stick your face in the crotch. Mom just sit there and watched. And she'd say, "How'd you like that you whore?" And I still all these years.

I turned 20 years old, I said "I've got to get out of this place. I cannot no do it no more." I had these visions of just cutting my throat, going out in the woods and just shooting myself. Anything to get out of that lifestyle.

When I was 20 years old I just took off and I just _____ wherever I could find a place to sleep overnight I stayed. And then for a year.

And then I met my husband. Didn't know nothing about this guy whatsoever, met him one time. And he was older, met him one time, and I was at my end's wits, you know, I never drank nothing before in my life, but I would come to the point that night before I met my husband, I started drinking. I didn't care, I just didn't care. I'd take any pill anybody give me, anything to get out of this world. Until the day I met him. We talked. Never saw the guy before in my life. And we talked. Second time I met him, we talked a bit more, and he says, ". . ., I can't offer you much, but I live in Florida, you want to go with me." I didn't know nothing about the guy. Just his name ... I said, "I'll go." I said, "I'll go." I didn't know what I was getting into, but just didn't care. I didn't care. I didn't know if he was a murderer or not, I thought even then when I got in the car, if he kills me, that's all right too. You know.

But after, and we took off down to Florida. Second time after I saw the guy.

But after I crossed over the West Virginia line, over into Ohio, I felt just felt this . . . it's over. It's over. You've got a life ahead of you. Just like that little voice, you know, and still I was kind of scared because I was in the car with a stranger, I didn't know where I was going. And didn't much care. I didn't care. But I heard the voice go ". . ., it's over. It's over. You've got a life now."

And I came to Florida, and I was with him for 25 years. But then I look back on it now, that was my way out, I survived, I look back on it now, I don't know how I survived all that mess. And the only thing I can say is God was with me. Because at times I wanted to die. I begged Him, I prayed on my hands and knees, "Take me out of this." And I tried it, tried it once with the aspirins, bottle of aspirins. And I went to the woods with a knife and gun and everything. And I asked my mom, I begged my mom to kill me, time and time again. You know. And but then after I got married, I said, with him I had 25 years with that man, you know. That's when I begin to live, when I was 21 years old. That's when my life began, you know.

And I look back on it now, no person in this world deserved to go through that. Nobody. Absolutely nobody needs to go through that. And if wasn't for God I wouldn't have survived it. But there was a plan somewhere. I feel bad at times, I think back on it, I was the weak one. But there was just pain, misery, day after day after day. They wouldn't feed me, day to day, I wouldn't go, I begged for something to eat. Didn't get it. And they drank, my mom and dad both drank real bad. ... There was all that going on. Sexual abuse, the beatings, then argument with them, you know. And they had all these animals that they tied up. Dogs and things. That they wouldn't feed. Wouldn't buy no food for them. Then in the wintertime I had to take care of all of them. In the wintertime the dogs would die of starvation. And in the wintertime they would go into boxes, (crying) literally freeze to death. You had to break them up to get them out of the box. ... they would freeze their legs they would stick their legs out like they were dogs and you couldn't get them out of that little burrow without breaking them. Would be outside like that. And you had to dig them up off the ground. They was froze to the ground. This was like this with dogs, chickens, had a horse had to do that. Just of starvation.

It was always 8,9,10 dogs tied up. One would die, they'd just go and get another one. And then I'd get beat for not taking care of the dogs that would starve to death. There wasn't nothing there to feed them. I couldn't feed them. When I didn't have nothing there to feed them, matter of fact there was nothing in the house to feed the kids and all the animals.

But the alcohol came first. . . .So there's just that nobody in this world that needs to go through that. But there's God through this, there's that survival thing there. Was inside of me that I really didn't know was there. Until I crossed that West Virginia line, and I heard that voice that told me ". . . it's over." It took me 21 years of my life to realize it was over.

I won't go back to that life. Nobody, you know.

There's so much. It stays with you. It stays with you. I got things, you know, stay with me till the day I die.

We had a shack. We didn't have no bathroom, no inside, no water, no nothing. We just had a little building outside over a hole. Had to carry water in buckets. ... No clothes hardly to wear. No nothing to eat. The house. My mom and dad's room was fixed up pretty good ... but the bedroom – there was two other rooms, one was for the boys that there was dirt floor for a long time. A pure dirt floor. You had to get a blanket sleep on the floor the dirt for a long time.

The roof just leaked like a sieve. And finally when they did fix the roof and put a floor in, I mean, fixed a floor in the house, it leaked so bad when it rained, the floor rotted out. And big old sewer rats – 'cause we had a stoop over basement and a barn down right below an old piece of a barn, sewer rats would come in at night, and just crawl into bed with you. Eat on your toes and things. They would be as big as cats sometimes. Biggest rats I ever seen in my life. You know. They would come inside and just eat on you when you was sleeping.

But you see they didn't go into Mom and Dad's room. 'Cause theirs was fixed up. They didn't care how the kids lived.

JR: Where did you end up in Florida?

C: Here in Marianna. . . . And I have no regrets about leaving up there. And I was gone for six years before I even told my mom where I was even at. But, even when I did call her she didn't care. I had a mom in name only. Then I have to be honest with myself, I never loved my mom, you know. She never ever showed no love. All I known was abuse, abuse, abuse. I didn't love her, you know. I kind of parts of me feels bad about that 'cause you're supposed to love and respect your mother. But the parents got to show some back. Towards you. If you don't receive some back from that person, how can you show it?

And I met my husband, and he showed me what the true meaning of love was, you know. Had 25 years with him... There's no way in this world I'd ever put my kids through that. I'll just disappear, won't even be a part of their life before I'll have to give them memories that'll stay with them till the day they die. You never forget it. I carry scars on my body that my mom put there. Just with the beatings she gave me. I wear dentures because my mom hit me across the mouth with a piece of wood like that because we had a stove, we heated by coal and wood? Little pot-bellied stove set in the living room? And all summer we had to put wood up on the porch around the house to heat with? Why she did it? I was sitting down and she come across, hit me right across there, right across the mouth with a piece of that wood. Why I don't know. Broke every tooth there was in the top of the mouth. My. . .begin to bleed, she didn't take me to the doctor or nothing. I deserved it. And I had no reason why. She hit me with that piece of wood. . . . And I kind of must have blacked out 'cause when I woke up I was just covered with blood and my sister was helping me wipe it off.

I'm 47 years old. But I didn't get even to live until I was 21. You know. Because that. But the main thing that we have to focus on . . . But there was that survivor instinct in there 'cause at times I wanted to kill myself, I prayed to God, just die, I begged my mom, kill me, just go ahead and kill me. I didn't want to live no more.

But I didn't [die] so . . . that survivor deal was in there somewhere deep inside. To go through some of the mess that I had to go through. Days without anything to eat, and abuse, the beatings, and all that sexual abuse, that just was it was in there.

Then she was ... always accusing me of being a wife to my dad and not his daughter. But I don't know. I can't remember, I can't seem like it that won't, won't come back. But I've talked to the psychiatrist, and all he said it's probably good thing it don't come back. I can't remember because sometimes the mind, the memory just can't ever just overload and mess you up too bad. Because I cared for my dad, I can't really say I loved him. I can't say I did. Because I would get beatings, he would beat me for things I know I did not do. My mom would tell him things that I did I know that I did not do. Or the other kids, we didn't do nothing. She would do it. But see my dad wasn't there, didn't know. But when he would come in, she would say such and such did this and my dad wanted us to tell on each other, tell him who did it. We wouldn't tell 'cause none of us did it. We tried to say that Mom did it. He wouldn't believe us. 'Cause see my dad was a coal miner. And he would beat us in one way. He ... had a big old belt, ... It's 5,6 inches wide, and maybe two inches thick, pure leather, it's leather all completely through. That he had to wear his battery on for his light on his head. And he would get that, and maybe two feet long. He would get that. And he'd keep telling us," Which one did it. Or I'm going to line you all up and beat it. We couldn't tell on each other 'cause none of us was guilty. My mom was.

So anyway, he just got where he'd line us all up in a row, and he would take that belt. And he would kind of get hold of the buckle and wrap it one time around his hand? And line us up and get us out there. He would grab us like this, put his hand on our wrist, and he would begin to beat, and he would beat. And that belt would just wrap you about twice. He would beat, he would beat. 15, 20 laps. And basically if you didn't wet yourself by then he beat you until you wet yourself. ...

(crying) And sometimes he would just seemed like how to forget quit beating. He would just beat and beat and beat. And if you didn't wet yourself, and the welts you know, it really left welts, and then when you wet yourself, it hurt that much more. It would just burn. But you wasn't allowed to cry.

Mom would be setting over on the side, just laughing. "Give her some more, give her some more, give her some more." And she would be laughing up a storm. But there would be finally let you go, you [weren't supposed] to cry. You weren't allowed to change your clothes. You had to wear them clothes till they dried. You wasn't allowed to change them or cry. You had to set there and watch the other ones get beat. Then if he felt like giving you more, you got up and got more. You know. And that seems like I got the beating three and four times a week. And we didn't do nothing to deserve it. But Mom would make up stories. We could not figure why we have to got beat for something we did not do.

I cannot say I loved my dad 'cause I'd be lying to myself. And I'm not going to lie to myself. You know. To be beat like that for no reason. . . . My mom was always right and us kids were always wrong. I don't know.

We could never go to him and tell him neither. I even tried to go to my dad at times, tell him what my brothers was doing to me. You know. It wasn't my place to go to my dad, to tell him that, but he didn't want to hear it either. You know. My brothers was using me as a wife. You know. So I just kept that inside. Nobody. When I was with my husband for 25 years, I never even told him. Because every time we tried to talk about some of what I went through, it would just make him mad. He was the type he wanted to go up there and cause trouble. And I seen how bad it was hurting him so I just kept it inside, I never told him. ... I never told him what all I went through. Because him with the temper he had, 'cause what I did tell him how there were days I went without anything to eat, and everything, be locked up in rooms, and spent the night outside. Sometimes, if I was lucky enough to get away from my brothers, I spent the night outside. In the woods. ... That was just on a lucky night, if I can get away from them before they could pen me up.

But I didn't tell him, my husband why, I spent the nights, but just with that, made him so mad, he wanted to go get revenge. I felt like I would have told him everything he would have went and – I couldn't do that. So I just clammed up and kept it inside.

How do you tell somebody? That you loved, and everything like that your brothers used you for a wife? That you couldn't even go to your own parents. Times you wanted to, you couldn't. They wouldn't hear it. See, my brothers were always bigger. ... Especially my oldest brother. He could come in there, he would just scoop me out of the bed, take me to his bed. Like he was a monster, compared to what I was. Tear my clothes off, crawl on top of me. He'd still at the same time be talking to my mom and dad through the wall. While he was doing that. . . . Gosh you've got nerve, you dirty old goat, you've got nerve. And talk at the same time. . . . He used (crying) the bathroom in you. Then he would pass out. ...

Sometimes it was both of them in one night. How disgusted. My parents were right in the other room. Why don't they come check on the kids? I do mine. And mine's grown. . . . Just to make sure your kids are okay. But, no, they sat there in the other room and he's talking to them through the wall at all the same time. On top of his sister? He had nerve. But one of them's still living and I hate him with a passion. I hate that boy with a passion. I don't care if I ever see him again. And again, I have to be honest with myself, I don't feel any sorrow for him. I can't. I cannot. And then the one is still living. I don't feel a bit sorry for him. There's no love there, it just somebody that I know. ... He's my brother, but he's not either. I wouldn't give him the time of day. He's still in West Virginia, I'm down here. I don't talk to him, don't want to talk to him. There's no need for him _____. They say blood's thicker than water, but in this situation, there's no way I don't even want to see that guy. You know. And the one brother up there and the other brother, the one that raped me that night that I got pregnant by, I feel the same way with him. I feel the same way. I don't want nothing whatsoever, I know them, but they're not family. I don't even want them around my daughter. I don't want them around my daughter, period. You know. I feel like if they ever tried to touch my daughter, I would just have to do something. . . . I'd kill them. There ain't no ifs ands or buts about it. 'Cause no woman needs to be robbed of her dignity at that young, at no age, at no age. They don't deserve that, that's something that takes. ... Even when my husband was alive, and we try to be intimate, I'd have flashbacks then, you know. I could just, and I'd try to knock them out, but I'd still have flashbacks, I'd see my brothers on top of me, you know. It was just. . . . My husband never raped me, nothing like that, at times, I'd have these flashbacks. And it wasn't my husband, it was my brother, you know? I never told my husband, he understood. He completely understood, and he says, you know, "We don't have to." He never questioned it, you know. Which I felt bad because I felt like I owed him a reason why? But he didn't question it, and I felt glad he didn't. 'Cause I don't feel like I could've told him. You know. Because he was the type he would've made a trip to West Virginia and you know, I wasn't going to let him do that. Because like I said, he gave me a life. And if it wasn't for him, if it wasn't for him, I thought about it, thought about it, thought about it. If he wouldn't have come in my life when he did, one way or the other I was going to kill myself, there wasn't no ifs ands or buts about it. 'Cause I was not going to live that lifestyle no more. I couldn't. I couldn't live that lifestyle, I wasn't going to live it no longer. . . . He was a perfect stranger to me, saw him twice in my life. Met him one day, the next day here I was loading up in the car with him, took off with him. You know. But I heard that voice say, ". . ., it's over." You know, and I look back and that survivor was in there. You know. But I didn't see it. The only thing I can say right now for any woman out there that's going to have to go through what ... strive for that [survival]. God knew it was there, but I didn't. But I look back on it now and that was survival, it's the only way I lived through it. . . . Twice I tried to kill myself, you know, and I begged my mom time and time again, you know, to do it, and that's pretty bad when you beg your mama to kill you. But you know back then I thought it was the only way out, I thought it was the only way out, you know. But I look back on it now, it wasn't. I wouldn't have had a life, but now I says I had 25 years with a man, two grown kids. . . . And since I've lost my husband times are hard, but I know I can make it, I survived through all that, you know, I know I can make it now because I'm older and wiser, I know I can make it now. I know I've got that survival in there.

Any woman has to go through that. You see you're supposed to go to your parents, go to your mom. . . . Sometimes you can't. I didn't have no . . . we had neighbors around, but they was all drunkards and everything. I didn't tell them nothing. There were things said that I never told a living soul before. Keep it inside, all these years.

And it was hard, you know, especially when I got pregnant and miscarried, but I knowed in my heart. I didn't want that baby. I could never have loved that baby like it should've and I would've mistreated it. I thank God I went and miscarried. I thank God every day for that, up to this day. I couldn't have raised my brother's baby. It wouldn't have been the baby's fault, but it would've been to me, I would know whose it was.

JR: Oh yeah

I: And I couldn't do that. And the two I got I thank God for my son and daughter now, that was a blessing right there, 'cause neither one of mine was planned. They just happened. My daughter wasn't planned or my son, they just happened. And it was meant to be. . . . It turns out they would have had an older brother or sister if I carried it. How would I explain that to them? You know. Hey you all have got a half brother, half sister here and such and such is the dad. How could I broke it to them? You know.

I'm glad it happened when it did, that's what I said. There was a reason in all of this. But now, just getting through the healing process. I don't think it ever goes away. Does it? It never goes away. So when I see somebody, some young girl or something like that that you know, and any woman that's ever been through that, my heart goes out to them. 'Cause I know what they went through. And they say don't judge a person until you've walked a mile in their shoes. 'Cause you can't look at somebody and see how bad they're hurting inside. But if you went there through it, you know. . . . Sometimes it just overpowers you at times it hurts so bad. And I got so much hurt and pain in my heart, that I don't know if I'll ever be able to forget and heal. It's bad enough when a stranger do it to you, 'cause I met a guy here a year ago, two months, but he was after I lost my husband and everything and I was just I was at a vulnerable stage and he knew it. And he more or less, he come right on in. And there wasn't no sex or anything, just it was like a companion, but I didn't know he was a drug addict at the time. Till one morning he snapped, and I mean I got it big time. You know, I got it big time. He begin to slap me across the face, he slapped me 25, 30 times across the face, his whole hand was taking my face. . . . I was bruised up pretty bad. So,

But I found out he just he hates women. So I don't know.

But all got to know is let other women know there's people, other women who have been through the same thing. That we can heal as a group. You call me I can help you, you same way we both heal at the same time. Because going through it by yourself is no fun whatsoever.

I'm done.

Elizabeth Nance

Elizabeth Nance is 49 years old. Born and raised in Bay County, one of five boys and three girls. She experienced abuse at the hands of her family and her husbands, where she was made to feel at once special and damaged. She lives in Washington County, Florida where she works in retail, and is learning that she too can lead a happy and safe existence.

My childhood was filled with a lot of work and little affection. The only thing that we had lots of was kids. I was number 8 out of 11. My mother could not read or write. She signed her name with an X.

There were several incident of my being fondled as a child. One was a neighbor who used to buy me . . . and little presents.

In some way I knew that what he was doing was wrong. I now know that I was just wanting to be special to someone. I would feel guilty and dirty but at the same time it filled a need in me to be more than just another kid to be accounted for.

I never told my mother or father what was happening to me. I always felt my father did not want anything to do with me except when there was work of some kind to be done.

There was also an Uncle ho stayed with us for a time. He would be out back with me and some of the others. He used to hug me a lot and his hands would be in all the wrong places. But again I felt the need to be special.

My mother never talked to me about sex or anything connected to it. One of my older sisters showed me what to do when my periods started.

The fondling continued through out my childhood. My oldest sister was already 16 when I was born. Her children were like more brothers and sisters since we were close to the same age. I would spend the night at her house and sometimes my brother-in-law would come into the room where I was sleeping. He would be rubbing his hands all over me. I would pretend to be asleep and try to roll away from him. I'was afraid to say anything to my sister or moma. That was the only place that I was allowed to stay overnight. He really made me feel dirty and guilty. I always felt him watching me when I was with my sister.

Later in my childhood my next to the oldest sister's husband took me to town with him one night. He went through the back roads. He stopped the truck and took hold of me and begin to tell me how pretty I was and that night he had sex with me. He told me that if I told anyone he would say that I was lying and that I would hurt my sister badly. I felt the guilt and the shame that it had been my fault. I must have led him on somehow. I have never told anyone of these things until a couple of weeks ago.

I got married for the first time when I was seventeen. He was thirty-one at the time. My second husband was 18 years older than me. Both marriages took place because of guilt feeling that my mother could raise in me. I would do most anything for my mother. I wanted her love and approval more than anything. If moma was happy that made me feel good. I guess I was trying to make up for some of the awful things that my father put her through.

As the years went on I managed to create an escape from my life through books. Through reading I could be someone else, see new places in my mind.

My second marriage really got to be a nightmare. Charles really knew how to get in your head; He was so charming and nice to begin with.

It wasn't until we had been married a few months that I began to see the lies that he told everyday. He began to keep me away from my friends. Telling me that they were trouble and that people would think badly of me if I continued to see them. Charles drank a lot and would disappear on the weekends. He would come home on Sunday afternoon and tell me the most ridiculous stories. Of how he had been in a hospital somewhere, or got put in jail, or stayed with friends and could not get to a phone. He began picking on our son. He would tell him how lazy and no good for nothing he was. He would come home late at night and wake our son up just to tell him he was no good.

At the same time he was telling me that I had better be glad that he had married me because I was fat and stupid and could not do anything right. Even though I was the one working and paying the bills.

He sat around during the day and was always telling me how sick he was. But come night time he would go out and get drunk. I was constantly accused of cheating on him.

I finally got the courage to take my kids and leave after he had been pointing a gun at my son.

Friends began to tell me that I should give him another chance and they were afraid he might hurt himself. At the same time he was begging me to come back. Promising that it would be difficult. I finally let myself be drawn back in. I had always been someone's property. Being on my own with kids to care for was very scary.

The promises he had made hardly lastly lasted a week. It was back to the abuse and mind twisting in no time.

Before the final break from him he had raped me and put a gun to my head and told me that he would kill me. He threatened suicide and that he would have someone come after me. That I would have broken arms and legs. After I had moved out again he moved into a trailer almost right behind me.

One night as I was going to my car he came out from behind a tree, grabbed me by the shoulders and slammed me up against the side of the house. All the time telling me that he would kill me or hurt me in some other way.

This is not a complete story. I have left things out. But I have tried to tell you some of the things that I think others that read this might see a pattern in their relationships and try to change things for themselves.

I would not wish my childhood on anyone or most of my adult life.

It has been only the past couple of years that I have learned that you can be happy and safe.

PD

PD is 51 years old. She was born in upstate New York, but lived all over the country and in Germany as her family followed the father's military career. PD was a victim of abuse in her family and in subsequent marriages and relationships. Throughout these relations, she has battled severe depression. She lives in Jackson County, Florida.

JR: Jan Rosenberg
PD

On growing up
PD: Well I grew up all over because my dad was in the military. So, I've lived, I'd say half the states this side of the Mississippi. And in Germany, lived in Germany for three years. And my mom and dad got divorced when I was, they separated when I was 11. And were divorced when I was 12 I think, and I was a daddy's girl.
JR: Uh huh
PD: And I was so much like my father, I mean I followed him around like a puppy dog. He'd go to scary movies at the drive-in and I'd go with him just to be with him. And then I'd want to crawl in bed with my mom and dad at night because I was afraid to be in bed by myself. (laugh)
So when he left, things starts, that's really when things went downhill. Other than my grandfather. I had abuse there.
JR: How so?
PD: It was sexual abuse. And I really don't remember when it started. I don't remember when it wasn't happening. So and that went on till I was about 15 and I finally threatened to tell, but I was scared to death to do it, you know.
JR: Was this your grandfather?
PD: Yes. It was my mother's stepfather. And I didn't you know, I thought it was something that I was doing something wrong. You know. And then I finally figured out that it wasn't normal, you know? But I think it was, I don't think my life was normal from the time we came back from Germany when I was nine years old. Because I guess that's when my mom and dad started fussing and fighting each other. My mother has a very violent temper and she'd get mad if she couldn't reach you to hit you with something, she'd throw something at you. (laugh) It didn't make a difference to her as long as she got you.
So when my mom and dad divorced the last time I saw my dad was when I was 13. And that was before he went to Korea. And it was the only time my mother let him see me. But in the meantime, it was always "You're just like your father." And I think I got very low self esteem from that because my mother was always cutting my dad down. And I don't know, I guess I just got it in my head if he was such a bad person and not worth anything, and I was like him. I had to been, you know, I wasn't worth anything either. And I was told that till I graduated from high school, "You're just like your father."

And my mother remarried when I was 14, no 13 and my stepfather was also in the army. And it was like my mother just turned care of all of us over to him. And the man didn't have a clue because he didn't have any kids.

JR: How many of there were you?

PD: At that time there were six of us. And we ranged in age from 14 to two years old. Yeah.

So, the youngest one is ten years younger than me. And of course she was spoiled rotten. My stepfather had very funny ways. Of course my first reaction when I saw him was I don't want anything to do with him. He's not going to take my father's place. And I think that, and I told my mother that. I didn't like him. I didn't like him at all. And things just went downhill from there because he was very strict. I wasn't allowed to have friends. I wasn't allowed to talk on the phone. Went to school, I babysat, and I wasn't allowed to baby-sit during the week if I didn't go to church on Sunday. They wouldn't go to church but they would drop us outside the church door, me and my sister Denise. And wait for us to go inside and pick us up when church was over. And if we didn't go to church no babysitting, which meant no money. And I bought or made all of my own clothes from the time I was in junior high. It was like my mother went from being married to a warrant officer making, having good money, to an E-5 which is there's no way and E-5 (laugh) can support eight people. It's ridiculous. But she went from having it all to having basically nothing. And she took it out, took a lot of frustration out on some of us. She had her favorites. My oldest brother, and then Denise was the one that my mother was constantly pitting us against each other. And because I was just like my father, and Denise was her favorite, she always sided with Denise. That no matter what it was, no matter whether it was right or wrong, Denise and I have never gotten along.

What you want me to tell you?

JR: You're telling me.

PD: I went through high school with I guess I would have to say most of my life from junior high on was just kind of like being a third person watching my life go by. It was at times it was... My stepfather was abusive, we actually got into fist fights. I was at the time five foot and weighed 100 pounds and he's like 6'3" and weighed close to twice what I weighed. But we would have physical fights. When I was 17 he broke my nose. My mother was there, they wouldn't take me to the hospital. They didn't want anybody to know it. And so I was out of school for awhile, sick, my whole face was black and blue. They wouldn't take me to the hospital and I couldn't even see anything for several hours after it happened. And you know that's just the way it went. Do what you're told so you didn't get smacked around. My mother was very good at that, I mean, if you even looked at her wrong, she'd smack you. I don't mean just smack, she has used fly swatters, not the little flappy part, but the handle part. She has used wooden spoons, she's used belts, she's used coat hangers. Like I said, if she couldn't reach you, she'd throw something at you.

And like I said, she had a very hot temper, and it was like I never could please her. And I tried, I tried to please her till I was like probably 35. And finally, I just gave up. There was nothing that I could do was going to make her like me. And I think most of it was because I was so much like my father. And I didn't realize that until I met him again.

But the day I graduated from high school, I moved out.

JR: Where did you graduate from?

PD: I graduated from a little tiny town in New York. We moved there six weeks before my graduation. I had been going to school in Texas, we were at the naval air station there in Corpus Christi, and I turned 18 the day we left there and I was not allowed to stay. So I had to go, I went to New York, which was okay, that's where my family was from, and I moved in with my aunt the day, I mean I had my stuff packed, and Aunt Bette and Uncle Bill I was scared to death to tell my mother. . . . All hell would break loose. And it did. She yelled and screamed at me, cried and went on, and yelled and screamed at my aunt and uncle and I just, we left.

But I did okay at my aunt's house. I had the first summer vacation that I actually had from the time I was in junior high. That I got to have for myself instead of working. Because I worked every summer, babysitting full time to make money for school clothes and stuff. To pay for my stuff for graduation, to pay for my lunches at school, whatever. I bought, I had to get my own. My brother who was in the same grade with me all the way from kindergarten to six weeks before graduation in the same class. It was like my mother was totally different with him. It was just whatever he wanted, he never had to get a job. He came and went as he pleased. I was not allowed to go anywhere. I was not allowed to date, I had no friends. I got very withdrawn by the time I was in high school. Kids thought I was snobby. But I (laugh) wasn't snobby, I was just, it was just too hard to talk to somebody.

So things were going okay at my aunt's house. I got a job, I liked my job, I had a boyfriend, first boyfriend I had. And we were together for two years and he had gone to college, and I let my mother talk me into, actually I didn't let. She didn't talk me into it; she told me I had to do it. My grandfather took my car, signed my name to the title and sold it and bought two plane tickets, one for me and one for Denise to send us back to my mother's because my grandmother and grandfather couldn't handle Denise because by the time she was 14 she was flat wild. And I think, and I still think to this day it was because my grandfather molested her too.

JR: So Denise lived with your grandparents.

PD: She did for awhile because my mother couldn't handle her. She was just . . . She was very promiscuous... From what I understand, if you are sexually molested as a child, you go either one of two ways. You could close down, shut out everything and basically that's what I did, and Denise went the total opposite. She was just, you know, she was too much for my mother to handle so she sent her to my grandmother and she wasn't there very long when my grandmother told my mother she had to go back, she couldn't, it was just too much on her.

So my grandfather sold my car and bought us plane tickets. My mother called crying "You have to bring her down here she can't come by herself."

JR: Now where was your mother living?

PD: In Texas.

JR: Was she back in Corpus Christi?

PD: No, by that time they were stationed, my stepfather were stationed at Fort Hood.

JR: In El Paso?

PD: No, it's in Killean ... close to Waco.

And I got back down there. I never should have, I should have refused to go. Because it was just the same, the same thing I went through in high school.

My mother had two men, two guys from my step dad's company, from the base waving for us when we got off of the plane. I guess she was determined to marry us off. When we got down there in April and my sister Denise was married in June. And I balked on the idea big time. (laugh) I had a boyfriend, and she finally, she, my mother is very good at getting her way. I don't want to say brainwashing, but it's just like, it's constant, never lets up until she gets her way and it's just, I didn't even like this guy. I didn't even like him. And I had never had sex, you know, my grandfather had molested me, but he had never actually penetrated me. And so I had had my boyfriend for two years, we had never had sex because you know we were waiting. And we had plans. And I just let my mother just. I knew better than to go back down there, but I did.

Any ways, the night my sister got married, everyone was pretty much lit, drunk and I just didn't drink, I hadn't. And so it didn't take but a couple of beers for me to be, you know, just out of it. The one, Roscoe, was his name that my mother wanted me to marry, and I had told him no, and my mother just kept on and on and on, but anyways the night my sister got married. I haven't told this to Janet even. He forced me to have sex with him that night, and I was drunk. We're in the middle of the living room floor, and I was supposed to have been sleeping on the couch and they were still, you know, him and Denise and her husband are all partying 'cause it was all at my mom's house. And I decided then that I wasn't, you know, I was used, I was damaged goods, you know.

So I married him. I didn't even like him. And I gave him back the ring, he gave me a ring, I give it back to him once and I wasn't marrying him, I was going back to New York and my mother just, you know, "Look at all he's doing for you. He'll provide for you, and you will have a good life and this is what you're used to and you know, and I married him. And it didn't last. Six months before I moved out. Because we were just totally different people. I was very shy, he liked to party. He did drugs. The guys in the company partied all the time. He would bring guys to the house from the company and that's all it was, it was just all the guys and they were at my house. We were the only ones that were married of the younger people in the company. And he would just come in and here would all the guys come in too, and there would be drinking and be doing drugs and everything else, and it's like the guys didn't bother me. They never made any advances or anything, they were all very respectful of me. Except for my own husband. He'd get drunk and he'd just start, he'd start shoving me around and stuff and his friends would make him quit. And when his friends were around, weren't around was I actually liked having his friends around because I felt safer when they were there, than when they weren't.

He had come in one day, we just moved into a new apartment, was on the second story, had an outside staircase up to it, and I was unpacking, I was hanging pictures up and stuff, and he would come in and he said "I'm changing clothes" and went into the bedroom, and I was standing there hanging up a picture on the wall, pounding with the hammer. And I heard a clicking noise, and I turned around and looked at him and he had got a nine-shot 22 long barrel pistol in his hand pointed at me. And said, "I ought to just blow your brains out." And that's how he would do, and I think some of it was the drugs, but he did have a mean streak in him too.

That wasn't the only time. One of my younger sisters threw stuff to get him off of me when he had me down, well he had me down several times, he had me down on the ground outside of the apartment with a broom handle across my throat trying to choke me to death.

And the last time I saw him and my mother for a few years was my mother had called me, I had filed for a divorce, I had moved out, went to my mother's and that didn't work because my mother had told me you know, I had been gone, for the day to a friend's house and came back and she said "Roscoe's here and he wants to talk to you" I said "I do not want to talk to him. I've had enough of him." Because it was just a constant thing, the whole six months we were together. You know, physical abuse, trying to choke me, trying to kill me, whatever. Yelling and screaming, and my mother talked me into going into her room to talk to him. "You need to talk this out, this is a marriage. You need to decide what you are going to do." And I told her, I said "I'm afraid to go in there with him." "Nothing's going to happen to you, I'm here."

And I did. He no more got the door closed before he hit me upside the head and knocked me down on the bed and just started beating the hell out of me. And I grabbed the phone trying to call the cops. My mother's standing outside the door, I'm hollering at her "Mom call the cops, Mom call the cops!" And she's saying, "But he's your husband, you need to work it out. You need to stay married to him." And I don't think I've ever really forgiven her for that. He was just, I was just black and blue. He had not hit me in my face, he'd hit me on the side of my head, I had a pretty good hand print. But he had taken the telephone cord and had it wrapped around my throat and was trying to choke me to death with it. And it was one of those ones that had the really long cords on it? And I just kept pulling on it until I got the handset in my hand and I hit him as hard as I could upside the head with it, and it was enough to get him to let go of me and I ran out of the room. My mother's trying to stop me in the hallway and I just kept running and I didn't go back, I went to my friend's house and stayed. And I filed for a divorce and moved to Kentucky with some friends.

He threatened to follow me. Gave me a hard time about me getting a divorce. Took me awhile, but I did get the divorce, and in the meantime I had met my second husband. Was actually my friend's brother from Kentucky. And we got together and of course I didn't have a job, after I went out there. And, right away we got married and I got pregnant. And with him there was never any physical abuse, one time I thought he was going to hit me because he. I got very upset, I was five, six months pregnant, and I got very upset and I had been sitting on his lap in a chair. And we were arguing about something, and he shoved me out onto the floor and I got "You shouldn't do that to me, I'm pregnant." I went crying into the bathroom and he came storming behind me, busted the bathroom door down and "Don't you ever do that to me, lock me out of a room again." But that was the only time he ever did it. I said, "I've already been here and done this, I'm not, I will not take it. If you touch me I'm leaving." And he knew it. He knew what I had been through. And I just told him, "I will not take it, I will not have you beating on me. I will leave first." And he apologized, and said he would never do it again. He never did. Never hit me.

But with him it was just constant emotional, all the time, "I'm going to leave you." "Well, fine, do what you want." "I'm going to leave you." He started that while I was probably, we moved to Indiana right after I got pregnant, and then I just couldn't stand living out there. I was being, just because he worked nights I was terrified to be there by myself at night time. And so I just wasn't handling it. I had told him, "We have to move back to Kentucky." And I guess was about three, four months pregnant with my son, my oldest one, he said "No we weren't doing that." And it got to where we were fighting constantly and "Well, then you just do whatever you want. Go to work, get you a job, take care of you and the baby. Because, he says, "I'm going home." So I went and we stayed there until after my daughter was born [in Kentucky]

JR: Moved back to Kentucky, okay

PD: And, I had a hard time getting him to stay on a job. He was, and I should have known better because when I met him he didn't have a car. He didn't have a job. He smoked a lot of dope. I had never smoked any. I didn't drink, I didn't smoke. I don't know where I ran into these (laugh) guys you know? But it was like that was his thing. He was a pot head, is what he was. And that's all him and his buddies did. But, you know, I told him I didn't want it around the baby because my son was only 12 months old when my daughter was born. And he would finally, he had gotten into a school through a state program and I mean we got food stamps, we had been on food stamps since we got married, we'd been on state assistance, I had been on Medicaid for both the babies. It was just, you know, I wanted a real life, you know? (laugh) Not being stuck back in the head of a holler somewhere and never ever seeing people. The only people we ever saw was his family. Except when I went to town to go to the doctor's office. Church was mandatory. I had that problem at home, too, didn't I? His grandfather was a minister. So we went to church most every weekend, whether I wanted to or not.

JR: What denomination?

PD: It was Primitive Baptist. Which was a whole 'nother world to me. Not what I was used to.

JR: What were you used to?

PD: I had been to several different churches, I was baptized in the Episcopal Church, and I went to it mostly and the times that my mother sent me to stay with relatives, I went to Methodist church, I went to the Catholic church with cousins that were half German, so they were raised Catholic. And you know but this Primitive Baptist was a whole new thing to me. And, you know . . . I got used to it and it was okay, I did enjoy going after I got used to it.

But it was like we lived there for three years and that was it. And I never thought of him as being you know, that was just the way it was. I stayed at home, he went to work, if I had to go to town with something, groceries or whatever, I had to bundle up both the kids in wintertime, or carry them both. When I was pregnant with my daughter, here I go along with my one year old to the doctor's office. And I always had to go with his grandfather who was the only one in the family there who had a car. And it was six miles into town, and you went whenever Papaw got ready. He would call you and say "I'll be ready to go in 20 minutes." So, you know, you better be ready or you got left behind. And you didn't come home either until he was ready to come home. When I went I would spend all day, and I'd have to carry enough bottles and diapers and stuff with me to do me all day until we got back home. And then on the way home he would take me to the grocery store. And we lived way up on the side of a hill. Had a little dirt path to get to it. Way up on the side of a hill. And that's what life was like for three years.

JR: What was the name of the community?

PD: Hazard, Kentucky

JR: Hazard?

PD: Uh huhm. Actually we lived on Lower Second Creek about six miles outside of Hazard. Closer to Grapevine though.

So when we. He was working in the coal mines and kept getting laid off because, or they'd go on strike or something. So he was actually out of a job more than he had a job for that entire three years. And finally, I told him, I said "You've got to do something, you've got two kids to take care of." I'd threatened to go out and get a job. Let his mom watch the kids. And that was when he decided he would call his aunt and uncle in Indiana and see if his uncle could get him on where he worked, which he worked at a big meat packing place in Logansport. So he wanted to go out there and get a job and work for awhile and get enough money to find us an apartment. And leave me and the kids there. And I told him "No" I was not doing that, that was not could work. His mother didn't like me at all. Tried to pay me to leave when she found out I was pregnant for my son. (laugh)

JR: Oh my God!

PD: She wanted me to go to the Welfare Office and tell them I didn't know who the father of the baby was.

JR: OH!

PD: So her son wouldn't have to pay child support or, you know, so I could get state benefits. I said, there is, "I am not going down there and telling any people that I don't know who the father of my baby is. " So then she offered to pay me to go home to my family, I mean we really didn't... I just did my best to ignore her.

But anyways. After three years we went to Peru, Indiana where his aunt and uncle lived. And lived there, I got a job, and it was the first job I had in three or four years, and I just, you know, I loved it. I had money. I bought me a car.

(laugh) I had his cousin babysat the kids for me and I mean really, really cheap. And we were doing okay, and he got a job, he went to work at Wilson Foods, making really good money and of course that is when I should have seen a warning sign, he didn't want me to get a job in Kentucky. Because I had just, you know, I got the job and was liking it and everything and I had money to buy what I want, and then it was like he started in on me, "You need to stay home with the kids. I think the kids will be better off if you're home with them and you don't really need to work, I make enough money" and all this. Which he did, he made really good money. And for the time.

So I did, I quit working.

JR: What was the job you had?

PD: I worked in, actually I worked in a couple of different places. The place I was working at then was the name of the place was Cofabco and what they made was metal and vinyl seating kitchen sets and barstools and stuff. And my job was to screw the holes into the bottom of the bar seat to go onto the or screw the plates that attached the bar on.

Anyways, I let him talk me into quitting my job and stayed home with the kids, and I never realized how isolated he had kept us because it was, it was like, my car constantly stayed broke down. He'd work on it and it'd run for awhile and then it would be broke again. So his aunt. We lived in Peru for awhile before we moved to Logansport and his aunt lived about three blocks from us. And the kids were three and two years old and so I'd walk them over to her house, and at first he didn't say anything. And then it started getting to where he would, "What did you do over there? Who did you talk to? What'd you talk about? How long were you there?" And it was just like, every time I went somewheres it was more and more and he, I don't know he just. He wanted me at the house, with the kids at the house. Marion and Marie, his aunt and uncle would come and get them and take them to the store and whatever, but I was supposed to be at home. And then after awhile it got to where the kids were supposed to be at home too. They needn't going and spending the night at Marie and Uncle Marion's house. And he just did everything he could to keep us at home. And I never realized how jealous he was. It just didn't hit me. And then finally his aunt, we had started fussing and arguing because I was not used to being tied to the house. I had been in Kentucky. But I was allowed to go to town, but I went with his grandfather. I could go visit, you know, his mother, his grandmother, all everyone all there on Second Creek, but it was all his family. But then when we moved to Indiana, there were other people around. And his aunt's the one who finally clued me in. She says, "Look at how you live." She says, "You don't go anywheres, you don't do anything, you don't even have any friends here." After five years of being back in Indiana. And she says, "Haven't you figured out why your car is always broke down?" I said "It's just because I got an old car." She says, "No," She said, "It's because Butch is tearing them up. He doesn't want you going anywheres so he keeps tearing your car up." You know. And it's like the longer we were there, it was, if I go to the grocery store, you know, and you grocery shop once a week. You take, he had never kept the kids, he never even had anything to do with the kids really. Like he worked nights most of the time. If I went anywheres I had to take the kids with me. Saturday mornings usually, take the kids, go to town, and go grocery shopping, we didn't have a washer and dryer so I had to go to the Laundromat. If I needed anything from like KMarts, which was the only place in town to go shopping, I had to go there. But if I weren't back it got after awhile where if I wasn't back in a couple of hours, he would start calling around the stores looking for me. And I was supposed to do all this stuff with a two year old and a three year old, or a three year old and a four year old, in two hours you know. And get back to the house. And it got to every time I went to Marie's, took the kids over to Marie's house, it was a fight. His sister moved up there, and by then we had moved to Logansport, so I wasn't seeing Marie as much. The kids wasn't seeing her as much. She would come over to the house, and still he'd wind up "What'd you do, what'd you talk about?" And if I went to his sister's, he would do the same thing. He got to where he didn't want not want any of us leaving that house.

Now the kids were allowed to have friends come over there and spend the night. And but he didn't want them going anywheres. And I didn't realize, you know. It got, even going to his mother's house, unless he was with us we weren't supposed to go anywheres. And we lived out in the middle of nowhere. We had no neighbors. It was like, you know, a mile to a neighbor's in any direction.

And so, by then, by the time we left Indiana and came down here, we were still together. We had divorced once, when the kids were like five and six, because of that. I wanted to go to school, he didn't want me to go to school. He was afraid I would meet somebody smarter than him. He told me that. He didn't want me to meet. He said, "You're already smarter than me." Because he never graduated school. But we weren't separated we weren't divorced long when the kids were little, until I let him talk me into coming back. And it was a whole lot easier, I had been trying to make it and I had been working third shift in there and had five and six year old and I am trying to keep babysitters for them so I can go to work and it was like I wasn't getting any sleep because I had to go, I worked third shift, come home, I had to get them ready to go to school. My daughter was going kindergarten half a day, and so you know I was sleeping about like three hours four hours a night. And or a day. I would get them off to school. I'd go to bed. My daughter would come home at noon and it was, you know, she'd have to beat on the door because I'd be sleeping and "Mommy, Mommy, let me in!" Or the school would call, "Your daughter is being sent home in a cab, please let her in the house." You know. Because I couldn't stay awake.

And I was taking them back to Logansport. We had moved to my mother's of all places, which was two hours, two and a half hours away. He never once in the year we were apart came and got the kids or brought them back. I had to take them to him and then go back or stay there for the weekend or go back to work and then go back and pick them up to bring them back home. And so things just kept getting worse and worse, so I went back to him. And we got married about a year later again. If it doesn't work the first time it sure doesn't work the second time.

So in the meantime it just kept getting worse and worse and worse, and we got to where all we did was yell and scream at each other, and it was like just – Every time I would get a job, I'd tell him, he was still pulling the same tricks … But he was sick, now when he was out of work. So he still had his job, he had that job for 14 years, and but it was like every year he was something wrong with him, you know. He was hurt, or he was sick, or something. He had to have surgery or whatever, and, you know, we didn't have any savings because we had two kids, we were trying to buy cars, we were trying to buy house. We really had no money or savings. And we're young and dumb, to boot. So every time he'd be off I would go get a job. To do us, you know. And it was like I wouldn't have a job very long before he would miraculously be all better. He couldn't stand the fact that I was out that I was meeting people . That I actually had friends at work. That wasn't allowed. And he would go back to work, and "Okay, I want you to quit your job" And it got where we were fighting about that.

I lost a lot of jobs I liked. But it was in the meantime it was like everything if he didn't get his way, okay, fine I'm leaving. So, you know, and that's scary to have two little kids and be 24 years old and not know, you know, and nobody, none of my family there. I had seen none of my family. We didn't go, we went one time to my aunt and uncle's house in New York. And it just got to the point where we just argued and went on and argued, and the kids were of course right in the middle of it all the time. And we moved down here when they were about 14 and 15. And several times I had said okay that's it that's enough, I can do this myself and I'd leave. And wouldn't be a year I'd be right back with him, let him talk me into going right back. And I did that several times, I think three or four times. In all the time we were together. Altogether we were together 16, 17 years.

And we moved down here, I got a very good job, I loved it. I was manager at a convenience store, had freedom. I was making more money than he was making. And he got jealous about that. And it got to where he just wouldn't go to work. He just quit. And I was paying all the bills. I paid a down payment, I paid the down payment on the house. I made all the payments on it. He didn't pay anything. And finally I had worked, I don't know how many days it was straight in like 12-hour shifts, and I was really tired. And I finally got a day off at work. Well, he wasn't working, he wanted me to stay at home with him that day. I said I'm not doing it. I got shopping to do, I'm going to get my hair done, I am meeting Renee, a friend of mine, for lunch, and I'll be home when I'm ready to be home. I had just had my fill. (laugh)

And anyways, I came home that evening and the big thing with him was he never lifted a finger around the house. He never did a thing to help with the kids, to discipline them, that was my job, take care of the kids. When we moved down here it was like my job to go out and earn the money to pay the bills. If he felt like going to work one day, he'd call up somebody he knew that was painting houses, he could work a day. If it looked like it was cloudy outside, well it might rain, I'm not going to go in. So he got to where he was averaging maybe one day of work one day a week of working and then not even that. And I just had my fill, you know? Hey, I've been doing it myself here for six months or longer, without his help. I did this on my own. And I went home that evening, and he was in a sour mood 'cause I left him sitting at home all day, he was just pouting and of course the kids had got home from school and my daughter at the time was 14. And my son was 15. And we had to eat supper, hadn't spoke a word to each other, he just kept giving me that pouted look and that's how he would do, he would just clam up and wouldn't say anything to me when I was mad and he would be that way for days at a time, not speak or anything. And he say, I told him we got to talk and we went in the living room, sat down, and you know it kind of escalated into an argument, and then, my daughter popped into the living room, and sat down in the chair right between me and him, I was on the couch, he was in another chair and she set down in the chair, and she just sitting there swiveling and looking from one to the other of us, and I says why don't you go in the other room, bedroom for awhile, study, do homework, whatever. I said because Daddy and I got to have a talk. And she kept, you know, just looking at us, from one to the other, and she says "But I've done my homework, I don't want to go in my room." She knew something was up, she was curious. And I said "Sissy, please go outside or in your room or something." And she just kept sitting there and…

We had calmed down some since she had come in there, I thought, well, you know, maybe it'll be all right. And he had said something nasty to me and I told Sissy, I said, "Sissy go to your room, please." And she said "But I don't want to." At that time he jerked her up out of that chair and hit her right across the middle of her back with a steel toed work shoe. And when he did, I just blew up. I just literally saw red.. And it was like I could have killed him right then. I mean I just I was out of control, was how mad I was at him because he had never, all the time we were together he had never done a thing to help. Never cooked a meal, never did a load of laundry, never changed a diaper, never, you know, nothing. Never kept the kids when I went to the store. Never disciplined them. And he was mad at me so he jerked her up and hit her like that. He did, I just, I went berserk. I just started pounding on him. And when I first hit him he raised his fist to me. And I told him right then, I said, if you hit me you better kill me. I said because one of us will die before it's over. I said I am not going to. … He raised his fist to me and I told him I said, you better, you, if you're going to hit me then you better do something. And he just stood there and looked at me with his fist raised up, and I just started pounding into him, I was so mad, I don't know how long I did it. And in the meantime, my son had come out of the bedroom, I guess, because. … I finally told him, I mean I was even had taken a cue from my mother, I guess, and I was throwing everything I could lay my hands on at him. And in the meantime my kids are standing there watching all this. And finally I told them, you go in the other room. He says, "Well, what do you want me to do? Leave?" And you know all these years I'd heard that, well fine, I'll leave. And I tell you what, I said you go in there and pack your shit, and I said, I want you to leave, and I don't want you to ever set foot in this yard again. You've done nothing to help me with these kids, and I just went off on him. And he left the room and I mean I was just shaking I was so mad. And my daughter and my son were just standing there just looking at me, you know they're just stunned. And it's like...

And then he comes out. He's got his bags, throwed in a duffle bag and he comes out and by then I had gone into, our bedroom was very big and it had the bed in this part and then it had like a huge sitting room where I did my sewing and everything, and he came out and he handed me a loaded gun. And I come this close to pulling the trigger. He [ ] it to me to shoot me to finish it off. I was still so mad at him. ... I would have done it. Except I looked up and saw my kids standing there in the doorway. That was really hard. (crying) I could have gone to jail. I wanted to do it. And if my kids hadn't been standing there I probably would have. I just had all I could take of it. Constantly fighting and bickering and putting me down, keeping it ... I couldn't take it anymore.

So he left

JR: You got divorced.

PD: We got divorced and I decided I was going to need something more. I wanted more. I felt like for the first time in my life I actually had a little bit of freedom. And 'course by then my kids were teenagers and it was like . . . having two teenagers at home and I had changed convenience stores. I was working with the same company but they put me in a different store and it was more complicated that store than it was at the little store I was at, so you have more employees, you have more chances for theft at a bigger store and everything. And so I wasn't making as good money there. And I decided to quit there and go to school. And I went, signed up for school and decided to go to nursing school, decided to be an LPN at Wallace College in Dothan, and things just went from bad to worse, I guess. Because I went to school all day, I went to work until. ... I left my house at 7 o'clock in the morning to go to school. On days I had clinicals I had to be there at 5:30 in the morning.(laugh) So that was a really long day for me because I worked as soon as I got off of school, I went to work. I didn't even have time to go home and see my kids. I would go straight to work after school and I worked in a convenience store and I was making minimum wage and you know, got home 10:30, on weekends at 11:30 at night. I had a part time job too to go with that. So I was working seven days a week, going to school five days a week and so I didn't see my kids much, and my daughter go to be a pretty good cook during that time she'd call me on the phone at work, Mama, (laugh) what do I put in chili? How do I make this? So, but it got to be where it was more than I could handle and I just wound up in the hospital I got to where I got very very depressed. Which I had periods of depression off and on since I was a kid. And, but I had gotten into a very deep depression where I was hospitalized because I was suicidal. And so one of my kids wound up one of them going to stay with my sister and one of them going to stay with Marie. Their father's aunt who had moved down here in the meantime. I moved down here, she moved down here and half of his family moved down here. (laugh) When I divorced him I think his whole family did. Bu t . . .

I was in the hospital for about five days and I was going to therapy. I missed some of my clinicals, of course then I was even more upset because I knew, I thought, I was going to get kicked out 'cause you could only miss three days a semester. And you have to take the semester all over. And I was on a grant, and I could not afford to pay to go to school. I had a grant, a Pell Grant. And that was how I paid for it.

So I quit my part time job and I had my schedule arranged at work so, you know, I could at least see my kids. I lost my house because I couldn't afford the payments on it. I lost my car because I couldn't afford the payments on it. Trying to get through school and there was times I didn't think there was no way I was no way I was ever going to make it, but I did and I graduated at the top of my class. And I cried. I stood there and just cried when I graduated. There were times when I didn't think I was going to live to graduate. But –

And then I had met Robert, my third husband. And I had met him before I got out of school. And he had actually paid for my daughter's wedding because her father didn't. He sent $100 to help pay for pictures. And Robert offered to pay for her wedding and I let him, and we were together, well we lived together for about six years, Robert and I did, and it was like… I worked as a nurse for awhile and then I let him talk me into quitting my job. He was farming, he was farming at the time, I think 1400 acres. And I was the gopher and I carried lunch to the crews and I took care of the house and I did all the yard work and everything at the house, we had a very big yard it was almost like seven acres yard, six acre yard. And which I enjoyed doing it, but it was in I didn't mind doing the housework and that stuff, it didn't bother me. I guess I was just used to doing it. I'd been doing it since I was a kid. But he got to the point and I saw some warning signs but I didn't recognize them as warning signs at the time, I mean, little things would click in my head like this isn't right or something. But I didn't pay attention to it. And I should have.

He was very controlling. He didn't control how much money I spent, like that, but I really kind of was never one to spend a lot of somebody else's money and I still considered it his money, you know, we were living together a long time. And I took care of the check book and I could write a check when I wanted to. And he very rarely said anything about it. He didn't mind me going anywheres, I had a friend that we went to the Country Music Awards one year, and we were gone five days four nights. He didn't care. I went to Germany for three months when my daughter was pregnant. And it didn't bother him. But I never wore my hair the right way, I never wore the right kind of clothes, I had too many flowers everywhere, I don't like that person, that's a low class person, He liked to think that he was, you know, better than damn near everybody.

So it was pretty much, you know I love to listen to music, I don't rarely watch TV. He had to have the TV on all the time. I think some people get so used to the noise from it, that they don't even watch it they just, it's there. And I liked music, so when he was gone, I always had the radio on, I'd get up, he'd leave in the morning and I always had the radio on once I was at home. And he'd come in and the first thing he would do is turn the radio off. And I'm like why do you always do that? I was listening to that. Yeah, but I don't like it it's rock and roll gives me a headache. Or country music just makes me so depressed. And you know, it was like unless it was something he wanted or he liked it wasn't the right thing. I , he always knew better.

Like with vehicles. He would tell me "Go look at and [ ] what kind of vehicle you like. But then if it wasn't a Chevy, you know, well you know that's not going to last or that's not. I want you to look at a Chevy. And it always had to be whatever, and it always wound up being whatever kind of vehicle he wanted to be. Never what I wanted it to be. And it was supposed to have been my vehicle, you know? But the vehicles were always in his name, everything was in his name.

I left him several times. I seemed to do that I seem to be able to stay with him and put up with it for awhile until, okay, I've had my fill. And Robert would say I'd get a wild hair and I'd take off. And I kept going back to him and it the same thing basically with all of them. I'd just keep going back and going back. Janet says that's because I was still trying to please them. And there was no pleasing them.

We were separated. We'd been together about six years and I finally said, okay, that's it, I've had my fill and I left. And I went back to work and I met another guy who was a lot younger. Robert was 13 years older than me and Eddie was 13 years younger. And I just really really enjoyed being with him. It was like he didn't, you know, tell me how to dress, tell me to quit my job, whatever. He just let me be me. You know.

And then I had another good depression, a bout with depression. And I started getting – I quit my job, I started sitting around the house all the time. I isolated myself, I didn't want to go do anything anymore, didn't want to – quit going out to dinner with him, I quit going doing anything with him and his son. And I would just sit at the house. I would just sit for days and cry. He would get upset with me. He didn't know what to do for me. I didn't know what to do for me. I didn't realize, you know, my bouts with depression were getting worse every time. And . . .

Finally I started coming out of it. And I started looking for a job. Had a hard time getting a job, kind of sunk back into the depression.

On the day of his birthday. We'd been together about six, seven months. His birthday. I had friends over, I was so excited. I got me a job, a good paying job, one that I liked. And you know, I thought everything was going to be okay. But then I found out that when he, you know, with these fits of crying and everything, he didn't know what to do for it, and one of his old girlfriends had called him up on his birthday and offered him a birthday piece. And he took it.

So right back down I went (laugh) and I think about three months later I married Robert. By then I didn't care about him. And we were married about three years total. ... I told him I would marry him, but I wanted a house with my name on it. So he sold our house and I told him I wanted to start my own business and it was like whatever you want, whatever you want. And after about a year I did start a business and he offered to help me get started and everything and it just kind of grew, you know? Took off and he thought, he called it my "play house" from the very beginning, go into your play house.

JR: What was your business?

PD: I had an antique shop and tea room. And was doing very good at it, and he, then we started getting into it because he thought I should go up there a couple of hours a day and come home. Had to hire somebody to do all the jobs I was doing. And he didn't like that. So he said, why don't you just get somebody to come in there and do it. Well, Robert, I can't afford to hire somebody full time to come in full time and do... And you know it was my business, I wanted to be there. I felt like I needed to be there. And it wasn't . Let's see, that was in July, July of '99 I started my business in February 2000 he moved out. We had bought a house in Graceville, my name was on it, you know, and we had spend six months re-doing this house. And in February he says I want to move back to Malone. And I want you to quit this business. And I told him, I asked him, I said are you going to put my name on the house? He said no, I've already bought it. And he said I just don't want to do that, I don't feel comfortable doing that right now. And he said it was all the business, it was all my business that was causing the problem. By this time he was farming 4000 acres, in the meantime I had helped him you know. I was doing the banking, I was doing the bookkeeping, I was doing the gophering, I was picking up parts, I was picking up chemicals. I was driving a tractor out in the field, you know? To help build his business up. All this time that we'd been together.

Well, you know, I thought I should have got some consideration for that. All I wanted was my house and my business. And I would have done anything, but he was absolutely determined. He thought if he could shut me down, shut my business down that I would go back to him. You know. Go back home where I belonged. But I just absolutely refused to do it. And we wound up getting a divorce and I wound up without a house and basically he had enough money to fight, to do until I couldn't fight anymore. And I just took whatever he offered me, which wasn't a whole lot. And in the meantime I was starting into another depression and didn't realize it. It's like when I would it was like you know afterwards I can see it, but during the time it's like I was in a frenzy constantly it was like I was making really bad decisions. It was like I was so hyper. I wasn't sleeping, I wasn't eating, and I was going from eight hours at my store to like 14 and 16 hours. And just physically just becoming exhausted from it. And I wound up having another really good depression, and literally, just let my business go, destroyed it. Just let it go, quit going, just wound up selling all my inventory. Like $27,000 worth of inventory. I wound up selling it for $2900 at auction. I just couldn't do it. I mean I was sitting crying all the time, everything again, and just could not do it.

And in the meantime I had gone back to   . . .after Eddie found out that Robert and I was getting a divorce – he moved out in February and in July I started seeing Eddie again. And I moved back in with him and was there with him till November of 02. And I decided to go back into nursing, and I went and I got my credits and got my license and everything, had a job. I was on orientation at the Medical Center, I was making good money. I guess I was trying to pretend I had no stress in my life. And I just got up one morning and set there and set there all day long: I didn't go to work, I'd sit there and I'd cry. I wouldn't get off the couch all day, you know, I wasn't doing nothing. And had a major major breakdown.

Eddie didn't know what for me, I told him I said I can't live here anymore, that I can't live with me. Let alone you. And he didn't know what to do for me.

So but I just kept putting moving out, I just kept putting it off. I didn't want to. And he and I started arguing. And he physically threatened me before I did move out.

And in the meantime I was not functioning at all. It was like I don't know how to describe it. It was like my world was ... And I went to the doctor's. My daughter made me go to the doctor's, she took me. And they wanted to hospitalize me. And the nurse practitioner that I usually saw, I had gone back several times and she tried putting me on medication and I was and I was just not functioning. And I hadn't been. And I told her I didn't want to go in the hospital that I didn't need to go in the hospital. And she was asking me about thoughts of suicide and I told her yeah, I had them but I wasn't going to do it. And she was asking me all these questions and she asked me what makes you think you won't do it? I said because I know it will get better, it always does. But this time it hasn't gotten better. (crying)

They put me on medication, my daughter had to call me all the time at home to check on me. And make sure I hadn't hurt myself. And I stayed that way for about four months. The only time I left the house was to go to a counselor and I did that once a week, my daughter took me to my counselor and I went home. And I didn't do anything. And in the meantime, I'm on medication, they kept changing it, I finally started to get a little bit better, I thought. And I started seeing Eddie again and I moved back in with him, I was still going to a therapist, my daughter was living in Alabama and at Christmas time she moved down here, I moved in with her, and so I started going, I was going back and forth to my doctor getting my medicine changed because it wasn't doing me any good. And every time it would start helping a little bit, you know, I'd go back to Eddie's and it was like back and forth, and back and forth, and I moved in with him again, and finally it was summertime last year . . . it was after I started therapy with Janet and going to therapy and seeing Janet every week and going to see Dr. Gray and seeing him every week. Because I had a really hard time getting my medicine right and still I have days when it doesn't. ...

And in the meantime I'm sitting over there at Eddie's, days crying again. And that was just it. Finally he told me, he said I can't do this anymore, you're going to have to leave. And that was it up till now. Eddie and I had our times. Good times and we had bad times to where we got into it and I would just not talk to him and just I've just been, Eddie [ ]. I didn't see the signs in him of being an abuser. But since going to therapy there's been a lot of signs that I have seen in him that I didn't realize that were there. And I did the same thing, I was isolated out there, I was the caregiver, I took care of everybody. I did, you know, and pretty much it was I didn't have friends. It was the same thing all over again, I just I've done the same thing three times and this the same thing running back to him. You know, several times before I could break loose of it.

And I haven't talked a whole lot about my childhood.

BS

BS was born in 1944 and raised in Cleveland, Ohio. She now lives in Washington County, Florida. She experienced abuse from her father at an early age and experienced a string of marriages to abusive men. She speaks animatedly, with laughter and tears, reflecting on a desire to be loved unconditionally.

BS
JR: Jan Rosenberg

Growing up
BS: In Ohio, Cleveland, Ohio in Valley View. Dad and Mom had me going to a school. When I was a bigger kid when we lived in Cleveland, Ohio we lived with my mom and my mother in-law, not my mother in-law but my dad's mother. And I was approximately, me and my cousin, my dad and my mom, my grandmother, my aunt and my uncle lived in like one big house.
JR: Oh my goodness
BS: It was getting pretty congested there.
And I was born in 1944. December 29th, four days after Christmas.
JR: Wow, what a Christmas present.
BS: Um hum.
My mom was a . . . there's a picture of Mom and Dad on the wall there.
JR: Uh huh, I saw it.
BS: And Mom and Dad. My dad was very very strict. I had real long hair, I can remember this. My sister and I, we both had long hair, and my grandmother that was owning the home at the time. My grandmother despised me having long hair, and she took me downstairs in the basement, put a bowl on my head and cut my hair to about that size.
JR: Oh my God, she cut it below your earlobe?
BS: Yeah. So I looked like a little Dutch boy.
JR: Uh hum, where's your can of paint?
BS: That's exactly right. And then after that this little girl started to change into a tom boy. 'Cause if you want me to look like a boy? I don't want to dress up. And I started being . . . I'm not a rebellious little girl. Just a person all her own self. And sister and I we got along to a certain degree, but I was the first one born, and she was two years under me. And her name was Carol, and her name is Carol, she's still very much alive. And Dad and Mom, my mother had to go to work at W.J. Schomberger's, making these bombs. And I can remember a lot of things. Still today, which is really amazing. ...
JR: What was she making?
BS: Bombs in the war time.
JR: Oh, okay.
BS: [laughs at dog]

And Dad was a foreman at the W.J. Schomberger's [ ] shift. . . . And Mom worked in the shop along with him. Doing all, I guess like piece-making things. Bombs.(laughs) That's what I was told.

So Grandma watched us. And that's where I had these real long, like I said, she had done my hair. So I became a child of, oh what would you want to call it? I was a good girl, real good little girl. I was sugar and spice and everything nice, but a tom boy on top of it. If that makes any sense to you.

JR: Uh huh

BS: And my grandma would always yell at me. Why she'd yell at me, it was beyond me, but my sister was treated just the opposite. And my cousins were treated just the opposite. So I felt like in a growing up situation, that I was the black sheep in the family.

JR: Uh huh.

BS: Does that make sense?

So I went to Grandma and asked her why did she hate me so much? And I asked her, "Grandma, why do you hate me so much?" And she goes, "Well, I don't hate you; it's just the way you are." So, okay, what is the way I am? She said, "You don't want to listen like a little girl." Well, I started thinking why should I listen like a little girl you got me made into an image of a little boy even though I'm a little girl. You see what I'm saying?

JR: Uh huhm

BS: And Dad would yell at me a lot: "Where the heck is Beverly at?" I climbed trees. I loved to climb the highest tree.(laugh) And I loved the hiding spots. I liked to climb up in the highest Bing cherry tree and just hide out. That was my escape plan. As a girl! As a tom boy. And I never forget.(laugh) He goes where in the heck is she? But he didn't say that. And Grandma says, she's probably talking to the neighbor down the street. Oh no, Grandma, I'm up here in the tree, I was playing Hide and Go Seek. Here I am! Here I am!

And when I got down, I got the beating of my life. I was a little girl. And I hated growing up in that factor. 'Cause everything that I did wrong, I mean that I thought I did wrong, I'd pay for it.

And then later on my dad got to be really more more abusive and to my mother, and we'd seen a lot of abuse my dad to my mom. He'd slam the table. The dishes would fall off the table and grab my mother by the hair. He'd slap my mother and we'd just sit there at the table. Is like, oh my gosh. Daddy please stop, please don't hurt Mama, don't hurt Mommy.

And me, I would see all this stuff and . . . I hated kissing my dad and my mother because they both smelled and they drank, they both smoked and they drank. Dad drank more than Mom did. Dad would come home as a foreman and have a foreman's attitude. I could relate with that now today more than ever. Very stern, very strict, very abusive. To me in my years right now, I would say child abuse because that's how I can actually relate with it, you know? He used to take my sister's and my head together, if that's not child abuse then I don't know what that is. Later on when we got older there was a white glove tester, the military man? Call this clean? You call this clean? Get over here. Pow. Why? Come here, come here to my sister. Bam! Take our heads together.

So I grew up with a lot of family feud fights in family. And I went into my own little world. 'Cause I'd seen how families would fight and I hated it. I remember we had this little hallway part in this old house, old house of ours, matter of fact it's still, it's an estate given to my brother now, my baby brother. And I'd go in this little hallway that had a, you know you can look outside on the back front porch? It's like an old brick porch that you'd see here in Chipley. And there were these windows, glass windows with the prisms like a crystal type? And I put my nose up against it and I'd watch the rain drops? I was very imaginative, very imaginative child. And I thought that God was having His angels crying for me when I was crying inside of me. . . .

And I went to, I'd go up on the hills in the backyard when I didn't want to work in the house as a growing up little girl. And I'd hide out in the graveyard. And I'd pretend that those people were alive.(laugh) It's strange, it's strange I know it was. And my dad he would tell me and he said, "Where in the heck did you go?" And I'd tell him, I said, "I was up in the hills." And he goes, "What were you doing up there?" And I said, "I was playing." Because you know we. And he said, "Well, you're supposed to be helping over here." I said, "I will." But to me that was my imaginary, that was my good side. You understand what I'm talking about? I lay down in the grass and watch the clouds up above, pretend that they were angels and sheep and all kinds of lovely things in my life. You know? I played with salamanders.(laugh) I had a pet salamander, I named him Sammy and later I brought him home, brought him home in a big glass jar. I used to love lightning bugs. I was a child of nature, I think, a nature child, outdoor child. I didn't like the indoors that much because there was too much abusiveness going on and I seen that and I hated that. So I'd go outside and enjoy the outdoors! Escape from this mad world. Or the bad world.

And my dad would tell me, "You're strange." And I'm like, okay! I would bring home butterflies and I was a happy little child inside of me. And he'd just tell me he said "You're just really. . ." Called me an asshole one time. And I didn't know what an asshole was at that time I was growing up, right? I said, "Okay!" Shrugged my shoulders, run off, go play. Overlooked that. You know, whatever, you call me an asshole, whatever. I'm gone.

And then, I was very very scared when my uncle come home from the service. He had black socks on.(chuckle) And an umbrella. And I would get terrified. Terror terrified. Scream my head off. Until my uncle had to either take his socks off and put the umbrella in the corner. It was freaky to me. It was the scariest thing that ever existed in my life.

My mama told me I used to sing in the playpen, Chickety chick chelak chelak, and then sit back in the playpen and walk back with my little shoes and I still have my little shoes today.(laugh) They're not bronzed either, they're little shoes. And she said I'd walk back in my playpen and be a happy little girl inside of my own little world.

And Dad would come home and I would kind of like get scared of him, you know, like growing up and always wanted to be away from him. He'd tell me, "How's Daddy's little girl?" and I'd look at him like, I'm not Daddy's little girl, Carol is which was Clicky in his life. She was named Clicky, nicknamed Clicky.

So he seemed like he favored her more than he favored me. You know? Even though, being the oldest.

And then we moved, like I said, from Ohio, Cleveland, Ohio to Valley View. We lived in this house, like I told you out there in the farm yards and that. We had a pet raccoon, we raised rabbits, we raised chickens, we even had, oh gosh, a big apple tree that I could climb up into.(laugh) And hang upside down and swing by my legs. Just like I didn't care, it was fun, the best thing that could ever have happened to me. I'd walk on top of the swing set, that's how daring I was.

JR: Goodness gracious

BS: And I would just, I was a very little girl that liked to do daring things.

And then my mother would always tell us, "You gotta watch, someday you're going to learn how to cook." I said, "Noh, I don't want to learn how to cook." Later on in school years, I majored in home economics. Minored in arts. So I had some good qualities about me.

Dad was never supportive to me in school. Never. I came home with the worst grades. I think I had the best grades of my life, I thought I hadn't come home with a B or a C. And I thought I had some of the greatest grades in classroom. And I'd come home with my report card, and he threw it on the table and look at it and he goes, "What do you call this?" And I said to him, "Why?" "Pshew, you can do better than that. You're so stupid." And I'm like Okay! I'm so stupid so I'll try harder next time. So I did. And my grades got lower and lower. As hard as I tried.

I can remember growing up, sitting at the table, trying to do my homework one night, later on. And he told me, he said "Everybody's gone to bed. You need to sit here at the table and do your homework till you're done." And he whacked me across my head. I'll never forget that.

He did not support me when I graduated, he was the type of a guy who was very, what do they call it, domineering? Tell you, don't tell you what to do but you have to do it anyway. You know what I'm saying?

. . . Like I said, I was a strange little girl, you know? And I had pets, that little salamander I had him named Sammy. I even played with my brother when I was older, on my hands and knees. In this playroom part. He knocked a hall tree on my head. Cut my head wide open when they were remodeling the house. I had to have 12 stitches ...my bone was sticking out of my head and everything. And I had to wear this big bandage around me. And you know what kind of goes back in my head at that time? It was Easter, and you had to dress up in like these little dresses you know? They were like chiffon dresses? And went to church, I went to Sunday School, my sister and I, my brothers, we all went to Sunday School, right down the road from us. And I went and had to participate in a Sunday School class. And I had this big bandage on my head and I looked like the fife and drum person. I didn't care. I really didn't care. To me I felt good 'cause I could stand pain. Yeah, I can take pain. I was getting hit in the head and having bone sticking out of your head was nothing and getting hit in the back of the head. You understand what I'm saying? (laugh)

And my mom passed out from the sight of the blood and Dad couldn't remember the number. And they were modeling the house and everything. And I'm like, okay, I said, when the Dr. Copeland sewed up my head it didn't even hurt. It didn't even hurt. I come home, and I lay on the couch and I didn't want to lay on the couch. They kept telling me they said you need to lay down, I said no I didn't want to lay down. I don't want to be having no pity on me. You see what I'm saying?

So I've lived with a lot of pain inside of me. I wasn't a rebellious child. Dad was the one who made me rebellious to rebel against him. And my sister too. You know my sister could get the better side of my dad. I was jealous of my sister after awhile because my sister Carol seemed to be the smartest one, he'd say "Why don't you do things like your sister. Beverly, you're so damn stupid! You're nothing but an asshole. (crying) You're stupid." You know, I mean I grew up with that. Plus the beatings. Plus the hits in the heads.

But I loved Daddy. I loved my dad no matter. I didn't want to kiss him, but I loved him. And Mom, I loved her dearly. I loved my whole family. But the family didn't love me. (crying)

I'm sorry

JR: It's okay.

BS: So then, when I graduated, I graduated 1964. I was a pretty girl, I had real long hair. And my sister fixed my hair up in a French Twist, like a real big high French bouffant. And she stuck hairpins into my head. (laugh)It was kind of funny. I'm like why am I sitting here in this chair and feeling lightheaded? She didn't mean to, she remembers this still today. And I say "Wow!" She goes, "Oh my gosh! Your head is bleeding!" I'm going my head! She goes, yeah. "I probably stuck the hairpin right into your skull." So she goes and gets a whole bunch of wads of toilet paper(laugh) and sticks it in my head. Absorbed the blood from the hairpin. "Don't tell Dad, don't tell Mom" I said, "I won't" And kept that as a military secret between sisters right. And her and I were just talking here a little while ago. She remembers that in her own little ways. (laugh)

So it was graduation day. And we went to my graduation and I got my diploma. I don't thank my dad for my diploma, I thank my counselor, my guidance counselor. He gave me the inspiration, he gave me the motivation, he gave me the determination, he gave me the desire to go ahead and grow ahead in life.

I wanted to be an airline stewardess. I really did. I wanted to parachute out of a plane.(laugh) Which is kind of weird, isn't it? For a girl. (laugh)

And I had a lot of girlfriends, I had a lot of girlfriends, but if I go to parties prior to this I had to be home at a certain time. And I did not, and I repeat, this is the God's truth as of today, which is April 13, 2004, I never had sex with a guy until I was 21 years old. That was my first husband. I was a virgin. I was real proud of me. Then that was a bad situation there.

And I had this pink dress, I can still remember this dress ... we didn't have panty hose, we had nylons. So get your dress up real real pretty, right? And little stack white shoes, high heels. And I thought that was very pretty. I never wore glasses or anything at that time. And I was having my classmates come to my party, my yard party, graduation, and my dad came up to me, we had this big lounge chair, I can still remember this today too. And it's a reclining chair that you push back, you know? And he said, "Beverly" he said, "Come over here." Said, "I'm so proud of you." I says, "Thank you, Dad" You know, I respected that. And he said, "You made the grade, you got your diploma, I want to treat you to something." "Okay. What do you want to treat me to?" "I want you to try something, just a little bit." "What." "Just a little bit of Cold Duck." "Okay." Poured it in a little glass, about that high [half a middle finger] . I drank it real fast. I think I was a dead duck. I really do.(laugh) I sat down on that chair in the lounge chair and the lounge chair and I seemed like to collapse before my friends had arrived, and I was so embarrassed. So embarrassed. I tore the knees in my stocking, and my dad was telling me "Now you are a real [ ] girl. That was my first taste of alcohol and I never liked it. Never. My graduation party.

So, what I had in my mouth, I ran in the house, I washed my mouth out with toothpaste on my tongue and everything to get rid of that smell, the bitter smell, it was, it was uch, it was terrible. But I drank it, you know? Why I drank it, Jan? I don't know. But I just did it. I guess to make Daddy proud of me. To make him feel love me? I don't know. I often wonder why I did it, but I did.

After that, never alcohol in my life. Until I got older. And I did try alcohol again. Later in my years I drank screwdrivers or bloody Marys. Never liked beer. Until I was pregnant. Then I liked beer. They always told me it would be good for your nursing situation. And that was a strange husband, that was my third husband. Telling me I drink beer I would have more milk for my baby. Which is Otto. 15 year-old now, going on 16. I despise that after awhile.

I was very very gullible. Naïve. Believed everybody that anybody would say things, I believed it. Except my guidance teacher. I truly believed in him, I loved him dearly. Mr. Frank. His name was Mr. Frank and he told me said "You can do anything, Beverly, you can do anything in your life. 'Cause you have a lot of guts." And what did I do.(laugh) Had a lot of guts to get messed up in lies with bad guys. But how did I know? I thought that was love. And I was always looking for love in all the wrong places. (laugh)

So then, like I said, I was I loved outdoors, I was a nature girl. And after my graduation party and that, I did not know how to drive, Dad never taught me how to drive. I went to live with my grandmother in Ohio, Cleveland, Ohio. And I became a, my first job that I had, that I can recall, was still back at home was working in a doughnut shop. And me skinny! I was only like 118, 119 pounds and five –six and a half, almost 5-7. You can imagine that picture that. So I looked like a skeleton (laugh), but I was proud of myself. I got this job in a doughnut place,(laugh) and we had this lady came in there, I took the orders, and I was never good in math, I can honestly say that. I was never good in math. 'Cause Dad never give me the encouragement ...

So I just left it at that. But I liked working with people, I found that out, 'cause I got away from everything, you know, it was, another thing I got to tell you Jan is when I was 14, I babysat for seven kids. Including a little baby! And taking care of that baby. Cleaning up that baby. Just to keep away and get 50 cents an hour. 50 cents an hour, which today everybody's like what! I wouldn't even take that kind of job. Seven children.

So that showed me right then and there that I loved children. I mean I seen that. I had somebody that I could relate with growing up that loved me and I loved them. Even though they were neighbor kids up the street and everything. And my sister and I we used to go to... we sang, we harmonized together. We'd sing together in a church and we'd sing at home days or fairs. And that was my inspiration, that was my rejuvenation. I loved that. And we'd dress us as flapper girls and sang for a home day. Five foot two eyes are blue, here I am blue eyes, I'm 5 foot six almost five seven and I'm like the hoochy koochy girl. My sister was a little bit hefty here [points to hips] but she, I always thought my sister was prettier than me. So we were kind of. And she was telling me she was all jealous of me and in my own ways I was jealous of her because she developed more than I did. I looked like an ironing board. And she had bigger bust than I ever had when she was growing up, and I'm like how the heck does this come about? Where did this come from? You know? I kind of like felt like a loner,(laugh) a female? And I was very athletic too in school, very, very athletic. I loved to jump rope, liked to shoot bow and arrows. Liked to run track, loved to jump what do they call those, high jumps? And with a pole, broad jumping and high jumping, where you stand on the ground and you go like this and then you jump so many. I loved that. I was very gymnastic. I liked to climb ropes. I could climb the highest rope in the gymnasium, all the way to the top, like a little monkey, thank God for that. That was my tom boy deals coming out of me. And I still would climb trees, even after I graduated, I'd still do it. To me trees were a beauty, and it was a secret, you could go up in a tree and you could sit up on that tree and you could feel safe, because nobody else could climb up there. And when I come down I felt very unsafe, I wish I could go back up in the tree. (laugh)

And then, getting back to my job, I come home and I was happy, and I was telling Dad and Mom, talking at the table and telling them this and that, and they said, my dad would "Well, how was your day?" I said, "Oh, it was great." He goes, "Did you work a lot?" I said, "Yeah."

Then later on when we got to doing the doughnut making, I thought that was fun, but I got paid in doughnuts, I think. 'Cause then I was starting to get sick on the grease smell, you know?

There was a truck driver that came into the building. Big, big brawny guy. Parks his big semi out in the front drive. And this was like a little, just a dinky little doughnut place, right? Comes in and asks for 48 dozen of doughnuts. I'm like is this for real? I mean my math was like 48 dozen of doughnuts. And my heart was throbbing inside of my chest. And there I'm like, oh my God. I said, "Is there anything else I can get you, sir?"(laugh) to be polite, and he says "I need some coffee." I got the coffee, "I need some orange juice," I got the orange juice. But 48 dozen of doughnuts. I don't think we had that many in the place. So he looked at me kind of like rough, in a way? I went back and I told the lady I was working with. And she said well we just keep making doughnuts and tell him to come back. I went back there and told him, I said, "Sir, you're going to have to go back, come back in awhile. " And he goes to me, he says "Okay, I'll be back in a little while." And then that's the day they let me go. 'Cause I couldn't pick up the racks fast enough and all that stuff. And that was my biggest let down, getting let go from a doughnut shop. With 48 dozen of doughnuts. (laugh)

And I come home and I told Mom and Dad, and my mom said, "Oh, that's okay." You know. My dad, puts up a drink, goes, "You're so damn dumb. You're so stupid." Just a remark behind the drink. You know? I can remember this. "You're dumb! You can't bring out 48 dozen of doughnuts.?" And I'm like, "No, I couldn't." "You had to lose your job, your first job." And I mean he dwelled on that, he [ ] on that until he was making me the point where I was "Dad, you hate me for this? What else do you hate me for?" You know?

So I told my grandmother which was my safety net. And she said "You're being too harsh with Beverly." She was my inspiration, she was my salvation, she was my lifesaver, she was my rescuer in life. She said "I'm going to take Beverly on a vacation trip." My dad says, "To where?" "To Chautauqua, New York" "For what?" "For vacation. She put up enough with your bull crap." That's how my grandma would talk.

So I got really oh boy Grandma, you're my sole inspiration, right? So I went with her to Chautauqua, New York, and she got in with a religious group.(laugh) But I love Grandma, 'cause she loved to bake this stuff it was called puschicke, it was a Polish dish, was a bakery. She loved honey, and I loved honey. I still love honey till today. She loved certain things, and I became a health freak later on after all these commotional things in my life, in my marriages. I never could eat bananas at the house. Dad wouldn't let us have bananas in our house when we were growing up. He would tell me it's like precious. You know, if it was Christmas or something we got to see an orange or something. You know, that's the kind of life that we lived.

My dad wasn't rich but they lived by. . . I loved oats, I loved cans of oatmeal. Just go into the can and eat oats. I thought maybe I was a little horse in disguise. I loved carrots, I loved carrots, I loved broccoli, I loved cabbage. But I didn't love what my dad did to me. He'd make me eat the fat, the bone of the meats. And tell me that was the best part of the meal. I'm so skinny. And that I need to eat more. And fat and the bone. Fat helped me. Today I won't look at a fat or bone, and I don't like pickled pig's feet. With the gel and all that stuff. It was gross. I finding myself on peanut butter cookies one time. My mother was making them.(laugh) This was shortly before I graduated. And Mom was working was going to a woman's club like auxiliary thing? That she made this peanut butter cookies and this Danish biscuits, rolls. And she said, "Beverly, said I made some peanut butter cookies and I'm going to go up to the store and you and your brothers and sister could have a few of them when you come home. " You know, later on. "Thank you, Mom, I love you." She had them sitting out in a big box on top of this piano, I went in there, I ate three, I maybe ate three more, I ate three more. I ate 36 cookies. I consumed that much. I fonded myself on cookies. Peanut butter cookies.

And she come home that afternoon. I had to lie my way out of this deal 'cause I was so sick.(laugh) And she didn't know there was that many cookies missing in the box yet.(laugh) And then when it was after suppertime, she asked me if I wanted a peanut butter cookie, I'm like oh God. I'm going to be sick. I laid in my bed that night and it was nightmares of cookies haunting me, big peanut butter cookies coming down and picking me up in the bed and making me eat more. And my sister, I told my sister, "Carol," I said, "I think I'm going to be sick tonight." And she goes "From what?" and I said "It's the supper Mom made and I think I'm going to be sick" And run down to the basement steps, we had like a big basement down there, and she goes "Where you going at?" I said "I'm sick, I can't go to the bathroom" Because you know, I just felt that I everybody could hear me throwing up and everything from these cookies. I mean I was so sick. Oh God. For two days after that, Jan, I didn't want to see a cookie in my life. 36 cookies is an awful lot of cookies for a teenager to consume.

JR: That's a lot for anybody.

BS: So, that I finding myself on cookies. And I don't like peanut butter cookies as of today. Still don't.

And then I went and went to Chautauqua, New York with Grandma. Had a great time, great time. And she was in a singing group, and I loved Grandma, the way she sang. And I said, she always told me, she said "You know what? Maybe someday you're going to be a little singer." And I said, "Why is that?" And she goes "Because you love to sing, just like I do." And my mom sang too. And my dad liked to sing, and she, but my mother was on a radio station. When we were growing up, my sister and I we went on Uncle Jake's program, and we sang "Davy, Davy Crockett." And our knees were knocking, we went down there to get some Bosco, which was big jars

JR: I know what Bosco is [chocolate sauce]

BS: And Spangbanker doughnuts. Huge box of them. And my sister and I were standing together, moving like this [swaying] and we were supposed to go on the magic elevator, that's how we got conned into this. We wanted to get on television to sing "Davy, Davy Crockett". And we started singing that song, "Davy, Davy Crockett" and it was like "born on a mountain top, born on a mountain top in Tennessee"

JR: Yeah

BS: And when we started singing Davy Crockett, and her and I were looking at each other, but we were scared, and we messed up with "bought us a locket" and something else, we got lost in the words, I mean totally lost. So but we still got our Bosco and got our Spanbanker doughnuts, come home that day.

But we had to ride in this magic elevator, and all you do is walk into a little closet, and all you doing is this up and down. That was the magic elevator in our life. Got our Bosco and our Spangbanker doughnuts, so we were happy.

My family had a lot of family doings, you know we would have a lot of clambakes, steer roasts, we raised chickens so we'd have steer and chicken. We'd have a lot of that cookouts, you know, hot dogs, hamburgers. There's one thing that I can remember that my dad had done to me. I was approximately about, let's see, had to be maybe around 10, 12 years old, and I didn't get new clothes, we hardly got new clothes, we got a lot of borrowed clothes. And I loved borrowed clothes. I loved the hand-me-down clothes. Matter of fact there was "Hand-Me-Down Rose?" To me there was a neighbor across the street who was just as skinny as I was? And she had some beautiful clothes. And the neighbor across the street brought them over for me? And I could wear them, my sister couldn't. And I felt like a queen! With the clothes, right?

And Dad and Mom had given me a coat that was a cashmere green, cashmere coat. And it was a day like this, almost a cloudy day and everything but it had rained a lot, I mean it rained. And it had froze before this, got real real cold, ice cold. So my dad was determined to take me, my sister, and my brother Chad back home, because it was a flood on the Canal Road in Ohio. And he worked at his, in Cleveland, Ohio still, and he told my mom that he would pick us up, my sister and my brother, and take us to the gasline, the new gasline in the back, pipeline they called it, a gas pipeline, and bring us home. So my mom says, "Ted, it's awfully flooded," he said, "Don't worry we're going to come home the back roads." So she did, he told her that. And Dad went shopping prior to that before, you know, we got home. And bought a big French bread, I can remember this, a six-pack of those RC Colas drinks, big bottles. 16 ounces. A chicken, a fresh bag of chicken. Tomatoes, all kind of stuff and he made us individually take certain items out of the bag and carry it home.

Well, we're coming home through the gasline, and it was real mucky and muddy but frozen, right? And my dad says, "Beverly," he said, "get on this [ ] here, stand on this side, trust me, it's okay. And I said "Okay, Dad." And I've got this cashmere green coat, white bobby socks, the black and white shoes, the oxfords. The long skirt, you know, which [ ] wore in those days, and my sister said to me she said, "Beverly, be careful so you don't fall." And I've got these six bottles of RC Cola in my hand, carrying it over the log. Huge log. Well he tells me to get on this side and I go on the same side and I sunk down up to here, my chest, in muck and water. And I held on those bottles like you wouldn't believe, that case of pop. That's what they call it up North, pop, not sodas.

And I said, "Daddy, Daddy, Daddy, Daddy." And he goes "What the heck's wrong with you! I told you over here!" And it was the exact same spot he said to land on, and he made such a mockery out of me, it was just . . . And my sister said, "Oh my gosh Beverly, you're in quicksand or something." I mean it was like muck quicksand.

So I here my new coat my neighbors had given me and everything, just totally muddy, wet, everything.

So we got home that night, and my dad bawled me out. Told me I was so stupid, dumb, why in the heck did you do this? Then I had to wash out my bobby socks that night, my shoes were ruined, totally black and white oxfords ruined. My coat was totally damaged. There was no dry cleaner there that would ever get it clean. And I hated that. That was the saddest thing in my life, growing up as a teenager.

JR: When did you meet your first husband?

BS: I met my first husband in '66, yeah. I was working as a sportswear model. I had a job with putting tags, these price things in this, it was called Lampels. And I worked with a bunch of Jewish people and Black people. And the boss came up to me and asked me, he said, he was checking me out, I know he was checking me out. And I was wearing jeans and everything. And he said to me, he said, "How would you like to be a sportswear model?" And I'm like, I see these other girls walking around the floor and I'm like yeah, they look really pretty. I don't think I could ever get into something like this. He said to me, he said, "Well, meet me after work. Come downstairs, my name is Marvin Cutler, and I want to talk to you." I said, "Okay." And so I went downstairs and I got me a job as a sportswear model. Along with being a pricing person, putting little tags on things.

So, it's kind of a long story how I met my first husband. But my first husband, I fell in love with a puppy, a puppy my grandma told me we could have in the house, okay? I went to the store, and I don't know if you've ever heard of stuff called pirroges? I loved them. And I had a plan, I had an escape plan later on afterwards, later in my life, how I met him, and what I did. I did not fall in love with the puppy downstairs in the basement at this lady who turned out to be my future mother-in-law, which was a witchcraft believer later on. That's my first life. That's underneath the trailer.

I went into the store, it's Fisher Fazzios, I can remember that. I was all dressed up and everything and there was this little lady standing in front of me, maybe about 5-2, and she's trying to buy dog food cans on food stamps, and she can't talk a word of English. But I understood "ponty poske" I knew some Polish words from Grandma. And I said "Ponty, nima" you can't buy it with this" And all I had was a package of pirroges, I wanted to get home to my... So I seen all these dog cans foods and I told the girl, cashier girl. And she said to me, "Lady you can't buy this stuff," you know. ... And she's telling me, oh, this little puppy she has at the house. So right then and there, my little ears perked up. I ran home, I told Grandma, I said, "Grandma can we have a puppy in the house?" She goes, "Yeah." The landlord? She said "Yeah." I went over to this person's house, total stranger's house and seen an Air Force picture on the wall. And fell in love with that Air Force picture. That was my first husband to be. I ran away with him later on. To Miami, Florida. I didn't think I was running away, I thought I was going on vacation. That's how naïve and gullible I was.

I took all of my money out of the bank, I had over $1000 saved. I had a plan later on.

He called me up on Valentine's Day, February 14th I didn't know the man didn't have, I didn't know what the man really looked like. All I know is that I wanted to meet him. 'Cause it was my heart throbs. You know, you see a man in a beige Air Force thing with a cap and everything in blues, you know, and stars on his arms and everything. Like whoa! This is my first love I guess you would've called it.

I met him later on, I told Grandma, brought him over and he smelled real good and when he had called me that evening he told me, he said, "I'm not like what you see on that picture." I said, "You're not?" He goes, "I got a scar over my right eye" and this and that. And I'm like okay I can handle that, 'cause I got a scar on my head and you know we got something in common. And if you don't like what you see, don't look at me. That's how I was in those young years. But I knew I was pretty. Because I could wear almost anything, real thin and I had pretty legs, and I could wear high heels. And in my own – I didn't wear makeup, but in my own image when I did put makeup on when I got older. Just as pretty as my mom. In fact my dad told me one time, "You're prettier than your mother." Which was really a strange blow to me, but whatever. As much as he hated me. That I was prettier than his wife.

And Dad was very crafty and everything, so I said to him, his name was Bill, too. So he called me up and I was all heart throbs. First love. And he said to me he said "I drink." And I said, "Okay, it's all right. I don't." He said, "You don't drink?" I said, "No, I drink frosties and I drink orange sodas, and I like pickles" and all this other stuff. Just a girl growing up! Young girl! So he said, "we're going to go into meet my mom." I said "I've met your mom."

So I went over to his house, as I was there before, that's how I seen that picture, right? I seen his dad sitting in the chair at the table and it was disgusting. Had newspapers on the floor and the man was sitting in his underwear, like in one of these old t-shirts, sleeveless things that old people wear. And spitting on the floor. And there's newspapers on top of the table. Metal table. But I'm not interested in this, I'm interested in this guy, right? Bill. So he talks to his mother in Polish, which I don't know Polish too well. Now. He's got me, right? He says, "Mama?" He said he called her "Mama" so I knew that was ... He said "Me and Beverly are going to go on a vacation." And she helped us. She helped us get away. And she gave him money, and we ran away in the middle of March or April. When it was real real cold. It was like 29 39 degrees in Ohio, and I got boarded the plane and was landing in Miami, Florida a couple of hours later. Fontainebleau. Here I come.

And I found out he liked to gamble, which I did not know that. Play the race, you know. I took him to my mom and dad's. My mom and dad thought he was a good looking guy, he really had the scars on his face, and whatever, but Dad and Mom kept thinking, he even told my mom and dad that he would like to marry me. So my dad told me at one day he said, "You need to wait." I said "Okay. I'll wait." I did! Maybe three, four months later I waited, then I went away with him.

Well, that was a trip. I got down in Miami, Florida, never being in another state, except with Grandma, in New York, Chautauqua, New York. And it was so hot down there! I mean people were walking around practically naked! And I'm like tanned and bikinis like you wouldn't believe. Jewish people and all kinds, all kinds of people on the beach. I'm like whoa! Is another side of the world I've never

JR: So you were a virgin
BS: Uh huhm
JR: And you were 21?
BS: Yes.
JR: And you ran away to Miami.
BS: Uh huhm
JR: What happened in Miami?
BS: We went to the Fontainebleau. Which is Frank Sinatra's deal?
JR: Yup
BS: And he told me he had a girlfriend down there, that was his old school chum. And I said "Really?." He goes, "Yeah. I'll introduce you to her someday." Okay. Whatever. I'm just young and innocent, right? I don't know. He's ten years older than me, by the way. He's 31, I'm 21.
JR: Yeah
BS: So he takes me on the beach, and I get, I'm very very fair complected, very very fair. Never been on the sun, nothing like that. And they would sit on the cabana parts with these high umbrellas and everything. And he bought me a bikini. 'Cause he told me said I had a pretty body. I felt pretty good about that, you know, I'm telling you, you know, wow. And I felt pretty naked too.(laughs) Because bikinis are pretty skimpy. But here I am long legged and got long hair and everything, whatever. Go in the ocean, play around in the ocean and everything. Then he goes to the cabana and he said he's going to have a drink, he said do I want a drink, no, I don't drink. He said "Well I'll get you a fruit drink." I said "Okay."

So I was feeling like the cat's meow. As a young girl. This was a vacation time, As I thought, right? No ideas of marrying this man. No ideas. No plan.

He took me around town, we rented a car, 'cause he didn't have no car or anything, and he took me to places and whatnot. Then at night it got late at night, and we'd seen a lot of stars up in the sky and everything, and I thought it was beautiful down there, totally, totally beautiful. And the ocean, you could see the ocean in the night time, and everything. Still a virgin. Still a virgin.(laugh)

And he said "I'll be back in a few minutes." We got in a motel. So he turns on the TV and I said to him, I said, "Bill, where you going?" And he goes "I'll be back in a few minutes." Okay. So I set down on the edge of the bed, and I gotten a chair and I propped my legs up and I'm sitting there, kind of pushed myself up against the bed and everything. And he goes, you know, he came back and he goes, "You know you are a beautiful girl. You are beautiful. You are beautiful, beautiful, beautiful. You have the prettiest blue eyes. Got the prettiest fair complexion. You're kind of pretty burnt now." And I said, "I hurt." And he goes, "Yeah," he said, "I got you some of this cocoa butter cream." Okay. Puts it on my arms and my back and everything, drop you straps off my little blouse dress, you know? Okay. He says to me, he says, "You know what? Have you ever had sex?" And I'm like sex, oh no.(whispers) And I got scared inside of me. Totally scared. And he said to me, "Have you?" I said, "No." He says, "You got to be joking me." I said, "No." He said "You got to be kidding me!" I said, "No. I never had sex." "Hmmm, that's the first I've ever heard that. You got to be lying!" Said "No" I mean I'm innocent, just totally innocent with this guy. He goes, "Wow! This is amazing. So in other words you're a virgin." "Yes, a virgin." "Ha. How 'bout that!"

I said to him, I said, "Why?" He goes "Well, I just asked." Okay.

Well the man was very like my dad? Dominating? Very cunning. Very coy. Very persuasive. And me naïve and gullible? You know we two of a kind? We clashed, came together. So he kissed me. And boy oh boy he kissed me and kept French kissing me and everything, and I'm like whoa! I'm getting like flutters in my ears and everything and I mean, this was my first kiss! I mean I'm and he's starting to kiss me around here [neck] and everything, and I'm like pushing him away, pushing, pushing him away. I mean just totally pushing him away. I said "No, Bill no." I said "I can't, I can't." He goes "You're kidding!" I said "I can't. I can't. I'm not married, I'm not." I'm very, very smart in that aspect. He said, "You want to get married?" "No." "You don't want to get married." "No. Don't ask me ever again."

He was a con artist, too, Jan, which I didn't know, see. I said to him, I said, Bill, can we just do something different, you know just stop?" and everything, and he goes "Yeah." I said "Let's go downstairs and go see what the shows are at night time or anything" He says "Why?" And I said "'Cause I don't want to do anything." And I didn't. So I had the upper hand in that department. (laugh) And so, that's okay. I had the upper hand in that department as I thought I did. And then he says, "Okay."

So I was down there about a week or two with him.

JR: Wow!

BS: Still not going to bed with him. Still not going to bed.

Then he called his mother and told his mom, talked to her in Polish, which I couldn't understand. And I think he said something about a ring. And I'm like, oh boy. What's going on? So he told me, he said "Let's go into this store." It was a big, huge store down in Fontainebleau, Miami. And he treated me good, I mean he made sure, he treated me like a queen. So I was falling in love with him, seriously, more and more and more. But I wasn't going to have sex with him. Seriously, I wasn't. As far as I can help it. As long as I can help it. And he said, "Let's go in this store and we're going to look at some rings. " Rings. He wants to become engaged to me or something. You know, I'll come back home, I'll be engaged, you know, Mom and Dad will like him better and everything. And at least we waited. 'Cause my mom and dad had to run away in Kentucky and get married, and that's where I came in the picture. 'Cause I'm going to tell you a little story about that later on in this department.

So, I had stars in my eyes, sand in my feet, the wining and dining, the eating, the good food. Falling in love. Not having any sex, that's the God's truth. Just maybe kiss in my ears and whatever. Get to fondle me a little bit. Whatever. Felt pretty good. Those soft touches that I never had.

So he went and he said "I got you a surprise." I'm like oh boy, what is it? He goes, "I got you a ring." "You got me a ring!?" And he got me this ring that was like gold and silver, put it on my finger. He said, "Let's go get married." I went and got married. The following day. In the courthouse. Then I knew I was doomed for it. 'Cause then my heart was, my heart was in my head, not in my chest. And I felt like a proud princess. I got a ring on my finger, he's buying me pretty clothes, I mean he treated me good. Everything. He hasn't abused, he hasn't hurt me, he hasn't so far.

That night came and I'm now married to him, right? Now I really got to think fast. I got my period or anything and even though I don't have it, you know. (laugh) I've got to think fast. So I go to the bathroom and he follows me in the bathroom. And goes "Hey babe," he said, "Hey baby." I said "Hey Bill" He goes "Why don't you call me "honey'?" I said, "I don't know," I said "I want to be left alone for awhile." I was very very – what's the word I want to use? Scared? Inside of me now? 'Cause I only got a ring on my finger. Which is pretty. And I know I'm a pretty girl. But I think I'm going to have to come up with a pretty good lie. To outdo this deal.

He says "Do you love me?" I said, "Yeah, I love you." And he said, "So, you're a virgin." I said "Yeah." He said "Well I got something I want to give you." I said "Something again?" He goes "Yeah" he pulls out this pretty pretty like a see through, it's not a negligee, but a almost like a chiffon thing, and I'm like oh my God.(whisper) So he had his ways with me. He wined and dined me. He pushed me on the bed. And he was stronger than me. And he had alcohol on his mouth which I you know, he was drinking before that. And I said, "I don't want to kiss you." And he goes, "Okay, I'll go wash my mouth out." So he goes in the bathroom, closes the door, and comes back out, he's stark naked and I'm like oh my God! I'm scared. I mean inside of me I'm like freezing up. And he goes, "I'll show you what we need to do." And I'm like "What?" And he goes, "Well first of all you have to lay down" and do this, and I'm like "I don't want to." And he goes, "I want you to" And I said "I'm scared", and he goes "I'm going to not make you scared. Trust me. I'm not going to hurt you." I said "I can't" and he goes "You can. You're my wife now." I said "I can't, Bill, I can't." And with that he spread my legs, he grabbed a hold of my hair, and he pulled me down on the side by the bed and he smacked me on the side of my face. And he inserted inside of me. And he kept jamming and jamming and jamming. Until it was actually hurting so bad, hurting so bad. Then turned me over on the side of the bed, and all I can remember is like a slap across my face and that slap, I just gave into him after that. Totally gave into him.

The next day, the next day was the most embarrassing thing, I couldn't hardly walk. I was hurting so bad down there, hurting so bad. And I felt so ashamed. Because how I was done, you know? It wasn't, it wasn't right to me, I hated him already. I really hated him. So I went downstairs and I got some money from my pocketbook and I went and called my parents. You know, I was crying on the phone, long distance call, this is costing a lot. My dad answers the phone, oh my God, that didn't help matters. "Where in the hell are you at!?" And I says, "In Miami." "Why are you crying?" I said, "Dad, can I talk to Mom?" "She's not here right now." "Dad, please let me talk to Mom, please, Dad let me talk." He said, "Okay, she just came in the house." Came on the phone, "Beverly, what's going on?" I said, "Dad, Mom," I mean "Mom, Dad, (crying) I want to come home, I want to come home, come home." My mom says, "What's wrong, Beverly?" I said, "I'm in Miami, Florida, I want to come home, Mom." She said to me, "What are you doing in Miami, Florida?" She talked to me real nice. My dad's yelling in the background get that little dumb little ass bitch and all this other stuff in the background yelling. And after that it didn't hurt no more. (crying) Because I said, I got married, Dad, I got married Mom." "Did you have to get married!?" That's the first thing I heard. "No. I didn't have to get married." "You're lying." "No, (crying) I'm not lying, Dad, I'm not lying, I was a virgin, I was a virgin!" "Yeah, right. Well you guys better straighten up your act." I'm like, what the heck does that mean? "Let me talk to him!" I said, "Okay." I said, "He's not here right now, could he call you back?" "Yeah, tell him to call me back."

So he talked to my dad and my dad told him, he said, he kind of talked with my dad, my dad and him talked it out, and he said, you promise you won't hurt me no more. And you better not do anything to her, you better not hurt her. He said "Well I've had sex with her," he told him, you know, over the phone. (crying)And I felt so humiliated, you know? So, so hurt, so humiliated. Like everybody in Miami knew what I had done. Because I was still hurting down there. From the abuse of intercourse.

And the last thing my dad told me, he said, "Let me talk to Beverly." I said, "What, Dad?" He goes, "Well, congratulations. We'll have a little party when you come back home. But you made your bed, you sleep in it." And I did. And I did. And I put up with it. Put up with it. And I became pregnant. And my mother-in-law was a witchcraft believer later on. We lived with my mother-in-law.

And we came back up north, I mean to, it was Cleveland, Ohio on the [ ] Road. That was our first place. We lived at with my mother-in-law. And my father-in-law. And she'd go out in the night time and peer through the windows and everything, and go on praying on her knees. In a white gown and red babushka. And then I became pregnant a year later after that. That's when Mike came into my life.

And then Mike was born and Emily which was his [Bill's] mom's name, she just died here recently. She saved the baby's navel, the cut of his hair, and everything. She was weird. She put salt and garlic in my clothes afterwards. Pushed me down the steps, I almost had a miscarriage. But it was thank God for my sister there. And I didn't lose the baby, I had all my babies full grown birth and everything.

Then after awhile I put up with a lot of abuse with that husband. Smack me, lie to me, tell me I was a little whore. Where he was messing around instead. It was just a pattern. Pattern, pattern, pattern. Dad's pattern. The way he treated me? I kept going on and on. I married a man 10 years older than me. My second marriage. I worked in a plant I was an overcast girl. And Mike was not five years old, six years old. And my husband, Bill, which was soon going to be my ex-husband? I still had him in my life, and he stalked me a lot. Stalked me and stalked me. And then I had the permission from the prosecutor that I can beat him up! And I did. 'Cause I hated for what I was put through. Beat him up with a baseball bat. He was drunk. Come over the house, tried to crawl through my back basement window. Where the dogs, they had – the screen was cut and I told Michael, I said, "Mike, I think your daddy's across the street." And he goes, "What're you going to do about it, Mommy?" And I said, "Well, first thing I want you to do is if I'm not back here in five minutes, come here I'm going to show you something." And he goes, "What?" "Put your finger in this little hole in the receiver" The phone? You know those type dial phones that you go like this?[dialing a rotary phone] "Dial "O" for "Operator" and let it ring back? And tell them you want the police." He did that. If I'm not back in five minutes.

So Bill came up to the house, "Hey baby! How ya doing?" Drunk as a bat. And in the meantime I had the baseball bat, steel baseball bat behind my hands. And he was drunk as a bat. "You got a lighter on you?" "No." "What are you doing? Go out on me?" "No" "You cheating on me?" "No. But I don't want you here." "Why? I still love you. I still care about you." "I don't" "What do you mean you don't care about me?" I said, "I don't. I want you off my premises. Before I have to call the police." "Oh, you won't call the police." "No I won't." I said, "Don't trust me, I can't trust you." I was saying this to him face to face, drunk as he was. I said, "I can't trust you Bill." I said, "I have a life to lead, live now by myself." "Well you're not going to get a divorce." I said, "Yes I am. Watch me. " He goes "Oh, so you want a divorce, huh?" Say "Yup." He said, "Well I come over here just to get a light. For my cigarette." I said, "Well, come here closer. I got your light." I messed his shoulder up so bad. I dislocated his shoulder, his wrist, his elbow part, beat him till he was down on the ground. And Mike went and called the police. They hauled him off in a police car, black and white police car.

Then I went to the prosecutor, filed a warrant against him. Trespassing on my land. Stalking me. The whole nine yards.

Two weeks later, Jan, he calls me. He don't remember a thing. He don't remember a thing. "Hey, Beverly, " he says, "I got something to tell you. Man, my shoulder's still killing me." I said "What!?" He goes, "My shoulder," he said, "Somebody broke my shoulder in some kind of rummage or something." I says, "You're kidding me. Who would do that?" He goes, "I don't know," he said "I was drinking." He said, "I was so drunk, you know how I used to get drunk." He said, "I got served papers to my house, my mother's house for divorce. Is that true you want a divorce?" I said, "Yeah." He said, "You really want a divorce?" I say, "Yeah." I says "Why?" He said, "Well somehow along the line," he said, "I don't remember anything. I had some blackouts." And he did have blackouts. He used to have seizures too. Which I put up with that, too. And sinking in the tub. Had to grab a wallet, put it in his mouth when he was going down underneath the water. I mean I saved his life. That was my husband. And I tried to save him many a time. But then after that when I seen what he was calling me a little whore, or call me a tramp. Come home. He'd come home one day before we got divorced and everything. He'd come home and I was staying by my parents with Michael at the time, and the landlord came over the house and told me my door is off the hinges laying down on the ground, and I'm like what?! My landlord came over, he's Polish and I said "What's going on?" He goes "You have to come to the house right away." I went to the house, sure enough my door's laying on the floor half-way down. "What the heck happened here?" The bed all messed up, bloody and everything. He was having sex with another girl in my bed.

Dad, he said, "I told you about this bastard." That's what he said, "I told you about this bastard." Who's a bastard, Daddy. But I said, "Dad, I love him." He goes, "Beverly, you need to get rid of him." "I love him, Dad, I love him, he's my husband." "You need to get rid of him. He's nothing but a crook, he's a con artist, he's everything." See?

But Dad, I love him, he's my husband." I'm telling you: whack! On the side of my head. When I was married already. My daddy! Not in front of the police officer, but just inside. "Did you hear what I said?" "Yes, Dad."[ ] Rather than go through a living hell with two men, now against me, my dad and my husband. Plus I found out when I went to bed the last time before this had to happen.

He told me to use protection on himself all the time so I don't have to worry about getting pregnant or anything like that. I was taking birth control pills left and right. But I got a vaginal disease so bad. It was so unreal. From him. Because I didn't get it from myself.

JR: Yeah

BS: So, that was my first ordeal.

And Mike's seen a lot too, Mike would see when he was sitting in a high chair, how daddy would dump the food out and slap me across my face and all that good stuff. Pull my hair. Call me a no-good for something son of a b and all this other stuff. And tell me I was a little whore in front of my kid. Tramp. But really it was the husband that was doing it to me. And he was the one that always: whoremaster.

JR: Uh huh

BS: So . . . I got married in February, I got divorced on Valentine's Day. And I felt free and really good about myself. Because now I'm going to become a whore. Seriously. Now I'm free. And I'm going to become a little tramp. Like Daddy wanted me to be, like Bill wanted me to be. I started partying. Started doing my thing. I started being a free for all little girl. My parents told me that you don't need to get involved with anybody else for a while. Okay! Fine. I'm not. I started going out with a lot of girls. Going to bars, bar hopping. Doing all kinds of little things here and there. Working though, got a job. Got me a job at J.J. White, Incorporated. Tires, tire liners, over caster.

I had wild parties over at my house. I had my own home. My grandmother gave me her home $75 rent. That was pretty cheap compared to what you're paying 350 nowadays? (laugh) Two bedroom house, upstairs and downstairs. Hey, I'm wild and I'm free. That's exactly what I turned out to be. And then that's when I met Dennis. Jeremiah and Dennis' daddy. At the plant.

And he was ten years younger than me. But I didn't act ten years older. I acted ten years younger. If that makes any sense. (laugh)

JR: Yeah it does.

BS: And I told my kids later on, Jan, about all this stuff, you know, how Mom was and all these good things, so, I'm not ashamed to, you know, I'm not ashamed to tell the kids, my life story, you know. Because they needed to know what's going on.

JR: Uh huhm, well that's good, that's good.

BS: And Dennis which is going to be 26 in July, he admires me. He admires me and so does Jer. So does Otto. And Mike? He's kind of eh today. He's the oldest one of the bunch and he kind of like, you know Mom, you used to do this, you used to be free and everything, but whatever. And I got grandchildren by Mike's side, little boy, four years old, little granddaughter. And I love children, I love children. I love children.

And then I guess I became, I became really really free and easy. And I even gave into my own boss.

JR: Hmmm

BS: At the plant. I went to bed with him one time. And I kind of fell in love with him.

JR: Uh hmm.

BS: So I was being, what do they call it, mischievous? Uh, promiscuous? The whole nine yards. Go for it. What my daddy made me, told me I was, what Bill told me [claps hands] yeah buddy, here we come! Got to go sow my oats.(laugh) And I did. And I met this young guy, Dennis, Dennis and Jeremiah's daddy? Loved me to the max. I had another guy that was bigger than Dennis, he was wanting to become engaged to me. And I played him, and today I hate myself for what I done, because I probably could have been married to the guy. Was decent, beat him up, everything, when I was drinking one night. And then I started seeing, I drank Zombies, I let my hair down,(laugh) I really let my hair down. I went in the bowling alley and started wearing the tightest outfits I could ever wear. Yeah buddy! (laugh) I'm free and I'm evil.(laugh) I'm going to enjoy everything I've got. I was going to be that little tramp that Daddy always wanted in his little life. I was no damn good, I was going to be everything you could imagine. And my grandmother even said, "Beverly, you'd better settle down." No no no no. I got my wings and I'm free. I'm divorced. Bill called me a whore. Bah! Don't want to hear anybody's kind of stories.

And I loved to dance. I love to dance! Jan. I still dance today. And my kids said Mom you just a spunky little woman. Hot mama.(laugh) But I went into go-go girl. That's how far I went! Got a job as a go-go girl.

JR: My goodness

BS: Up on a table. In bars! Hey! With the little white boots. These boots are made for walking, [clap] and that's exactly what I'm going to do. Let these boots just walk all over you.

And Dennis had seen that. I guess Dennis' dad had seen that a lot in me. I mean I was just a wild child. Nothing's going to stop me now.

He came into my life, and I got exactly what I wanted. I had kind of wrapped him around my finger. And ... let's see. I was 35 and he was 25. So went to bed with him. Whow! That was fantastic. 'Cause I didn't have to worry, we used protection and everything, and I was just a little Evel Kneval.(laugh) Get all the taste of the honey I want. And I'd make him beg for it after awhile because that's exactly what I was done to in my life. If you know where I'm coming from. You know? I just turned just 365 degrees tables around. I became mischievous, promiscuous, sexy, sexy wasn't the word. I mean just you know, these girls are pretty, but I'm pretty prettier than them. You know.

And I did. I mean I really was pretty, I really was. I'd have all these parties at my house. And I would not drink. I would not drink. This is the thing that's kind of hard to believe. I loved to be promiscuous, but I wouldn't let my hair down after I'd done to that one guy, Dave, was his name. Oh when I had went to the bar and it was on these bowling machines, and I was like wiggling and everything and he told me "I think you've had enough." I'm like "Let's have another one, let's have another one." I went into the bathroom and I couldn't even stand up. With these Zombies, had these little umbrellas on them, I remember how the umbrellas like they seemed like they were spinning around my head. And that night he took me home? And he tried to kiss me, and I pushed him like that [both hands], I said, "Don't kiss me. Nobody kisses me. I'm too good for everybody." That's exactly how I put on that trait.

And he worked for the Cleveland Press Department, so he taught me how to drive. And I mean I used him to the max. Not sex

JR: This was Dave

BS: Dave. I used him to the max. He bought me things, he was, he loved me, he loved me right from the get-go. But I also had Dennis on the line. Which was my bed partner. And he was bigger than Dennis, he was almost like 240 pounds. So, and I was only 125 pounds. Okay? So I was a mighty fine piece of meat to have, but no 240 pound man's going to lay on me because he's going to kill me. And it probably suffocate me and then I wouldn't have any sex. That's in my mind.(laugh) But Dennis, yeah buddy! (laugh)

I went and got me a car after awhile, I worked in the Sheriff's Department afterwards, 'cause I had a you know those saying "tote that bar, lift that bale"? I did that in the factory job. Plus I wigged that tail. Wagged that tail. I overcastted, big huge rolls of tire liners. But in the night time, on the weekends, party hearty. But not drinking. Just go for it.

And I made my house into like a little party house. And my kid was there, and then I'd take him to my mom's, have my boyfriend Dave, I'd tell him "You're my best boyfriend." I mean I used the best tricks in the books. And the guy was, I introduced him to Mom and Dad, and Mom and Dad said "Man, this is the guy you should marry." "Nah, I'm not going to get married no more. I'm not getting married. I'm going to be exactly what I want to be. Free."

But then later on I got married to Dennis later on. We got married in a through a mayor. ... Valley View, Ohio. And Mom and Dad didn't approve of him, but, whatever. Dad mostly didn't like him. But I loved him. Then I found out he was a bad guy too.

And he had a mother that when I worked in the sheriff's department, I had Dennis later on about a year later after that. And he brought his brother from Pennsylvania to see if that was his baby. Can you imagine that? After I conceived Dennis. All the way from Pennsylvania. Ask me if that little bastard's his. Then it started hitting home again, and then Jer was born, Jer and Dennis are two years apart. And I thought I, you know, I was working as a correctional officer, I had a home, I paid on the home, we had not a home, we rented a home in Valley View. And he didn't hit me yet, yet, but he was abusive in words. Verbal words.

Then one night I come home late from correctional job, which is a graveyard shift, and that was the scare of my life. 'Cause Mike was living with me too. Which [Dennis] considered his stepson, my real boy from Bill. And I come home one night from the graveyard shift early, I went upstairs, and here he's laying with pump gun across his chest. And I didn't know that.(crying) And he called me a bitch. And I didn't pay no attention to the, I've been called worse than that, whatever.

And I tried to tell him that he was drinking and everything, because he was. And he held my little boy Michael, (crying) he wasn't too little, but he was my little boy in my eyes. And I. He told me he was going to kill him. And he said he was going to shoot me. And I said, "Dennis, don't hurt me, don't hurt my son. Please, please don't hurt him, Dennis." And he beat me. He threw the gun down on the floor, then he ran out the door. And he said he's got a whore, he's got somebody better than me.

And I accepted him back after that, kept going with him. And I had Jer and I had so many bad things happen in that life. (crying) He hurt me a lot and his mother hurt me a lot. Dennis was just a year old and I was working in the Justice Center and I come home early in the afternoon and he had my car. He's riding around with his girlfriends. And it hurt. And I seen him and he didn't pick me up and then it hurt even more.

(crying) And I come home to the house where his mom lived on a bus, and I seen the car go past the bus. And he's riding with two girls in the front seat of my car and then I it was running. And I come in the house, and my mother-in-law Flossie, she's smoking, and she puffed smoke into my baby's mouth. 'Cause of the hiccups. This child today occasionally smokes when he does drink on the side, he's not a heavy drinker, but he's got a life of his own, and I blame that on me. Because his mom putting smoke in his throat. (crying)

And then Jer was born. I found out I was pregnant with Jer, and he wanted me to have an abortion. And I had his mother living with us. And I worked at Fisher-Fazzios in the deli. He was a guy that, tells you he's working and he didn't work half the time. Nine times out of ten he never worked.

So I paid the price for that in a way. And when I found out I was pregnant with Jer, he said, he told me "I want you to have an abortion." And I went to see a doctor, and the doctor told me he said "You're too far gone." And in my heart I didn't want to have an abortion because I love children. And he told me, he says, "Who told you to have an abortion?" And I said, "My husband." He said," You know what you need to do?" I said, "What?" "You need to abort him." I'm like "What? What does that mean?" He said, "Get rid of him."

We had a yellow Mazda. And I was determined to kill myself that afternoon when the doctor told me that. Rather than go home and tell abort him? And I was gunning the car pretty good, going around the corner. And all of the sudden

I just put my foot to the brake, and I was big, pretty good size. And I says, son of a gun. I'm not going to kill me. I'm not going to go kill anybody.(crying) I'm not going to kill this baby inside of me. No way, no way in Hell. I'm going to go back to the house, I'm going to move his mother out of my house, and I'm going to move her fat ass out of my house. I'm going to call the Law. And my brother's a cop. I'm going to tell my brother to get him out of the house.

I went back to the house. I had the guts, I had the guts. I said "Marie, Maria, I want you out of my house. You do nothing but smoke here, you don't drink you're a diabetic, your son you've teamed up with your son all the time. I want you out of here. And when Dennis comes home, I want him gone." "Well, you can't put me out!" I said, "I'm putting you out." I said, "Not only that, I've called the Law." "Why'd you do that?" "'Cause I hate you." She said, "Well, I've been good to you." "You haven't been good to me." I said, "I can't stand you. You hurt my first child, Dennis." Well I went and I had Jeremiah, I had Dennis, little Dennis potty trained. Potty trained. Totally. I was in the hospital, in Marymount Hospital, having Jeremiah. He wasn't even there to come and see his kid being born till later on. I can remember this like it was yesterday.

I come home to the house, the house is all smoked up and everything. I didn't like smoking in my house, I never smoked to begin with. Told you about my dad and mom. I came home and I could hardly walk after I had the baby and I got the baby in my arms. And little Dennis runs up to me and he goes "Mommy, Mommy, Mommy." I said, "Hey! Dennis, how you doing, hon? How's my little boy? He's crying and I'm like, why is he crying? "Daddy beat, Daddy beat." Well, I didn't catch up on that, you know, didn't pick up on that yet. "What!" he says, "What did that little bastard tell you?" Sitting in the front room, playing his guitar. I said, "Daddy beat he said "Daddy beat, Daddy beat." I don't know what the heck the little guy is talking about.

I went to the bathroom, was off the kitchen part, and there was a pair of his underwear, little Dennis' underwear, all poopdied up and everything? And I had him potty trained, both ways. Go both ways? I come back out and I go, "What's this?" I'm weak, you know? "What's this?!" "Well, Dennis had a accident, and uh, you know, we just put his dirty shorts in the corner. His underwear." I mean he had little pants, little training pants. I said "You've got to be kidding me!" I was nice about it, I wasn't mad. You know because I was weak, just had the baby coming home. I said to him, I says, "What is going on here, Dennis?" I said, "This little guy is potty trained." "Well, the little bastard just shit in his pants." "What!" And I looked at Dennis, and Dennis goes, "Well, Mommy, Daddy beat, Daddy beat, Daddy beat." That's all he kept saying, "Daddy beat." Then it dawned on me, he's telling me Daddy beat me. Daddy beat me. I had to re-train him to go to the potty again, with a new baby and him. You talk about my hands full?

JR: Jesus

BS: Big time. And I remembered all that stuff, too. How he called him "a little bastard."

So that day when I went back to the house and I told his mom that day to get out, get going, go find herself a place, I said, "That little bastard? You called my son "a little bastard?" She goes, "I never called him a little ba." I said, "No you didn't," But I said, "He was a little bastard in Dennis' eyes? I want the big bastard out of here." I mean, I had the guts, I had the guts to say that. She goes, "Don't call my son that." I said, " I didn't." I said, "That's what your son called my son. "a little bastard." Those were his kids. They're little bastards. I want youse out of here." She said to me, she says, "I can't go just like that." I said, "Well, let me help you." And then I went and got her packed up. Then got her stuff in my car and took her out of here. Took her back to wherever she could find a place, I could care less. And I found me a place in Ohio again, in Cleveland, cheap place, and I called my grandmother, which I told you was my sole survivor, and I lived with Grandma there for awhile.

And then Grandma and I kind of conflicted a lot, you know, she didn't like Dennis when he'd call me on the phone. And I was making my way to child support division, you know, trying to pay child support on them kids? And then when I lived on my own and everything, I made my provisions to take care of my children, no matter what, if I had to starve – That's one thing I'm proud of today. I maybe had to starve, but my kids never, never, never. None of them, never.

And he played his little games with me and he told me he can't pay this, and I said, "Oh well, should have thought about it. " I went to the Prosecutor, and to court, got child support [snaps fingers] bam! Don't want to hear about it. "Well, you know I can't pay –" I said, "Well, you know, you shouldn't have done what you did. Those are your children, and I let my guard down, whatever." I started getting a little bit tougher. Little bit tougher. Little bit tougher.

Then I became a church-going girl. Changed my whole line of thinking. I got involved in church, sang in the choir. And Dennis and Jer, we lived in this old house. I still have a mark here, a scar. I had to pound on the wall one night when I heard rats in the wall. That turned out to be a glass door underneath. Glass in through the walls. I called the landlord and told him that I could sue them. But I didn't.

Then I met Dave. Otto's daddy. He went to a non religious church. And this is in Ohio again. And I met him in the choir. He's a nice guy. Had a real sharp car, he loved the way I sang. I loved the way he acted and treated me, you know, I mean it was just the total, total off the wall stranger, I mean my past was caught up with me to the point where I hated what I had done. 'Cause I felt that I had done something bad in my children's lives. You know, I realize that. I tried to kill my self. I did. When I was just before I became a Christian girl. I tried to slit my wrists, but it didn't work out. Instead I just cut my self little bit here and too scared to do anything more about it and took a bandage and wrapped it up. Whatever. Gave it to the Lord.

I had me an old car that was given to me from the church donation. And I was happy with that, I had my kids. Mike went to live with my mom and dad after I had got David in my life. Mom and Dad were taking care of Michael. I had Dennis and Jer, I was taking care of both those kids. Along with the child support, and he'd come over there, tell me he can't pay the child support, but that didn't go with the courts, you know, you don't play with the courts. He'd come over there and watch me. He'd seen my whole image change in front of his eyes. My second husband. Divorced already. And going to get divorced I had that in mind. I'm going to get divorced.

Dave helped me to get divorced. Dave helped me to find a good lawyer. And I got it through Legal Aids. A divorce attorney and that. And he worked matters out, yeah buddy, I got free from that. And I was doing great. I didn't have much, I didn't have much, but I what I had was good.
Christmas time was the hardest time for me to survive. 'Cause I didn't have much for the children, you know, even though I had child support coming in. I felt like I could do more for those children. I couldn't get a Christmas tree like I wanted to...
JR: Christmas
BS: Uh huhm
JR: Christmas was a hard time.
BS: It was. And didn't have a Christmas tree or anything. And Dave treated my kids, Dennis and Jer like wow. Totally, totally, lovable person. Very lovable person. Smelled clean. Looked smart. Very, very smart. He told me he says I was pretty, which I knew I was pretty, but in the back of my mind, it didn't feel pretty inside of me, I knew I was pretty. In the back of my mind, I say that again, In the back of my mind I know I was pretty to a certain degree, but inside of me I knew I was even I was beautiful inside of me. 'Cause I've already survived, this is the third baby.
JR: Yeah
BS: So I know I was a good mother, even though I might have been a fly by night and all this other good stuff in the past. Had my parties and wild child girl and everything. Still kept those kids going. Kept them happy, and they loved every bit of it. Went to church, took them to church with me, never left them by themselves, never locked them in the house. Never abused them. Never beat them. That's one thing I kind of like admire about myself. Because through it all, all the beatings, everything that I endured, I would not beat those children. So there had to be something good about me in my life(laugh). Even though I had some bad things in my life
JR: You had moments, you had some bad moments.
BS: You know
JR: You had moments.
BS: Yeah. A lot of the little things that came up. It was new things happening to me. Dave was treating me so good. He treated me so so good, I met his mother, she was so so nice. And it made me feel like a woman, like a real woman, woman. Bought me little things just not really pretty, but just little things. Took me in that car with the kids, well, Dave's got to go. I said Okay.
Come in the house, my house it was really cruddy looking... And I kind of felt ashamed of that 'cause here he's looking good, smells good. He even when he dressed up in a pair of jeans or something, I was kind of like ashamed of how the environment in the house was, you know 'cause I lived above people in the house were Lithuanians. And that's another experience I had downstairs in the basement one night with the old man, I almost killed the old man. With the light

bulb situation. The light just went off and I was downstairs washing clothes. And this guy comes up from behind and he grabbed me. He tried to have sex with me. And I let him have it. Like you wouldn't believe. 'Cause I wasn't going to put up with it! I had enough of that life and I was a church-going woman. So I'm looking out for my safety- ness. And I told his wife and she couldn't talk English, so we didn't have too much to relate with (laugh). But he had a couple of bruises and scratches on his neck that he had to change, tell his wife where he got it (laugh).

So as it so happens that Dave was in my life, and then he said that he's going to retire from I think it was a US Steel mills. Republic Steel in Ohio. And he asked me, was really a blow away situation. I took him to meet Mom and Dad, I've always taken them to meet my parents, everybody. That I've had in my life. My mom's seen him come over in a blue suit, a blue suit and a pink shirt underneath, dressed to the max. Nice sport car and everything. Talked intelligent to Mom and Dad. And figuring out all kinds of things in my head, I'm like what do you think, Mom, what do you think? My mom says, "Think so. Think you made a right choice. Good choice."

Well, he wanted to become engaged to me, Mom. Really?! Hmmm. Well, get engaged, and just leave it at that. Okay. But I didn't. I didn't. I didn't. Uh uh. 'Cause I've been there, I seen it, I don't know what this character's all about yet. He looks good, too good to be true, but he's a beautiful person, he goes to church in my eyes, in my image, in my mind. He's a great guy, you know, he's clean, he smells clean, he treats me clean. Well somewhere in the back of my mind, was a question mark, what happens if I marry this guy and he turns out to be like another guy? Like the first one. I was so easy going then. I'm a church – I'm going to start praying to God that if it's intended for me to have this man in my life, it'll go. If it's not, it won't.

Well, he brought up some issues, he said, you got a pretty shabby place here, and all that stuff, and I said yeah, I know. He said, "How would you like to go with me?" I'm like, oh boy, here we go again. Where to now? Newport News, Virginia. Newport News, Virginia, yeah. He'll go, I'll get we'll get an apartment and everything. I'll take the kids, I'll take care of the kids. They could call me "Daddy Dave." And they were. Dennis loved Dave at first. Dennis started picking up little traits, how to fold a hanky and all this other stuff, it was cute. He was only four five years old, he knew how to call on Daddy Dave's traits. And then I had to get rid of my car, my Skylark, had a Skylark, an old Skylark I [] just recently. And I took him back to my mom and dad's and they said, "Well, wish you the best," you know and "write to us," whatever. And Mom and Dad were pleased with him. They felt that their daughter had somebody safe in their life, to watch over and protect them, He was a church-going man, he was a runner, a health nut. You know, hey! Everything was honkey dorey.

We got an apartment in Newport News, Virginia, he introduced me to his brother in Hampton, Virginia that's married, I seed a new side of life. I'm still a Christian woman. He did let me get my nails done, my hair done. Buy me the best clothes, buy me the best cologne, Shalimar, I mean expensive stuff. Buy me my first suitcase that I could ever travel with, that cost like 35 40 dollars on a charge card. I mean treated me like a person, person.

Then we moved into an apartment in Virginia with the kids, and Jer and Dennis, he got Dennis enrolled in school, bought the best of food, had treated us good, and I had seen that he ... brought in good food in the house, never ate collard greens in my life, that's the first taste of collard greens, loved them. Never ate grits in my life, but I loved them. And then we, ...He talked about getting married later on, but that didn't enter into my mind.

I don't know if you've ever heard of Eckankar. I got married at an Eckist later on. Then things started different. Little by little, not much, but little by little, just teeny little things. First of all, he used to spank my kids. Which I didn't approve of. Mostly Dennis. Then I found out he also had kids of his own from a past marriage. And he had three boys, and I had three boys. Michael, Dennis, and Jer. So my three sons on both sides. One was a construction guy, another one was a policeman, and another one was in septic, working sewers and that in Cleveland, Ohio.

So I met the family, his side and you know my side, and hey Dad, these are cute kids and everything. 'Cause when we traveled back and forth, we used to go back and forth from Newport News to Ohio to see his mom periodically, 'cause she was getting elderly, and his dad was still alive, and they lived in an apartment in Ohio. And we just checked on them periodically 'cause they were elderly and everything. And his dad couldn't talk. His dad suffered a stroke later on. And all he could say was "Mama." Mama, Mama, all the time, all the time. And I loved their parents dearly, they were really good to me. They treated Otto, not Otto, but Dennis like their own grandchildren. We fell into that category, you know that kids were treated good you can see that. But when we got married, just little things I could nit pick here and there. And it was mostly spanking Dennis. And then Jeremiah peed in his bed one night. In a bunk beds, he bought beautiful bunk beds, bought beautiful furniture, I got pictures to even show of all this stuff. And he spanked him one night. And I hated that. 'Cause I heard that kid crying. And I got on the bed and he goes "If you're going to discipline him then there's no sense in me disciplining him." I go , well, where's this coming from? These are my children. See? He's already taking control of me over my children.

And then. He still treated me good, bought me stuff, whatever, treated the kids watermelon, go to Nag's Head, North Carolina, we did this. Buy the best of shrimp, all the best foods. We met his brother, his brother works on the Air Force base, Langley Air Force Base, Hampton, Virginia. Langley Air Force Base, Captain, he was a big guy, big tall guy. And met Jerry, Jerry treated me nice, and so did his wife, and kids were treated good, got to ride on doctor buggies and what not.

And I seen, we were going to Eckankar meetings, which was really kind of strange because when I was in Newport News, Virginia, I had a déjà vu. It's really unreal how that came about. We were at Williamsburg, Virginia and before we got into that area, on the cobblestone roads and that? In Williamsburg? I told Dave I said, "I've been here before." He goes, "You're

kidding me." I said, "I've been here before." In my lifetime, in my back lifetime I felt that I'd been there, a little pioneer girl. I could tell him everything inside of that building before it was inside that building. And it was true. That's what really blew my mind, because when I walked in the building I'd have never been in this place, never been in Williamsburg, Virginia. But yet I knew this place.
So he told these people that was in Eckankar. And they said, hey! She probably was here in one lifetime. Truly. You know? So I started reading Eckankar, and all this stuff and got into that. And we got married as Eckists. In 40 degree weather, barefooted, nice white outfit, all clean outfits and whatnot.

Came back, my kids, when Dennis came back to this apartment where we kept our kids, you know, in a safe place with a neighbor down the street, elderly lady, came in the house, and Dennis' eyes were all puffed up under here, red, and his hands and under his little arms, and I'm like what the heck happened here? This lady had an apartment full of cats. He's allergic to cats.
JR: Oh
BS: Kid could hardly swallow, could hardly breathe. Got him home, give him a shot of Benedryl. Washed him up real good. Got him all cleaned up and got him away from that place. Today he's still allergic to cats. He has to get shots. Today. And dust, and feathers, and God only knows what else.

So, and Jer, Jeremiah was scared of Sir Walter Reilly.[Raleigh] It's a big statue in Nag's Head. And he'd go up and touch it and cry.(laugh) The statue's going to come and get him. Just a little half-pint little kid.

And we would try and encourage him and take him with us all the time and give him the best of treatments. Back in when Jer was six months old, when I was married to Dennis, he had to have three blood transfusions, Jeremiah, 'cause he had jaundice so bad. So bad. That he could've died. And Dennis' daddy never even came to see the kid in the hospital. But we had him, he today, this boy is 6 foot six, 230 pounds, the jaundice is totally cured, and everything. Took him back to Children's [] Hospital, Dave was there for that little boy. When he came out of surgery. Not his daddy. So this is kind of like, you know, how this falls in his pattern.

Then, we moved around quite a bit. In that marriage. Plus I moved around in my first marriage, plus I moved around in my second marriage, so I mean, I moved from not out of state, but from Miami to Newport News, Virginia, that was my biggest move. Everything was in Ohio back and forth. We lived in Atlanta, Georgia, I mean in Augusta, Georgia when I was married to Dave, too. And then we moved back to Ohio, then he got a taste of Ponce DeLeon and then we moved to Florida, and that was my last place in Florida was in 1992. And then that's where I remember how the abuse was starting. I would have been married. If I would have stayed 30 days more in my marriage to Dave, I would be getting a widow's pension. As of this year. Social Security. I thought I was married to him 20 years, what I had to put up with him.

He was reverse psychology. If you've ever heard that. He'd tell you the sky is blue, and I'd tell him "No, it's cloudy." And he'd tell you you're crazy. That's how this all turned around later on. If he told you you were dumb, I'd say this is stupid, and he'd change me all the way around. He used to beat me too. Used to pull on my hair. I used to give him massages. We lived in Ponce DeLeon, Florida, and we moved from so many different places. And it didn't show so much down in Newport News, Virginia, his attitude was there, but it was not until later on when we got further into Florida, and then Florida it start coming out more and more. He start getting involved with drugs, drinking, he told me that I was my children was the cause of him having a nervous breakdown. Which was not true.

JR: Why did you move to Ponce DeLeon?

BS: Because from Ohio he wanted to move from Ohio he wanted to move back to Florida, to get into a Social Security disability? He had a disability coming. A long long time ago before I even knew him, he ran smack dab into a garbage truck [claps twice]. Fell asleep at the wheel, in a Volkswagen.

JR: Oh God.

BS: And he told me this, he hit his head and all this stuff, and he was manic depressive later on. So that's how that goes on with that department. And I went, we also lived in Beach Island, South Carolina too, Jan. I moved around with him so much it was unreal.

JR: Sounds like it.

BS: Big big time

JR: So when did you leave Dave?

BS: I left him in 92 or 93. I didn't leave him, but I had got in the situation where I got to drinking a little bit of wine coolers again? With him? And they were really nothing, nothing bad to me, but he would drink the best gin, Eagle Rock bourbon? And smoke the best cigarettes, and cigars. And then Otto came about by accident. But in a God's way. And he didn't want me to have Otto. ... Wanted me to have an abortion. But Otto came, 'cause his middle son got killed. In a 5.0 Mustang, that skidded, hit the road, icy road, decapitated him. And here I was pregnant already in Beach Island, South Carolina. And he did reverse psychology, and I went to Life Management. I went to Life Management in Augusta, Georgia, north Augusta and that. I started, he told me he said in Ohio he told me I was crazy. He'd beat me up. I couldn't see my kids for seven days, I had to move out of the house. I had to go live with my cousin down in Caryville, Florida, we lived in Ponce DeLeon. I mean it was just chaos after awhile.

He used to smoke a lot of marijuana, and have hallucinations. (laugh) When he had his last bout was when he went home when we had a big big fight, in Newport News, no it was in Beach Island, South Carolina. I kept going to the bathroom, and I'd hear this "Mommy, Mommy." And I'm like what the heck! Where's this little kid's voice coming from? And I'd go outside in the modular home we lived in, Beach Island, South Carolina, .. What am I doing? He told the Life Management in Ohio that I'm going through a change of life at the age of 43. That I'm crazy. Yeah. And here it turns out to be, I wasn't crazy. Later on I was very much pregnant. When he lost his son, I was two and a half, three weeks pregnant. So there was the answer from God.

But we lived from there in Beach Island, South Carolina, I went through that abuse there, then we moved back to Ohio, then we moved back to Florida. And

then it was in Ponce DeLeon that he told me "If you don't find a job, this marriage is on the rocks." And I said, "Dave, I'll do anything, I'll do anything, I'll find a job. If it kills me I'll go out and find a job. Just as long as we can save the marriage." I went to Life Management over here in Bonifay. And the lady met him later on. In Ponce DeLeon, and I came all the time and told her exactly, her name was Alicia, I remember my counselor's name. And I told her how Dave would abuse me with words more than anything. But then he would beat me too. He'd slap me. And she said, "Why do you put up with that?" And I says, "Because I'm crazy?" She goes, "No, you're not crazy." 'Cause I didn't have no other answers at that time. So she said to me she says, "Beverly, let me meet him, I'm going to find out what he's all about." (laugh) She said the next time I went to see her, she said, "Beverly, you are a survivor to the max." I said, "Why is that? I'm still married to him." She said, "Let me tell you something, honey, you are the sweetest, sweetest thing that ever came into this world. And a true God up above loves you. But you been put through living hell from Day One. From the first day you were probably born. From what I pick up. Now this man is your third husband, he's using reverse psychology on you to the max." And I didn't know what reverse psychology was. See all that time? I didn't know it.
She said, "Do me a favor. Go along with the program to the certain degree, but do not let him hit you. Do not let him do this to you.." I mean, she named numerous things, and I did.

Then one day I was driving the car, his Oldsmobile, and the mirror came down in front over [ ] in Ponce DeLeon. And when I seen that mirror, it showed a reflection of me, that, who is this person? Who is this person? It's not Beverly. It's not the Beverly that was born here, I mean born in Ohio. To the daddy, to the first husband, and the second husband, and the third husband. What does he hate about me? I'm give him the best oral sex, I give him massages, I do everything. Why does he hate me so much? What the hell did I do in his life that caused this? I'm the one that's been the good person, why me, Lord? Why? (crying)

And I seen this mirror reflection, and I look like a monster in the picture in the mirror. And I went home. And I told him, I said, (crying)"You know what, Dave, I hate you, man, I hate you. You made me out to be this. I didn't do this. You did this to me!" And he said, "You're crazy." I said, "I'm not crazy, man! You're crazy!" I said, "You've gotten me so twisted around, and you buy me these wine coolers and you tell me I'm still sick in my head! I just realized, realized, man you're the worst thing that can ever happen in my life, you're like a living nightmare in my past lives! You do nothing, you do nothing for me good, you treat me good and then you hurt me! You put hurt into my life, you pain me! You do all kinds of things, you screwed my life up, you tell my kids, you made my kid walk home from Caryville! That's child abuse! I could tell the law! But no, you said I was the one that did it, I was, and I took the blame! You beat Jeremiah, you left Jeremiah outside in my yard to brush his teeth with a toothbrush and everything! That's child abuse, Dave! That's child abuse! I've been there, Dave! And I told him all these things. I said, "That little guy that we gave birth to, I gave birth to. You're doing the same thing to him like you done to Dennis and Jer! And I'm not going to put up with it, man.

He got a lawyer. That was a trip. He paid almost $500 to get this lawyer. And I had not a leg to stand on, not a pot to pee in, nothing, and feeling really bad about myself, and yet I wasn't a bad person. You know? I liked to have my kids and I'm saying Man, this can't be like this again. All I want is love in my life.(crying) All I wanted to be was loved. All I wanted was love. Love me, Daddy, love me Mom, love me Bill, love me, Dennis, love me Dave, but not like this. I can't take this no more.

And with that, the counselor helped me to see the light more. Alicia. And she said, "You go home, Beverly, and you make provisions to make something new in your life." And I said, "I can't, I just can't, I can't live without a man, but you know he's good but he's bad, you know? It's all twisted. So twisted." And I said, "When I come home, to the house, and I got the job, I was going to look for any kind of job, Wal-Mart job, anything, I'm not smart, but I tried a chicken job, I was going to be a boner, a chicken deboner.

JR: Yeah, I know what those are.

BS: He wouldn't let me have the car. He wouldn't let me have the car. He told me he says, "You're so dumb." I said, "Why?" He said, "You're so dumb Beverly, you couldn't even pluck a chicken let alone debone a chicken." And with that, you know, Jan, he hurt me verbally, more than he hurt me physically. He said my emotions were really out on the limb by then. And you know, and now he tells me, I tell him, "You know, Dave, I love you, I love you, I loved you, and I've always loved you, but I can't see… Let's go get a counselor. A marriage counselor and try to work this marriage out." That's how much I put up with. I really did.

He said "Okay, I'll give you six months to clean up your act." Six months to clean up my act. Me? To clean up my act. Okay, make a list of things that you have to do. First of all, I said to him, I said, "Get a job. I can't support you all of my life. …" So I said, "Okay," I said, "I'll find me a job." He said, "Next of all, I want you to start thinking not so bad about me." I told him, I said, "Like what?" He said to me he said, "You got to trust me." I said, "I've trusted you, I trust you , and I kept trusting you," and I said, "We keep going in circles here."

And he says to me, he says, "Well, it's not circles, you're the one's that's screwed up, you got to realize that you're screwed up right from the get-go. Look where you came from." You know? And I'm like, maybe you're right. Yeah, look where I came from. And I started to give it some really deep, deep inner thought, you know, look where I came from. Look what I met up with, look where I'm at now. So I just you know [] what do they call it, "psychoanalyzing" me, so I said, "Okay. If that's the case, you're going to have to clean up your act too." I thought, okay, you know the old saying, "what's good for the goose is good for the gander"? And if you love me, it seems like you're saying you love me, we'll work this out. []

He went and applied for a divorce anyway. But I socked it to him on that. And this is how I wound up in Bonifay by myself with my three children. He went and told the attorney that I did this and I did that, and I'd do this and I'd do that, right, which I didn't have no idea about this. This is after he had this nervous breakdown. This is after he said he would be a better husband and a better Daddy Dave and all that stuff. AFTER. And I says to him, I said, "I don't believe everything you're saying," but I said, " I want to talk to my counselor and find out, you know, your feelings, my feelings, we got feelings for each other, still we do." And he said, "No." he says, "You got a job and everything," and he says, "It's not going to work out." I'm like, what? Huh. So everything that he would say, I'd take it in deep, deep, deep, deep, thinking, consideration. And I was like – it had me so screwed up, I didn't know if I was coming or going.

So he said to me, he said, "I got a plan." I said, "What's your plan?" He says, "We'll work this out on a six month basis" and blah blah this and blah blah that. Okay.

So I got this job. I was a dietary, dietician worker in a nursing home in Bonifay, Florida. And I would be a dishwasher. And then I'd work on the front lines, which is on the end line. And I met this fellow, I went up to him, and I told him, I said, "It's not that I am looking for a job, I want a job." That's how much guts I had. I want a job. I want a job. So he said, "Okay." Can you do this? I said, "Sure. I can wash dishes." I'd wash dishes at home, so what's the difference. I mean, I'm doing this for how many years already, and here I am. I can do that. So I went and I applied for the job and I got the job.

I come home, that day, I had the surprise of my life. All my stuff's packed up, all my children's stuff's packed up, the bedding's dissembled, everything. He's got a truck, somebody's truck down the road. He's got one of these trailers, you know like you haul like equipment on it? With side gates on it? All my stuff's packed up. Get out. "Dave, I can't do this." "Yes you can. I give you six months to get your act cleaned up. "But this is not a marriage. This is like going –" "Right." So I said, "Okay." And I was hurt. Took my kids, drove us down there to Bonifay. He said, "You got good credit because you've been with credit up here," and blah, blah this, and "You could probably, now that you've got a job, you could establish yourself a place" And I got a place, believe it or not I did. God must've been looking after me right then and there. Right from that day.

And I got into Palm Winds Trailer Park in Bonifay, Florida. I took my three children, and it was hard at first to realize that I'm going to be on my own, all by myself. Especially a working mother now. And I said, "Okay." This was a mind blower. Because, what is six months, it's not even six months.

Then I got the surprise of my life. When I'm working, starting to work this job, he comes over to my trailer, mind you, and he checks out my refrigerator to see if it's got food, see if my kids got the proper, you know he's going to pull something else on me, I felt that he was going to pull something on me, but I couldn't pinpoint it, right? And Otto was his kid, so I got every right to not turn him away, it's his child, and even though Dennis is growing up, 13, 14 years old, and Daddy Dave's done this and Daddy Dave's done that, you know, and Jeremiah's two years under him, and everything, so I said, okay. So Dennis would call me up at work and tell me, "Mom, Dave just came over today," or something, and I'm going "You're kidding me," and he goes, "No. Came right into the trailer. He came right into the trailer and checked around the house. And went into the refrigerator." I said, "You got to be kidding me!"

Well, in the meantime, in between time, when I did get home, and I was really whacked out for the first couple of days of work

JR: I bet you were.

BS: Oh my God. Doing dishes. Dishes? I thought I'd never get out of the dish room! These are shelves, these are carts. Take them out, scrape them off, clean them up, steam them . Whew. And get back and learn something else new and learn this and go back here and help the girls [] and all that stuff, and I'm like oh my God. And then I got to go home and prepare supper. And oh my God, you know, why me, Lord. But I love children and if it kills me I'm going to do it. Because I'm not going to get this divorce in the back of my mind, I'm not getting a divorce.

Then, I got papers served to me. Divorce papers. That's how fast he worked, like that [snaps fingers twice]. Boom, boom, boom. And that blew me away, more, 'cause it was not even six months! So I got up with Legal Aids in between time. And I'm like what the heck am I going to do? I don't know where to turn, I mean, I got a roof over my head, I got food in the house, I've got people helping me out through like not Tri-County but it's like a life place, like a church thing, they're helping me with food, I make sure that my kids, I got a washing machine in my house.. .. I could apply for anything, I've got credit like that. I've got a good background, I got a good name. Something good must be going for me. But what about this situation, still worried about what's going on up there. Why I got these papers.

So I talked to Legal Aids and they said well you have to do this and you have to do that, and blah, blah this, and I'm like oh boy, that's a lost cause. It's a lost cause. He's probably got me over right over where he wants me, you know, exactly. I get a letter from the attorney and the attorney's saying this about me and all this other stuff, and I got to be appearing for this, and I'm like how in the heck am I supposed to do this with this job?

So I told my boss, which was Richard, now this was my new husband coming up in the future. My last husband, my last husband. And I told Richard and he goes, "Well, what's going on with you?" I said "I'm getting a divorce." And he goes, "So you're still married?" I said "Yeah." He said, "Where's your husband at?" I said, he lives in Ponce DeLeon, and he was decent, young guy, much younger than me. I don't hardly have any teeth in my mouth, too, by the way, I hardly have any teeth, I don't feel attractive. My bottom teeth on the bottom, I have no teeth. 'Cause what he had done to me in the past, David. Messed me up and all that other good stuff. Then my other husbands too, prior to that. So I didn't have too much self esteem about myself. Period. I felt beautiful inside, more than I felt on the outside. You know I was still thin, whatever.

One night I went to bed on the floor for myself, not with Richard, nobody. My kids slept in regular beds, I slept on the floor on big white blankets, going to work back and forth. And I said to myself, Lord, if there's a God up above, please help me out of this situation. I don't know what to do, aside with Alicia, my counselor. I called my counselor and told her, she said, "Well, Beverly, you could get that divorce." I said, "I can?" She says, "Yeah." I said "I don't think I want to go through with another divorce. This is my second one, this is my third one." She says, "Beverly," she says, "You've got everything going on your side. You never done any abuse to him, you never done any kind. You got so many things that are going in your favor." Like what? you know What have I got to show for it? He's told the attorney this and he's told the attorney that, where have I got a leg to stand on? That's what I was thinking, Jan, in my mind.

Well, that day we went to court. And the attorney's all elegantly dressed up and so is he, sitting by his side and "pssst, psssst, psssst, like that. And here I'm sitting in courthouse, in Bonifay, like a big, long table, the bailiff's standing over there, the judge comes in the room. And I'm like oh my gosh. There I got to get my wits together now because I've got to really be on my toes. He's going to tell this attorney, he told his attorney that I was such a bad person, more than likely. I don't have a leg to stand on. As I thought.

And so I went and sat at the table, and very, very, like look around me, like who's going to help me now? And I took a deep breath, and the officer, bailiff, walked aside and I'm like God there's one two there's four guys and me just me! I'm here by myself, I have no representative, I have no witness, I have only have no nothing.

So he says," Okay," pounds the gavel on the table, he said "Okay, would you like to tell me, Mr. Mazhieski what's going on. He goes, "Well, I want a divorce." He said, "No contest." And he goes, "Okay, does she want a divorce." He said "Yes, she does." I mean, he's doing all the talking. I had no say-so, right? Nothing.

So, as the time goes on, he's asking all these questions, and I don't get nothing. He don't ask me nothing! And I'm feeling like I'm nothing to this room. Just totally, totally, that big [pinches thumb to index finger].

Then after that he said, "Okay, I want to talk to Beverly." You want to state your name? I said, "Beverly Mazhieski." He said, "How old are you," blah, blah this and that. I said and I told him. He goes, "Ma'am, do you want a divorce? " I said, "Yes, I do." He said "Raise your hand, right hand, swear to tell the truth, nothing but the truth" I said, "I do."

And I was squeamish inside of me. I said, "Your honor." I said, "I'm not very smart," That's the first thing I said. "I don't know if I have even a living chance here in this courtroom here, with you, the bailiff, my husband, and his attorney. But I want to make some statements here, if I may." He said, "You may." I said I was I thought I was happily married to this man, I loved him right from the get-go, beginning. I said he took good care of my children, he did this, he treated me good. And I mean I had my head down, I wasn't looking at him in the eyes 'cause I felt ashamed of myself, the way in front of this man. And I was nervous, and I said to him, I said, "I don't think I have a living chance here. But I'm going to try my best, and I'm telling you the God's truth.

I said, "He" I couldn't get it out. He goes, "Ma'am," he said, "What are you trying to say?" I stumbled and stammering, you know, I couldn't say it. I said to him, I said, "I, I , I've been abused." Oh he could care less. That's how he looked at me. He goes, "How do you mean abused?" I said, "I've been abused, I've been accused, and I've been used. He looked and he sat up in his chair, straightened himself out, and now he's going to listen to me.

Dave in the meantime is shrinking down in his chair like this [shrinks down]. Then I looked at the attorney across the room. And I took a deep breath and I said, "Your Honor" He said, "How do you consider yourself abused?" "Well," I said, "First of all, Your Honor," I said "I have a 14 year old child by a previous marriage." He goes, "Okay. How does that consider you abused?" "Well, that's my flesh and blood. And I want to say something. Is it fair for a child 14 years old to walk home from Bonifay almost to Caryville? Is that considered right?" He said "When did this come about?" I says, on such and such a date. "And I took the blame for it." He says," Do you have record of that? I said, "I do, in my mind." ... He said, "Go on." I says, " Dave didn't tell you everything the truth." He goes, "What's that?" "He never told you that he beat me." He said, "No, he didn't. 'Cause you wanted the divorce, right?" I said, "I do want the divorce, Your Honor, but" I said, "I have more to say to that." He says, "Such as" I said, "He's beat me from the time we got married in Newport News, Virginia." And he goes, "Well that's Newport News, Virginia. That's their laws. I don't know what goes on over there." And I mean he was real stern with me, real stern.

And I said to him, I said, " Okay," I said, "He put me" and this is the truth, "He put me, he beat me up in front of my two children, Jeremiah and Otto were trying to protect me on the couch from him beating me. He got me into a car, and he admitted me into Rivendale." And my knees were knocking. I mean just totally shaking. And he goes, "When did this happen?" I said, "Just last year." He said, "How did you get out of Rivendale?" I said "I called my cousin." 'Cause I was crying, he told everyone that I was crazy. "He did something to me in Ohio, too." He says, "Hmmm. Seems like we got some discrepancies right here." Pound the gavel on the table." I said, "Your Honor, I'm not finished." He said, "Ma'am, I hear you, everything you're saying." I said, "I have one more thing to say." I said, "Even a landlord gives you 30 days to get out of your home." Right there it worked a button. I said, "My husband told me he'd give me six months to save this marriage." And Dave was like to the attorney and the attorney looking at him sideways. And I said, "He just gave me a couple of hours after I got a job, to get out." And he goes, "Excuse me? David! What happened here?" "Uh, this wasn't you know, " I mean he's going eh, eh, you know like that. And he goes "Excuse me? We got a discrepancy here. Let's get it cleared up right now. It seems like we've got too many mistakes here. Too many depositions coming." This and that. "Order, I want order right now. Bailiff I want you to type this up, I want her out of here. I want him out of here. No divorce. Till I think it's right. I'm like oh my God. I don't believe this. I don't believe this.

I come out in the hallway in the Bonifay, Holmes Courthouse. He is blue, he is red in the face. His attorney said, "Dave, come over here. Don't you say a word to her." He goes, "You dirty bitch. You fucking bitch." Just like that. He goes, "What did you say to her?" He goes, "I just told her she's going to get her day." He says, "You don't say nothing to her. You don't say nothing to her." He goes, "Hey, I wanted the divorce, she wanted the divorce, I paid $500." He said, "I'm telling you right now, you are not getting a divorce until the judge makes a clearing on this situation."

I come home, Jan, I couldn't believe what I said. I mean I was just like. And Dennis come in the house, set on the couch, he goes, "Hey, Mama! How you doing? Did you get your divorce?" I go, "No." He goes, "Yeah buddy!" I says, "What I that all about?" He said, "Mom, you are going to sock it to him. You are going to sock it to him." Otto's not here, Otto's with Jer down at the playground. But, "Mama, you're going to get him. You watch and see. I know you're going to get him." I said, "Dennis, I'm not going to get him." He said, "Mom, you're going to get him. You're going to get him good. Did you tell them about me?" I said, "Yeah." He goes, "What did he say? The attorney." "The attorney just shrinked in his chair and so did Dave." He goes, "Yeah buddy! Yeah, Yeah!" I mean this kid was like wow. Mom is really coming through.

Ten days later I get a letter from the Cody Taylor that I have to make a decision if I want this divorce.

JR: Who's Cody Taylor

BS: He's like works underneath the judge.

JR: Uh huhm, Clerk

BS: Uh huhm. I go to the courthouse and I sign this paper, I write everything that was the truth, nothing but the truth, never lied. Calls in the court the next day, which is on a Monday. He's got his attorney all baffled and believing. He goes "Ma'am," he says, "We going to do this in a quiet way and I'm just going to very reasonable discretion. You got a divorce." I got a bluh, bluh, I got a divorce? You got a divorce. We threw the other case out. I'm like oh my God. Oh my God, Oh my God. Tears were just rolling down my eyes, I couldn't believe it. I couldn't believe it, Jan. Me! I couldn't believe it. He wasn't even there. Dave didn't walk in the room.

NOTES

A 64 Year Old Woman

A 64 year old woman speaks firmly. Her accent is distinctly Southern, reflecting her Florida Panhandle roots. She speaks of a marriage that was emotionally and physically abusive. The striking event in this story is when her husband became involved with her daughter from a previous marriage.

MJ: Millie Jackson
I: 64 Year old woman
JR: Jan Rosenberg

MJ: How did you meet your husband? Start from there.

I: I met him in '97, I was working for a lady in Graceville, and he was the maintenance man for her, did all her odd jobs around the house. I met him, he started coming on to me and making advances toward me. I really didn't want to get into a relationship because my second husband had just committed suicide, February of '97 and I went through pretty good ordeal there. I wasn't ready for any kind of relationship, but I put it off and I stood him up several times and put it up, and he kept advancing, and finally we just got to going out and talking, one thing led to another.

He moved in the trailer with me. I was self supporting, had a trailer, making good money. And he gives me a sob story, he's living at the Auction Barn at night, he worked there and he lives there at night. And so he moves in the trailer with me unbeknownst to me he's got an ex-wife down the road who he's living with, but he didn't let me know this.

So after he moved in with me, about three weeks later he married me. And his ex-wife kept calling the house and wanting to know my relationship with her husband. That was something right there. Anyway, that went on for a long time. And finally he kept on going back to her and finally he got her to move to Georgia and live with her sister. Guess he wanted to get her out of the way for short term. Why, I don't know. He was married to her for 20 years. Married her in '57, divorced her in '83 and was still with her in '97.
MJ: How did you feel about that? What was your emotion?
I: Well he got her to move and move in with her sister in Georgia. I said, "Well everything is going to be fine".you know? And the trailer she was living in, I gave my trailer up and we moved down there into the trailer she moved out of because my husband raised goats and he had goats down there. So we had to move there to take care of the animals.

So my husband and I did real good for about six months, she was up there in Georgia. But she would call, was calling constantly, was calling collect and I didn't pay any attention to it. But

Finally.

MJ: You didn't pay any attention to it?

I: No, really, I was married to him, I figured I had it made, I'm the wife and she's the ex. And it kept going like that and finally six, eight months later, she calls and she's fixing to get on SSI, get a big back pay. At that time I didn't know my husband loved money like he did, but I learned that real quick.

So when she did get on SSI and got a back pay of five, six thousand dollars, shit, my husband left me at the trailer and he goes to – she already moved to Jacksonville and live with my husband's brother.

And so when he heard she had gotten her big back pay and her SSI in and everything got started he went to Jacksonville and brought her back to Graceville. No, he didn't move her in the trailer with me, right then. He moved her in a house with a friend of hers in Graceville, lady named Mrs. Hart, he moved her in there. And she stayed there two or four months and they had. . . .

My husband and his ex at Miss Hart's had a suitcase. They said it was full of money and $60,000 worth of jewelry and her clothes, I don't know what all was in it. But his ex had it at Miss Hart's house. Well, it was stolen out of Miss Hart's house. And Miss Hart's daughter came over there and commenced to throw Pauline, which was the name of my husband's ex, Pauline, commenced to throw her out, so my husband commenced to go over there, and guess where he moved her? Right in the trailer with me.

JR: Oh my God

I: She was a 64 year old woman, she had a heart condition respiratory condition, she was just about as crazy as they come. She couldn't talk without cussing. Bad. She hated me from way at the start. She hated me. She wanted my husband, which was her ex- husband, wanted him back, wanted him all to herself, she put in to get him back.

So naturally we got along for a week or so and then things started to perculate. She started to get bad-mouthing me, she would accuse me of every evil under the book. I was stealing from her, I stole the suitcase. I got rid of all the money. If I did I don't know what I'd done with it.

But anyway, I went over to Miss Hart's. I stole the suitcase, the Law was brought in and so forth. And she accused me of everything under the sun, you can think of. She was right underneath me all the time. If my husband was in _____ there wasn't one second of privacy between me and my husband, her ex. If he went into the bathroom to take a bath, she was right under him.

And one night he went in the bathroom and he was going to take a bath, well she commenced to get his clothes up. I said, "Pauline, I'll get his clothes up and take to him." "No, I'll do it, I'll do it. I've always done it and I'll do it now!" So she did, she took his clothes back there to him. And I got back in the living room, I was holding a cup of Pepsi in my hand and I just about took all of her mouth, all I could take, and I turned around, and I said, "Pauline, I don't usually say these things, but you know what you are? You are one hell of a bitch!" And when I said that, she plowed into me, she grabbed the cup out of my hand, poured Pepsi all over my head and busted me in the head with it. There's still a scar on top of my head where she busted me.

JR: Oh my, I see it.

I: She busted me that night, And when she did that, I started fighting her back to keep her off of me and killing me and the floor was wet where the Pepsi had spilled, and when I pushed her she slipped down.

Well, I got back there to Cecil where he was, he hadn't got in the shower yet. I said, "Cecil," I said, "She's gone crazy." He just stood there, didn't make a move for nothing. About that time she grabbed me around my throat and my hair and pulled me backwards and I fell, we all went down in the hallway. And I got up and I pushed her back down, And he whirled around, he said, "Both of you, get your tails up there and behave yourself. I'll be out of here in a minute and I'll take care of this."

So we did, we went back to the living room. She set on the couch, I sat on the edge of the bed, we didn't say a word to one another, and he come back up there and he said, "I," he said, "You get in the bed" which was in the living room, that's where we slept, she slept in the middle room. He said, "Pauline, you go back there and get ready for bed, and we'' all just go to bed," We did. Nobody said nothing, we went to bed.

The next morning he went outside and he called me out there, he says, "I, here's a few dollars," he says, "Go up there to Hardees and I'll meet you up there," and he said, "Don't come back here," he says, "Go on to Amanda's house." I said, "OK."

So I went up to Hardees, he never did show up, and I went over to Amanda's. Amanda's my daughter. At that time she was with her husband, living across town. I went to her house, hadn't been at her house 10 minutes, here comes the Law. Police officer come in, female police officer, name Becky. She says, "Well Pauline says you jumped her first." And I said, "Well, that's not true. I called her "bitch" and she plowed into me" And she says, "Well, it's your word against hers." And I said, "Yeah, that's true." And I said, "I know my husband he ain't going to take up for me."

And Becky, the law officer came over and she said Pauline said I attacked her first, which was a lie, I said, "No, I called Pauline a "bitch" and she attacked me, and I defended myself." And I said, "She grabbed the cup I was drinking Pepsi out of [my hand] and busted me upside the head." And I showed her. She said, "Gosh! See you later."

JR: That's incredible.

I: Well Becky says, "Well, this woman's crazy." I says, "You're telling me?" She says, "Well, I'd advise you not to go back up there for a day or two." I says, "OK"

So I stayed at Amanda and Jimmy's house. And a day or two or three rolled into two or three weeks. ... Not one time did he try to contact me, I didn't try to contact him. He didn't call me, nothing. He was working at the barn [auction], but he didn't call me and I didn't call him.

I went into such a depressed state, I couldn't do anything, I'd just sit and cried. That's when I went to Life Management and that's when Tammy helped me. Remember I asked Janet if Tammy was still there? I called Tammy and I said I gotta have something done, I gotta have some medicine.

Well, two or three weeks went into a month, two months, three months, four months, five months. After about two months he'd come by the house once in awhile, throw me a dollar or two. Want to know how I was doing. I was doing fine. "Well, I'm working on it, I'm working on her, I'm going to try and get her out. As soon as I get her out, you can come back. I says "OK".

Well that went on five months. He come by. And we'd go off, we'd go out to the woods where he wanted one thing, sex, and I was his wife and I didn't figure I was doing anything sinful, so we had sex in his truck, in the woods. He'd take me back to my daughter's house, go back to his ex-wife to sleep. Assured me he wasn't sleeping with her, I'll never know whether he did or not.

But after five months of separation, I can't think of all the things she accused me of.

But anyway, he wiggled me back up in there. His excuse was her health was getting worse. She had a heart condition, she had a respiratory condition, slowly the woman was dying. Cecil knew she was dying, knew that nobody else would take care of her, family didn't want anything to do with her. So who was there to take care of her, and who did he try to wiggle back up in there? Me. The wife.

Yes I went back. And I don't know how he talked to her, but she accepted me back in the trailer. She never accepted me as his wife or liked me, but she accepted me back in the trailer. Her health was getting real bad now. In fact, two months after I moved back in the trailer, she became bedridden. She couldn't hardly get up, she was so weak, she was dying.

For six months, from January, February, March, April, May, about five months, I lived in the trailer with her and my husband, I did all the cooking, all the washing, everything, I took care of her. I bathed her, cooked her meals and took to her, I went to town, got her something to eat and I brought it back. She had to go to the doctor, I took her to the doctor and brought her back. She was slowly dying, I knew it.

And May the 15th, May the 14th, I put her in the truck, I took her to Dothan. She said, ". . . ., I don't know what I would have done without you. You've been a blessing." That's one of the nicest words she'd ever said to me.

I took her to Dothan to the hospital, and she saw her doctor, and he put her right in the hospital. Three days later she died.

Her sister from Georgia came down, and they got all the arrangements ready. She was buried in White City, that's a little town south of Fort Pierce, Florida, she was buried in White City. Well, my husband Cecil's brother, half brother, came over from Jacksonville and 'course all of Pauline's family was from Georgia, they went down, everybody met at White City. And she was buried the 21st, I think in White City, that's a little place south of Fort Pierce. We all went down there, laid her to rest.

I thought, well now. The ex is gone, I was good to her, I don't regret one moment of being good to the woman, I'll never regret taking care of her, I don't care how mean or ugly she always treated me, and dirty and cussing. I still took care of her. I don't regret it one bit. I saw her die. My husband he never really said anything one way or the other, about how I appreciate you taking care of her so so. Never said nothing like that . He was just there, didn't say much of nothing.

Well, I thought when she died and we got back home and everything got back down to normal and me and my husband was back in the trailer by ourselves, and just us and the goat herd, I thought, well, everything gonna get back to normal. Well everything did go pretty good until October of 2000 and one. My husband went into killing goats, he was working with some Muslims, a Negro from Chipley of the Muslim faith. You know, they kill goats and eat goat. The Muslims do. Well, they got a scheme going, where my husband had a herd of goats, and he started buying goats to kill, and sell, him and this other guy went in together and start killing goats.

September the 29th, was the day it happened. But it all started September the 27th. Me and my husband went over up in Alabama and bought some billies. Huge billies. We brought them back, they were to be killed. Well he put them all in the goat bin but one, one big bill, about a 150 pound animal with a nice rack of horns on him. He put in our front yard of where we lived. We lived in a house then, we've moved out of the trailer into a big house because the trailer was about to fall down. By the way, we lived in that trailer for that many months and no running hot water, no working bathroom, no shower, no nothing in there. But anyway, getting back to the present.

It's September the 27th and we went and bought some billies and he brought them home, but he put one male in the front yard. I said, "Cecil, this animal doesn't act right, he sort of acts crazy." I'd been around goats long enough, I knew how to tell one from the other, and I knew them as individual animals at this time. He said, "Oh he'll be all right, I'm going to kill him." I said, "Well how' bout tying him? Well, he did tie him to the fence. I says "Good. You tie him to the fence." Well, that was Friday night. Well Saturday morning, early Saturday morning we got up and went out and the bill had got twisted itself all up with the rope, just had it twisted around his durn front feet and wrapped up his hind feet, he was just all twisted up, and almost had the rope around his throat. I said, "Well, he ain't going to _____ out," what I mean, he's gonna kill his self like that, so we turned him loose. And it was my job to go out and water and feed the goats. I worked the goats harder than my husband did, I took care of all the watering, I kept the water feeders clean, I helped feed them all, I helped worm them every three months, I'd hold them while he wormed them. I'd fill the needles, I worked harder than he did, I kept the barn cleaned, I help bag 50 and 60, 100 pound bags of seed, and unload it off the truck and put it in the barn, and pour it up in the barrels.

Well, anyway, that day, that Saturday, I told Cecil that this goat don't act right, he's running up and down side the fence and he just don't act right, he acts crazy, let's tie him again. My husband said "No, no, no, we ain't going to tie him again, I'm going to kill him Monday morning. Well, this was Saturday. I says, "OK."

So I fed him Saturday night, went to bed Saturday night, and we got up early Sunday morning. And he says, my husband, "You going out to feed and water that animal?" I said, "I guess so." I said, "Don't you think you ought to go out there first and tie up that animal? I'm scared of that animal. "He said, "No, it'd be all right, just get some water and feed him, I'm going to kill him in the morning anyway." I said, "OK."

I bounced out there and already had some feed in his bucket, and with carrying the water bucket towards the place where it was to be set down, when the animal turned towards me and charged. He hit me in the right leg. He lowered them horns and he charged, and when he hit me I heard every bone in my leg break in two. And I went to the ground. Animal stood over me, and I started screaming. My husband didn't come running up to me. It was another man working, they were out there in the goat herd working. This other man's name was James Trim, he come running over there, and he said "what's the matter?" I said, "This animal has hit me and it's standing over me, get him off of me." If I had tried and gotten up he would have hit me again, I'm sure. But anyway, I knew to lay flat on the ground still.

So James came over there and got the animal off of me, and tied him to the clothesline post. And my husband come walking up there, "What's the matter? What are you doing? Bump you a little bit?" I said, "No, he hit me" I said "I think my leg's broken." "Well, what do you want me to do?" I said, "Go in there and call the ambulance." I said, "My leg is busted. Completely." He said "OK." So he ambled in there, I guess he called the ambulance because they came and they put me in the ambulance. I was in so much pain and shock, I don't hardly remember much, except the ride to Marianna and they couldn't give me nothing for pain in the ambulance and every turn that ambulance would hit a bump my leg would bounce off that dang table and I'd scream.

And we'd got over there to the hospital and they finally gave me some morphine and I blacked out.

I was in the hospital nine days. In surgery four hours. Doctor said it was one of the worst busted up legs he had ever seen in his life. Every bone in my leg was broken, one's still broken, he couldn't fix it. He fixed the two front bones that had been busted, with about eight or nine stainless steel screws and I don't know how many fiberglass boards he had to build the bones back together. But I was in the hospital nine days.

Amanda, during that time Amanda was coming to see my husband, and sort of doing the housework for him, didn't think nothing about it. Sort of doing the housework, sort of cooking, he was still working. And so they would come to the hospital, him and Amanda would come and see me about three times I think. But I didn't remember much of the first four or five days, I was out on morphine. Didn't care what was going on nowhere. Didn't think nothing anyway.

But after nine days the doctor he says now, I really didn't want to go home. But he said, ". . . you gotta go home. You can't live here in the hospital." I said, "I know." Because I knew deep down, deep down, I knew what was coming. I really did. What was coming at home. Well I did. They come and got me, Amanda and Cecil came and got me and they brought me home, and I was bedridden, I don't know how many months I was bedridden.

I was bedridden, I don't know how many months I was bedridden. But anyway within two weeks, probably within one week, I don't know, I really didn't _____ everything that was fixing to happen, and I saw was fixing to happen, I wanted to deny it, but I just put it out of my mind, and probably within one week Amanda and my husband was in the back bedroom doing their thing. And this is where it gets bad. I had been through so much hell and torture before, but that wasn't nothing to what's coming.

The house was a mess, there was wires strung all over the house. My husband had a dolly, a hand trolley, what do you call them, a hand truck? That Badcock uses to move refrigerators? He had one of those outside, it was tore up. He had it leaning up against the fence outside, we had a fence around the house.

Now my daughter has a baby with her. She's already left her husband and moved in with us, by this time. The day I got home she moved in with us, her and her little girl, her three year old, three year old at that time. Moved in with us. The house was all messed up, there was electrical wires all over the place, the house wasn't child-proof what I'm trying to say, the house was not child-proof. Was not two three year old child-proof. For a child that age. And that dolly's leaning out against the fence outside, I kept telling, I said, "Cecil, Amanda, get that dolly out there and take it down, just lay it down on the ground, or do something with it. It needs to be on the other side of the fence." I said, "This baby is going to get hurt on that thing. (This was a chain link, not an electric fence.)

The dolly was leaning there, it's got a sharp edge on it. And they had the sharp edge up in the air... I said, "Get that dolly on the other side of this, the baby's running around there playing, she going to get hurt on that thing." I kept telling them and telling them. They didn't do it. So one evening Samantha went outside and she comes in covered in blood, screaming her head off, she done got crawled up on that dolly and it fell on top of her. Cut her head, cut a gash it went on through to her teeth, through there and right through there (through her lip). Slam to the bone through there and slam to her teeth. All the way through now. You could see her teeth through her upper lip.

So Amanda and Cecil got her in the car and took her to the hospital. But they ended up in Dothan. The hospital in Graceville, which is a band-aid station, it was so bad they got them right on, told her get on up there to Dothan to Southeast Medical. And so they were up there till all hours of the night. And needless to say the surgeon that was up there, he wasn't up there at that time so they had to carry her back the next day for the surgeon to sew her up. So, I don't know how many stitches it took up here and I don't know how many it took down there. But anyway,

I didn't call HRS, I should have. Needless to say I couldn't think straight no more. I was just in a [was still in the bed from leg surgery]. I was still bedridden at this time. I hadn't even thought about my walker yet. I had a bedside commode, and I was using it. And I was in communication with the baby's other grandmother. Amanda has already left Jimmy that was her husband. But Jimmy had a mama and she and I talked on the phone a lot, and I was talking to her that day that they were in Dothan at the hospital, I told Miss Edna, that's the baby's other grandmother, her daddy's mama, told her what had happened. And then Dolly she went and called HRS. So, I didn't know this at the time, so this all happened in October. Let's see. Is the fair in October? Because the night they went to the fair, Amanda, the baby, and Cecil all went to the fair that night. It was on a Saturday night. I was laying up there in the bed, it was about 8:00, and there was a knock on the door. I couldn't get up hardly, and I hollered out the window, my bedroom was right up to the front, and I said "Who is it?" And the policeman said, called his name, and it was a policeman from Graceville. I thought, oh my gosh. And the policeman says, "Ma'am can you get up and let us in?" I says, "I don't know if I can get up or not. I'll try," I said, "I got a busted leg and I'm laying here in the bed." And wires all over the floor, I mean big cords, electrical cords. All over the floor. And I was scared I'd trip over them.

Well, I managed to get up, I don't know how I done it, but my walker, I managed to get up and get my walker and I hopped on one leg to the front door and I opened it. The policeman come in and HRS worker came in and he just stood there and looked at the floor and house. He said, I don't know what was going through his mind. I can't imagine. But he helped me get in the chair in the living room, sit down. My leg was in a cast, I had to hold it straight out... so he helped me. It had been bleeding, the surgery had been bleeding pretty good, and I couldn't bump it or nothing because it would start bleeding so bad, the surgery – I had about 22 staples in it, 22.

He said, "Ma'am, we got a report that there is a baby here, a three year old and she got hurt by a dolly or something that was in the front yard that shouldn't have been out there." And I said "Yes," and commenced to tell the man the whole story. He said, "Will they be back tomorrow?" and I said, "They should be back tonight, I reckon, they gone to the fair, should be back tonight." So he said they'd be back tomorrow or next day.

So he help me get back in the bed and they left.

So the next day HRS came. Well my husband is sort of the type, he don't like to be told what to do by anybody, especially the Law Enforcement or anybody in authority, which HRS, I'd say, is in authority. But Mr. Jackson begin to tell him that this house had to be baby-proofed. Those wires had to be got up, there's some electrical outlets in the house had to be fixed, there had to be a door put on the back to keep the baby from running out into a little side room back there with all of his electrical tools back there. Also I told him about the goats. My husband had been taking this baby right out there and putting her down in the middle of the goat herd. Didn't see nothing wrong with it. Oh yeah. He'd take this baby and put her right down, and me laying in that bed, just a-dying. Seeing that baby be put right in the middle of that goat herd knowing what a goat could do. I was laying up there with a busted leg from a goat and he was taking that baby out right in the middle. And I called Amanda, I don't know how many times, I'd say, "Amanda, get that baby out of there, get her away from them goats, blah blah blah." "Well he's out there watching her." Now my daughter's got a mind of about a ten year old, and that's the way she thought. Anything he wanted to do, fine.

I'm laying up there in that bed, dying, just scared slam to death, just fear. But anyway, my husband, needless to say, he got the house straightened up, and done what the authorities told him to do, but one thing. Mr. Jackson told him to build another fence, the chain link fence parallel with the goat herd. Here's the goat herd, here's the chain link fence, here's our yard. To keep that baby from going up to the fence and putting her hand through there and the goat could hit it and break it. Mr. Jackson told him to build a fence so many feet away, another fence so many feet away from the chain ·link fence, keep that baby separated from the goats. Of course he didn't do that, he said he wasn't fixing to do that.

So, _____ one thing and another, and it was hell

MJ: How did you feel about them sleeping together?

I: The first night, well they never did sleep together, they tried to one night. And that was one of the most horrible nights I have ever experienced. I was in my bed, he, my husband was in his bed in the living room, and had a bed in the living room, and Amanda and the baby was in the bedroom. But, during the night, unbeknownst to me, during the night he was going in her bedroom. I didn't know this. She got pregnant two or three times, and she said she aborted, I don't know if she did or not during that time.

JR: You OK?

I: Now this. And then they started drinking. Before that they tried laying in the bed together, they weren't sleeping together now, but they were going to each other's bedroom and I was still in bedridden in there in my bed. I was on antihistamine because after I got out of the hospital I had a bad case of the hives, started itching all over, and got fever. Called the doctor, put me on antihistamines, I was sleeping most of the time. Was on pain medicine, antihistamines, hives, and I don't know what else. I had infections and so...

MJ: But you could hear things.

I: Yeah. But anyway.

The first night they tried to sleep together, It's so much, it's just so much. But the first night I recall, I think they were both drinking. They... I was already up on a walker, I was just hopping around on one leg on a walker. And he always said that the bed I was in belonged to his son. My husband has a son by his second wife which I never met. And I never met him and he never come around and he was estranged from my husband, he also had that to worry about because Pauline his ex-wife said his son, his name was Matthew, he hated him, so if he ever come around he would kill him and anybody else that was around him, he would blow us away. I really didn't want to meet him.

Well that night they both got drunk, well I ... had gotten out of my bed and he gave me the bed in the living room and he start sleeping on my bed, which wasn't my bed, it was his son's bed, and he got mad with me one night and told me get out of his son's bed, he wanted it back, I said, "All right, fine. You can have it back." So I moved all my stuff in the living room, he moved all his stuff in the bedroom, he started sleeping in there. So that night they started drinking, I don't know how they ended up in the bedroom. But anyway, Amanda and the baby went in their, and crawled into bed with him and they shut the door. And I started beating on the door for them to get out of bed, I says "I ain't gonna have this, if I die tonight I ain't gonna have you all in the bed together, not with me around." And I started beating on the door. And I beat on the door, and I was standing there on a walker, on one leg beating on the door, and the only thing I could find to beat on the door was a grease gun that you grease automobiles with. It was the only thing I could find and I beat that door. And I beat that door and I tried to push it open, and I beat it. I don't know how long, this was during the night. And finally I just quit beating it and I set down. I says, "All right," I says "Fine, you all going to sleep together, that's fine. But I'm fixing to go pick that telephone up and I'm fixing to call HRS abuse line." ... That door flew open real quick and [they] come stepping out of that bedroom. "You ain't calling no .... " You all just stay in there and see if I don't" "I'll kill you all, blow your ass away." I said, "Go right ahead. I'm calling HRS. If I ever see you all get together with that baby right in there with you," I said "Not when I'm around. So he slapped me and pushed me around that night a little bit, anyway, that was that.

And the night Amanda went crazy? And started throwing everything. She threw everything in my bedroom, jerked everything out of the closets, jerked all my clothes out. I had boxes stacked up in the bedroom, she emptied everything out all over the floor. My husband took the mattress in there, brought it out and put in on the floor in the living room, and I went in there, I went in Amanda's bedroom and I turned everything of hers over. I took everything I could find of hers, I turned it upside down, then I went in there and I picked the phone up and I called the Law, and here they come.

MJ: [about the camcorder " and stuff..."

When the Law come over there that night, he could've taken both of us to jail, I reckon, and removed the baby. I says, "I don't care." But he says, he told Amanda he got on to Amanda real good, and he told her to settle down, and I set down and settled down, and the poor baby just a-screaming and squalling, she screamed and squalled constantly, every night it was something. They was hollering and screaming at me and getting drunk, and the baby was screaming and ... The two of them would get on the floor rolling around like two young'ns, pulling their clothes off, right in front of me, I'm sitting in the chair now and they was, and Amanda and Cecil down on the floor right in the middle, baby right in there with them, they pulled their clothes off ... One night he got real drunk. And I got the camcorder and I recorded everything that night. He was walking around naked as a jaybird. And I recorded everything. I was walking about this time now. This was October, November, December, January, February. This was around February, started trying to put some weight on my leg, February. Remember now, this went on from November, December, January, February, March, April, May, June, July, August. Ten months. This went on in the house. Just hell every night, every day. Hell, hell. I'd make a derogatory remark about his meat and he'd rub meat all in my face, and he'd rub it all over my body, fresh meat, liver, raw liver, he'd rub it in my mouth, in my eyes, steak, I don't care what kind of meat. HE had to have meat three times a day. I got so tired of meat, meat, I got so tired of meat. Cooking meat and seeing

him fuss about his meat and all, if I said one wrong thing he'd just rub it all over me and throw it away and go off and buy some more. He'd spend $40 for one piece of meat. Didn't matter to him. It was meat, he was obsessed with meat.
And one night, oh one night, the lady that I live by now, Miss White, her church called and Miss White called me and she was going to church that night, and she said, ". . ., I've got some homemade dressing over here, ' she said "I'll send you some," I says "Oh, OK." Homemade dressing. I hadn't had any homemade dressing or collards or turnips in a long time. And Miss White says "I'll have the church, I'll have the preacher's wife take you some" Well, she did, the preacher's wife come over and about that time Cecil had come in, and he saw the car driving up there in the front, he turned to Amanda, "Who the hell that is coming out there?" Amanda says "Oh, that's the church they're bringing something to eat over here." He says, "Well they're not neither." He marched out there, cussed the preacher's wife out told her to get that food and get her car and get off, never ever bring no food back to his house. He furnished all the food there, and nobody would bring no food there. And the poor preacher's wife left the house a-crying.
    And I'm laid up in there in the bed and oh there goes my dressing tonight. And the night they got drunk, laid in the front yard about half naked. And both of them laying out there all _____up now, out there in the front yard, I left the front porch light on, hoping the Law would drive by, but they never did. And they get drunk, they come in the house, and they fall on the floor and they'd hug up together, and he'd have his hand stuck out there between her legs, and Amanda got drunk one night, she just got about naked, pulling her bra off and she vomited in the trash can, and
MJ: How's all this making you feel?
I: And the morning, in the morning I got up, my bed was in the living room now, I'd done moved into the living room. The kitchen was right in front of the living room. And there was a mirror on this wall in the kitchen. I could stand up here, look in that mirror, and if there was anybody in the kitchen standing here, I'd see them. So I get up one morning and looked, and it was about 7:00, and Amanda and Cecil was standing in the kitchen just a-loving and a-smooching... and I just went off, man, I just went off. That was one of the last really violent outbreaks before they moved out. I just went off, I still on a walker now, but I was setting weight on my leg, this was back in July, June, July, remembering now. October, November, December, January, February, March, April, May, June. This was around June or July. Ten months of hell had done gone by, hell. Inside the house, I saw them kissing and loving on one another and it just sicko-ed me. And I got in there and I said, "You all ain't doing that, I guarantee you all ain't doing that, I'll kill both of you you not doing that in this house, not with me in this house." I says, "You all go to a motel (which they already had)..." They'd leave on a Friday go out to a motel in Panama City. Sometimes he'd cut the telephone lines where I wouldn't have a telephone, yeah, and one night he turned off the heat during the winter months, January, February, they left to go to a motel and he cut the gas off so I wouldn't have no gas heat. He cut the whole electricity off outside. At this time I still couldn't get around too good,

and Amanda made him cut it all back on. Because she said "If you cut out the lights, then everything in the refrigerator's gonna be ruined. And we won't have nothing to eat when we get back." That's the only reason he went and cut them back on.

But anyway, this morning I saw them hugging and kissing, I went in there and I went off. And I said something derogatory and all and he went over there and he started pushing me and when I got back into the living room he slapped me and he pushed me on the couch. But before he could catch me I picked up phone and pushed 911. Just like that. I had learned to move fast. Real fast. I had learned on my busted leg how to move after he slapped me and pushed me down on the couch. Hurt my hip bad.

Again, here come the police. Well, we got some great police from Graceville, I tell you they're just the greatest. I mean. .Got me off to the side, "What's going on?" I commenced to tell them, I say my husband and daughter are having a thing going, but as long as I'm in the household, I'm the wife and it ain't gonna happen in here. So he went and got my husband, back there and talked to him in private. And then he talked to my daughter in private. Directly he come back up there on the front porch where I was sitting in private he says, "What do you care? The man's sorry as hell. What do you care?" Why do I care? I says, "I know he's sorry but I ain't going to have them loving up on one another and doing all that in the house when I'm in here. "Would you?" He said, "No ma'am, I don't guess I would." I says, "Why, no you wouldn't." Crazy policeman. I said, "You tell them as long as they're in this house with me, they're not to have any physical contact with one another." He says, "Yes ma'am, I'll tell them that." He says, "You're right, I guess you're right." I says, "I know I'm right. As long as they're in this household they're not to have any physical contact with one another. Or there's going to be a death here or two or three deaths." Well, he went back in, he says, "Well you stay here on the front porch." He went back in there, he talked to both of them. And he said, he come back out there, he says, "Now ma'am, I told them that they're not to have any physical contact with one another as long as you're in this household. If they want to have physical contact or have sex, they're to go off to a motel somewhere." I said, "Yes, that's right." I said, "They been doing that" but I said they ain't gonna do it here. He said, "Well, I explained it perfectly to them." I says "OK".

So things cooled down after that, pretty well cooled down after that. And well, in February of that year, Amanda didn't have to get drunk to go crazy, she'd just go crazy, she's just crazy anyway, she's acting like a monkey most of the time and that night she was jumping up and down on the bed right over him. He was laying on the bed, she was jumping up and down, up and down. Well she got mad with him, something about $200. She had $200, two one hundred dollar bills. Gave it to him. Well she said something that pissed him off, he threw it back at her, so that night she took the two one hundred dollar bills, ripped them in two, glued each of them to the fan blades. And I watched thing go around with money for the rest of the night. Oh they'd get handcuffs and she'd handcuff him to the bed. Sick-o! Yeah, I still got the handcuffs. She bought some handcuffs, she cuffed him to the bed. He liked that. It was sick-o. I was sitting there and watching it. Couldn't do nothing. It was sick. And the poor baby right in the middle, just

He'd come back with all these sweet things things, you know, and say, "You're the best, I'm getting tired of her. All she wants to do is fight and have violent sex, I don't like violent sex, I like your kind of sex, peace and quiet, you know?" And so I'd give in. Because he's still my husband, I wasn't sinning, that was my husband.

...[Husband gets a job in Donaldsonville and commutes from Graceville]

So finally it's gets too much, driving back and forth from Donaldsonville every day and at night, back at night, with the baby, getting too much. So they give up the little hideaway, move back, lock, stock, and barrel into the house where I was. And he kept the rent up on my home, he paid rent where I was. Because all of their stuff was there, you see, his stuff and Amanda's stuff; all of it was there. The dogs were there. They weren't my dogs. One dog belonged to Amanda and one was Cecil's dog. So they finally moved back in to the house, with me, lock, stock, and barrel and gave up their little hideaway up there close to Donaldsonville. That was on July, August, very first of August.

Well, there wasn't any physical contact between them, that's for sure, but it was still abuse towards me. So Amanda got ready to get out again, so she went out and found herself a house up the road towards Slocum. Unbeknownst to me she. Again, Billy helped her get it. Well, Amanda paid the deposit on it, Cecil paid the rent on it. So they commenced to move into this house. And left me at the rental house.

Well, I forgot to mention that much earlier, I had already gotten a lawyer. I couldn't get Legal Aid because Amanda had her papers in before I did, she was filing for divorce from her husband. And I was going to file for divorce against Cecil. But anyway, I couldn't get in Legal Aid, and because Penny said there was conflict of interest. I said, "Well, Penny, what am I going to do? I've got to have a lawyer. He's left me here in this house, he said he was never ever paying another dollar here." I says,"I've been abandoned, I'm still half crippled, I've got to have some support." I couldn't pay the rent, I'm not drawing nothing, I can't pay the rent, light bill, water bill. Penny said, "I, let me work on this. I'll get back with you." So Penny called me back in a day or two. She said, ". . .," she said "The higher ups here at Legal Aid in Quincy told me I cannot take your case because Amanda got her foot in the door first. Be a conflict of interest." She said, "I got you one even better." She says, "I got you a lawyer in Marianna, free of charge, he ain't going to charge you one dime." I says, "Who is it?" She said, "Matthew Fuqua." I said, "Thank you Penny, because I gotta have a lawyer, I gotta have something. I'm here all alone, completely abandoned. They've done moved out. Gone."

So I went to my lawyer, and I met Matt. Within a week he had me in an emergency hearing before Judge Pittman, Judy Pittman. She awarded me $350 alimony, she awarded him to pay the rent on the house, the water bill, not the telephone bill, but she told him to pay the rent and the light bill on the house and give me 350 a month alimony, as long as I lived there. And so that was the emergency hearing. And also, Judge [sic] Fuqua ordered the judge to order him to pay $500 on his fee. And he got that too. He made Cecil give him $500 and Cecil give it to him, too. And he gave me 350 and paid the first month's rent and first month's light bill.

Well, needless to say the landlady that lived next door didn't like me, I don't know why, I imagine he told her all about, all kind of lies on me, I reckon, but she wanted me out anyway. So she come over one evening, which was about two months after they moved, and she come over, and she gave me a piece of paper ordering me to vacate the premises within three days, I had to get out. I says, "You'll have to see Cecil about that," I says, "He's been ordered to pay the rent here and you'll have to see him." She says, "I ain't gonna see him, I don't have nothing to do with him, and you better be out in three days." Well, I had the upper hand, but it scared me so bad. I didn't know what to do, scared me. So I bounced on my feet, I could walk now some, this is about eight or nine months later, I could walk a little bit, I walked down the road and got a friend to take me out to Cecil's house, where him and Amanda was living. And I told Cecil, I says, "Well, you're gonna have to pay that rent up there, and pay me my alimony. Or else I've gotta move in here with you." He says, "Well, I'll tell you what," he says, "how about you moving in here with us?" He knew what he was doing. He knew he wouldn't have to pay me a dime if I moved in the house with him. And I fell for it.

JR: Oh no.

I: I fell for it.

And I moved in the house with them. But I still didn't have any transportation at this time, had no way of moving, and this woman, this landlady was wanting me out, I had no way of moving. I could have probably made arrangements and got out, but anyway, I made the mistake. It was a mistake. But there was something good that came out of this mistake.

I moved into the house with Cecil and Amanda. It pissed her off big time, she didn't want me anywhere around, she never wanted to see me again, she hated my guts. He had threatened to kill me so many times, I got so tired of hearing it. We'd be going down the road, Amanda had a big car, a Ford LTD and it could go, man it could fly down that road. go off on a trip, and you talk about crazy. I'd be sitting in the front seat, Amanda'd be driving, the baby would be in the back in the car seat, Cecil would be right behind in the back seat, right behind Amanda. Well, Amanda's a fast driver, crazy, fast driver. She's like a young'n _____.

And then they start playing. She'll reach behind and grab his hand, they'll start jerking around, and directly he gets up and covers her eyes where she can't see a thing. 80 miles an hour down the dang road. And I'm sitting there eating that seat up.

JR: Oh God.

I: And they keep on playing and I start screaming and the baby'll start screaming, and I say, Y'all crazy! Crazy! And they keep on, . . . nothing bothered them. They're two little child in a world of their own. A 66 year old man and a 23 year old girl acting like 10 year olds. Playing. Doing 80 miles an hour down the road, and then Amanda starts swerving the car: "I'm going to kill everybody if you don't shut up!" talking to me. Starts swerving so I'd shut up real quick. And I sit there and just pray we get home, we get home. I'll never go out with them again, never never never never. That they just make it home. Oh. See why I tremble.

Now I know, there's so much more that went on

JR: That's OK

I: Oh, the time he took the mattress and put it in the living room on the floor and tore up the whole bed and before I moved out of the bed in the bedroom where I was. He took the whole mattress and put it on the floor in the living room. Had just enough room to walk 'tween the mattress and the chair, and me on the walker. I had to pick the walker up on the mattress, and trying to hop. And he took the box springs off the bed and twisted it completely around, no way I could fix it. He was pissed off at me, that's why he done that. But I'd never sleep in that bed again, he'd make sure of it. Thank goodness I had the little daybed up in the living room, up where I was.

JR: You must've gone through a whole range of emotions.

I: One day, I was... I took a picture of when he cut the lines, when he cut the lines from the telephone power, he cut the whole wire, from the telephone pole that runs down the side of the house? He cut the whole line. Cutting the telephone off on me, I took a picture of that. And while I was in a cast on a walker, I couldn't wear nothing but a moo-moo, a gown, a moo-moo, a moo-moo. You can't wear jeans, not with a big cast on. And one day, this was back during the early six months. I walk in the kitchen and he would do all the cooking, Amanda didn't cook, she didn't care nothing about cooking, he'd do the cooking. I was feeling abused so, I just couldn't stand it no more. I turned the garbage can upside down, and boy that pissed her off. He get my clothes off one night when I did that, he just took that moo-moo and just ripped it off of me, me on the walker. He put a knife, a butcher knife he had, fixing to cut some meat, he put it here, and here, and then threw it, and it stuck in the door. He said, "See that?" He says, "I'll throw it right between your eyes, just like that." And, you know, my mind had taken so much, I retaliated, that's the only way I knew. I'd hop around and I – there was a bowl of flour on the cabinet one time, I just turned it upside down on the rug. I said, "Now clean that up." And boy that piss off Amanda. She poured water over the top of my head....standing in the kitchen. And I found something and I turned it upside down, and she'd push me and I'd fall. And one night, I had been abused so bad, mentally, I just walked through the living room, by this time he put the bed back together, and I walked into the bedroom, and I just fall on the bed, I don't know, if I'd a had something that night I would've probably committed suicide, my mind was just gone, completely gone that night. I just blacked out, I just blacked out. I don't know how long I slept, or blacked out. When I woke up he was still sitting in the living room like nothing had happened. Amanda was washing dishes. And I lay there, I didn't get up that night, I my mind had been so abused, I just I was just

...

MJ: What I'm hearing is a lot of things I went through. There was almost that pull to want their love and attention...

I: Yeah.

MJ: Even sleeping with him when he'd slept with your daughter there's that pull and tearing, that you [that he would] change.

I: Change

MJ: And you kept thinking, you know, able to get better. You know when he would do the bad things to you.

I: Yeah

MJ: It was that thing was maybe I can fix it, or maybe I can make him see what he's doing to all of us.

I: I haven't told you all the bad part. Not yet.

MJ: Today you don't know where they're at.

I: I don't know where they're at. But getting back to ... August of 2002. I moved in the house with Amanda and Cecil in a different location out from Graceville, I moved in the house with them. ... Everything went pretty smooth. Through a long ordeal and another whole story I managed to get Cecil to turn his truck over to me, title, clear title in my name. And that's a long story that I'm not going to get into, but I got the truck. And it was pretty peaceful, Cecil would get up and go to work, come home and sometimes he'd cook, sometimes I'd cook supper. Amanda cooled down some. Everybody cooled down some. Well from August , I moved in with them first of September, October, November, December, January, February, March, April, May, June, July, August, September we lived in this house. The baby was in school at this time, now, pre-school. And when the baby started back to school in September. And the baby had seen and gone through so much, she was beginning to, in her class, in her pre-school class, the baby was beginning to act up inappropriately behavior with other children, And her teacher picked up on her behavior, knowing that she had seen things that babies aren't supposed to see and she had been in a situation, and my teacher was smart enough and trained enough to see this behavior wasn't normal in this child. So at conference, first conference, the teacher approached me and Amanda wasn't there, she was in the bathroom. Amanda was always underneath me, I never did have a spare moment to myself, all those nights I had quit calling Janet, and I wasn't in group anymore and I was right underneath her, Amanda was right over me constantly, if I said anything, did anything wrong, Amanda jump on me, cuss me and just to keep everything down and cool and to keep her from going crazy I just played it cool, kept calm, didn't say nothing. So the day at conference her teacher, while Amanda was in the restroom, her teacher approached me, and she [said] the child was inappropriately behaving, and she knew something was going on. And I commenced to tell her the situation.

I: I didn't know at the time she was going through that. Because I knew if HRS was called in I'd catch hell, which I did. And my teacher did call HRS and HRS called Janet. I had been praying all those months Janet wouldn't close my case out because I knew things were coming to a head. Well, when my teacher got in tough with HRS and HRS called Janet, Janet knew things were coming to a head then. And within three weeks, Amanda went and stored her and Cecil's material things, furniture she stored everything. I had the truck at this time, thank goodness, that was the only good thing out of those few months with them. I had gotten me some transportation.

And October the 10th they had everything stored in a storage bin at town in Graceville, I helped them with the truck, I loaded their stuff up and I took it to a storage bin and I helped them. October the 10th they put all of their personal belongings in the car, took the baby in Amanda's car, and he had just got off of a big job where he made almost $2000, he went out that morning and he got his money and he comes back and he gave me $200, he threw it in my lap, he said that would be the last dime I ever got out of him. I was happy to get that. I was so happy to get that. I wasn't expecting a dime. And they got in the car and pulled out, and that was the last of them, I haven't seen them since, haven't heard from them, don't know where they are, nothing.

I immediately got on the phone and started calling. I got me an application, turned into a HUD finance complex in Graceville, got me an apartment, I moved, moved all my stuff in, my son helped me. I went to court, got Matthew, my lawyer, to get me a divorce in December 10th I got a divorce before Judge Wright, he awarded me $3200 alimony, which I haven't seen yet because I don't know where Cecil is to get it. I have to find him first before I can collect any alimony. But I got my divorce, I am completely divorced from Cecil, and I'm back in group now, I don't know what I'd have done without group and Janet and Millie...

    I'm in my apartment, I'm all alone. I have my sons and my group and Janet. ... And I keep pretty busy... I live in my apartment, I eat what I want, I don't eat meat.... I eat out of cans. I don't cook, I eat out of cans. I eat cereal for breakfast, I eat when I want, I get up when I want, I manage my own financial affairs, and when I got divorced from Cecil I was drawing a Social Security check off of him. Well his check has stopped, and I'm going to start drawing some money off of my dead first husband, which'll be a little bit more, but right now that's Social Security dragging their feet on that, but anyway they'll come across sooner or later.

MJ: How do you feel about yourself today after what you went through?

I: I'm just happy to be alive. I feel that peace, but I'm still having some down moments, yes I am. I think about anticipated circumstances that could arise, for instance, circumstance could arise Amanda and Cecil get in a fight, she leaves him, comes back to Graceville, she comes to me, what am I going to do? What am I going to say? I don't know. Janet's going to help me through all that, I don't know. I don't know whether I can forgive her. I'm just living one day at a time. ... Without Millie and Janet I couldn't have made it, no way

NOTES

Patricia Rogers

Patricia Rogers was born in 1948 and spent her early childhood in New York City. Her father, a military man, was very strict and Patricia and her siblings felt like they were walking on egg shells around him.

The family moved to Florida in 1960 and Patricia's father left the family. This left Patricia to take care of her brother and sister. She moved to Panama City in 1984 and also lived in the Holmes County area.

Patricia has been involved with domestic violence for some time. She worked for the Salvation Army's domestic violence program. She experienced domestic abuse in her five marriages. The last marriage was physically violent and was the "crowning blow."

In 2004 Patricia moved back to Panama City where she works part time in a medical office.

Desperation

The kids were singing quietly,
That dreary day,
They were afraid he would waken,
But I told them "It's ok."

"It's raining, it's pouring,
The old man is snoring."
"He is not snoring," I
Wanted to say, just
Keep on playing,
He can't hurt us today.

"He bumped his head
Against the bed"
But it wasn't a bump,
It was a blow, instead.

"And couldn't get up
In the morning."
He'll never get up,
I've seen to that.

I left a note,
They'll take care of my kids.
I'm not sorry at all,
For the thing that I did.

Patricia Rogers

Scarred Love

How does he love me?
A bruise no one will see,
Endearing words of comfort,
Praise and support,
Are never spoken.
My spirit is broken.

His insidious ways
Bend me to his will.
Before I know what is happening,
He is in control.
My sanity, my health, my self
Manipulation has taken its toll.

My home is my jail,
There is no bail.
How does he love me?
I know I must be free.
I can stay here no longer,
I am getting stronger.

Patricia Rogers

Show Me

I am a prisoner in my
Once happy home,
No dignity is left,
My spirit is gone.

Oh Lord I pray,
Please hear my prayer.
If suffer in silence,
A victim of
Domestic violence.

I am afraid to speak out,
He threatens my family.
There is always a fight,
I can do nothing right.

Dear God, please guide me
My soul is in your hands,
I give you my life,
I will no longer be,
His wife.

As I begin my journey
To mend my soul,
Guide me, Lord,
Show me the way.
And as I heal and learn,
You will hear me when I pray.

Patricia Rogers

No More

A trusting soul, so full
Of life.
A target, a punching bag,
A doormat, his wife.

She is happy and looks at him
With such devotion,
As he zeros in, the trap
Is set in motion.

Her friends tell her
Something is wrong,
As she looks at them
With frustration.
She feels betrayed, and
Sinks, deeper in isolation.

The bruises begin to show,
Where once was a happy glow.
Her self esteem is no more,
Why did he call her a whore?

Her life once mattered,
But no more –
She is battered.

Patricia Rogers

Night

I sit alone in the dark,
Without a light
Alone with my thoughts,
Well into the night.

I let the night surround me,
I'm trying hard to cope.
Alone in the dark,
Without any hope.

The empty promises,
The lies and deceit.
The hurtful words,
I would never repeat.

What causes someone
To be so malicious?
Can no one speak kindly?
Must they be so vicious?

The moon and the stars
Are my friends this night.
There is always tomorrow,
Perhaps there will be light.

Patricia Rogers

Survive

The bruises are healed, and
The bones have mended.
I thank God every day
The torture has ended.

I am a survivor of
Domestic violence.
Be it physical , emotional,
Or torment,
It is not worth paying
The consequence.

Now it is hard to trust,
You can never give in to lust.
Be cautious and look for
The signs,
A partner should not control
Your mind.

Be confident and you will
Survive.
You will look forward to
Being alive.

Patricia Rogers

Why

I miss our times together.
Most were good, some were bad.
All our talks, all out plans,
They are no more, how sad.

We used to laugh at
Some silly little thing.
We turned on the radio,
And, you would beg me not to sing.

They said we kept the roads hot.
But, we stood our ground.
Who cares what they thought?
Remember the junk in
The dumpster we found?

Now all has changed,
My integrity is challenged.
I don't think I can fix it,
Why has this happened?

I am angry, I am grieving.
My mind can't comprehend.
What were you thinking?
You let our friendship end.

Patricia Rogers

INFORMATION GUIDE FOR
ABUSED WOMEN IN
HOLMES, JACKSON AND WASHINGTON COUNTIES

Printed by:

HOPE FOR LIFE, INC., 2004
With Donations from:
City of Chipley
City of Sneads
Bridge Creek Baptist Church

Reproduced from:

INFORMATION GUIDE
FOR ABUSED WOMEN IN MAINE

CONTENTS

Acknowledgements

The Hope for Life, Inc. gratefully acknowledges the Maine Coalition for Family Crisis Services for granting permission for the reproduction of their booklet *Information Guide For Abused Women in Maine*. This booklet has been adapted to reflect the current laws of the State of Florida and the Resources of Holmes, Jackson and Washington Counties.

This booklet is for abused women and anyone in a position to help them, such as social services personnel, law enforcement officers, medical professionals, clergy, neighbors, relatives and friends. The better we understand how violence is allowed in our communities and find ways to take individual and group action, the sooner violence against women will stop.

We recognize that this booklet does not specifically address the additional safety issues that arise for battered lesbians. As of this printing, the Lesbian Caucus of the Florida Coalition Against Domestic Violence (FCADV) is actively working on issues for battered lesbians. Issues unique to various populations, such as women of color, rural battered women, and formerly battered women, are also being addressed by FCADV task forces. For more information call Florida's Domestic Violence Hotline at (800) 500-1119

Our community has come a long way in working together on this issue, but we still have far to go. We hope the time comes when a booklet like this will no longer be needed.

FOREWARD

Victims of domestic violence are hurt and controlled by someone with whom they have been emotionally and intimately involved. Abuse crosses all lines of economic status, age, geography, race, religion, and sexual orientation. Some experts estimate that one in every two women in the United States will be the victim of at least one violent encounter with a partner.

For purposes of this booklet, we will refer to "he" as the abuser and "she" as the victim. Research suggests that 95% of abuse is male to female. However, we acknowledge that in intimate relationships there are women who abuse their male partners, women who abuse women, and men who abuse men.

You may be a victim of domestic violence even if:

- You are not legally married to your abusive partner
- You are in a gay or lesbian relationship with someone who abuses you
- You have formally and legally ended your relationship but your ex-partner continues to behave in an abusive manner towards you
- You are not living with your partner but he does abuse you
- Your partner abuses someone else in your household, such as a parent or child.

You are no less a victim if what you are experiencing doesn't seem as bad as what you've seen on TV or heard other women describe. Any type of abuse is hurtful. What you feel about your partner's actions or behaviors is the best indication of whether or not you are being abused.

YOU HAVE THE RIGHT NOT TO BE ABUSED!

BATTERED WOMEN'S RIGHTS

We have the right not to be abused.

We have the right to freedom from fear of abuse

We have the right to anger over past beatings.

We have the right to share our thoughts and feelings and not be isolated from others.

We have the right to privacy.

We have the right to be treated like adults.

We have the right to choose to change the situation.

We have the right to want better role models for out children.

We have the right to leave the battering environment.

We have the right to ask for support from our families and friends.

We have the right to request and expect assistance from police and social agencies.

We have the right to prosecute our abusers.

We have the right to develop our individual talents.

We have the right not to be perfect.

We have the right to happiness.

Amended from Region IV News
February 1981
Southeast Coalition Against Domestic Violence

We acknowledge that there are ideas in this booklet that have become part of our working knowledge in the battered women's movement and that the original authors have been lost to us. We thank anyone whose original works are printed here, and welcome hearing from you for any future reprinting.

AM I BEING ABUSED?

If you look in the mirror and see that your body is bruised and swollen because of the actions of your partner, you realize that you have been abused. But often we focus just on the physical abuse when trying to figure out if we are being abused. Some forms of physical abuse are not so visible.

Ask yourself these questions ...

- Do you feel like your walking on eggshells to keep the peace?
- Do you feel like a prisoner locked in your own home?
- Does your partner monitor your actions and time, making you account for every minute?
- Does he follow you or show up at work, school, or friends' homes?
- Do you feel forced to have sex when you don't want to?
- Does your partner refuse to practice safe sex and consequently put you at risk of contracting sexually transmitted diseases?
- Does your partner call you names or verbally threaten you?
- Is your partner violent with the children, property or pets?
- Do you feel powerless to make your own choices, have your own opinions or come and go as you please?
- Does your partner make all the money decisions, deny you access to money or make you account for every penny?
- Does your partner humiliate you through actions or words privately or in front of others?
- Does your partner frequently accuse you of having affair?

If you answered yes to any of these questions, it is likely that you are in an abusive situation.

Being abused is a frightening and lonely experience. You may wonder "Is there something wrong with me that makes him do this?" or "Am I the only one?"

It is not your fault! You are not alone!
Help is available to you!

Abuse and battering is a system of behaviors used by one person to control another's actions and feelings. One way to think of these behaviors is of tactics, actions which are chosen and planned. Your abuser is not "out of control"; he is trying to control you.

Physical and sexual abuse are not the only control tactics used; they are the power behind all the other tactics. If you are kept in fear of your physical safety, indeed, for your life, then you can be controlled. If he has harmed you in the past or you know that he is capable of physically harming you, then all the other tactics will work even when the physical and sexual abuse are not presently happening. Once someone has used violence against you, it increases the impact of threats, isolation and humiliation. If he "only" hit you once four years ago, it does not mean that you are free from abuse now, if he is threatening or isolating you to control you. If he has never hit you but you are afraid and controlled by his intimidation (shouting or throwing things) or threats of taking the kids, you are still being abused. In fact, your partner may control his physical abuse at times but use the other tactics even more forcefully and successfully to control you.

DOMESTIC ABUSE INTERVENTION PROJECT
202 East Superior Street
Duluth, Minnesota 55802
218-722-2781

A-7

- He put matchsticks in the door each morning when he went to work so he'd know if someone came to see me during the day."
- "He was always saying I was a lousy mother and that, if I left, he'd get "the kids and I'd never see them again."
- "When he came home from work last night, he threw the dinner I had made on the floor, then made me clean it up."
- "He used our money to buy beer and dope for him and his friends; then he would yell at me when the bills came."
- "I had been working on a term paper for school but before I could hand it in he tore it up."

HOPE

After you once raised your voice to me
Then your hand
Then your fist
I lost respect
 For you
 For myself
 For us ... what we once were
And never will be again.

I live in hope
 That you will change
 That I won't feel guilty
 That we will be happy
 That you will stop drinking
 That you will die.

My hope is a pipe-dream
I live in hope

From Say "No!" by Marry Marecek
Respond, Inc. Somerville, MA 02143
Used by permission

WHY DOES ABUSE HAPPEN?

Those who are unfamiliar with the dynamics of domestic abuse and violence are generally confused and amazed that women do not quickly and resolutely choose to leave the abusive situation. You may have been frequently asked the question, "Why do you stay?", as if by staying you "allow" the abuse to occur. This is an example of "victim-blaming", and it represents one way in which our culture suggests that women are responsible for the abuse. ABUSE DOES NOT HAPPEN BECAUSE OF THE VICTIM. The real question is: "Why do men batter and get away with it?"

Men batter because our culture says that they can and should control women and that women want and need to be controlled.

Until very recently, women were considered the property of men. They belonged to their fathers until marriage, when they were given to their husbands. Men had to right to treat property as they wished. Under British common law, it was legal for husbands to chastise their wives with any reasonable instrument. Laws were slowly changed to restrict this right. For instance, the "Rule of Thumb" term comes from an English common law which sad a mean could not beat his wife with an instrument larger than the circumference of his thumb. It was not until 1892 that the United States established laws abolishing wife beating.

For hundreds of years, men have been considered superior to women. If that superiority was challenged, physical force maintained that position. Men who batter are not abnormal or necessarily sick; they are carrying out a role defined for them by our culture. They are expected to get what they want by being aggressive and violent. The lack of immediate consequences for violent behavior in domestic violence situations is a further message that our culture accepts, expects and supports violent behavior.

Violence works for the abuser. It is effective in establishing his control over you and getting what he wants.

Our culture passes on these beliefs in male superiority through the media: television, magazines, movies, and billboards all give the message that men dominate women. The role set up for men is to be the "tough guy": strong, powerful, invulnerable and in control. Women are seen as "Cinderellas": quiet, pretty, needing to be dependent on men, and putting the needs of others (husbands and children) before their own. Our role as women is to keep everyone else comfortable and happy. Based on that cultural attitude, the assumption is that when a man is unhappy enough to hit his wife, she must have done something terribly wrong and therefore deserved it.

These beliefs are passed on through generations. Children learn from their parents what the rules of the culture are. Is it okay to hit? To feel? To scream and call each other names? Who gets what they want in the family and how do they get it?

These beliefs are also passed on by our societal institutions. "When the police come, they just walked him around the yard and then left. I was so bruised I couldn't move and was too frightened to speak up."

"My minister said I should keep praying for him, that he didn't mean to do it."

"The psychiatrist gave me tranquilizers when I described what happened. He said I was a nervous wreck."

"When I was with him I felt like I was in a box. I was afraid to move."

The result is when women go for help they often run into the same tactics used by their abusers to keep them in place. If you are encouraged to stay "because of the children" or "to keep the family together," or are given so little money on welfare that if you leave all you can afford is a one-room apartment for you and your children, or are threatened by a police officer not to ever call back unless you "mean to do something, then it is clear how the Power/Control Wheel is supported by our cultural institutions.

Many people in the helping professions want to "fix" domestic violence by blaming it on characteristics of the individuals involved. They may see a "profile" of battered women as individuals who are dependent, depressed, and isolated, with low self-esteem, implying that these traits make them vulnerable to battering or bring out abusive behavior in their partners. Many women end up in therapy working on ways to change their behavior to stop the violence. It is a mistake to view the results of abuse (dependence, depression, isolation, low self-esteem) as the cause. These characteristics are normal reactions to being victimized.

Another myth that is widely held is that abused women don't want help and won't take it when it is offered. That is NOT true. As abuse toward a woman and her children gets worse she will ask for more and more help. Women seek help, on average from seven different sources at least three times... 21 requests! Often these helpers are unable to provide the support necessary to enable women to leave.

There is also a perceived profile of men who batter as individuals who are insecure and unable to "express feelings", individuals who suffered from deprived childhood, have poorly developed egos, and lack impulse control.

But men who batter are as diverse as the women they abuse. They come from all backgrounds. They are also usually selective about whom they abuse and how they do it. IT IS NOT THEIR PERSONALITIES BUT THEIR BELIEF SYSTEMS THAT PUT MEN AT RISK OF BEING ABUSERS.

Stress is commonly noted as a cause of battering. However, women under stress do not beat up men in large numbers. Stress does not cause battering: many men may choose to deal with stress by battering because they believe it is their right.

Alcohol is also pointed to as a cause of violent behavior. For many women, alcohol may have played a major role in their battering relationships. Once again, women who drink do not batter men in large numbers and many men who drink do not batter. Most alcoholic abusers are not randomly violent. They do not assault bosses, friends, and neighbors; they do not usually assault their partners in front of other people or out of the home. Alcohol abuse may result in impulsive behavior, but the fact that women in the home are so often the targets represents a belief system that battering women is acceptable. Wives and girlfriends are selected targets.

Some women who have been victims of abuse as children may also experience violence in their partnerships. Women who are physically, verbally, or sexually abused as children, or who witness their mothers being abused, may grow up believing that they are worthless, that they are the cause of the battering, that their bodies do not belong to them and that abuse is "normal" behavior in families. Once again, these beliefs are the result of being abused and are not character defects that cause a woman to be battered later on. These beliefs do not mean that she enjoys abuse, attracts it or has control over it.

In summary, men batter because they believe they have the right to control women. Even though their individual motivations are unique, through battering men are making a statement about the superior position to which they believe they are entitled. Women stay for all kinds of reasons, but ultimately because they are controlled by the violence. Fear overtakes love, respect and trust in the relationship as battering continues and escalates.

The battered women's movement is working to change attitudes about domestic violence in our culture. The abuser must be seen as the cause of violence and the one responsible for stopping the violence. Our societal institutions must take action by responding to his violent behavior with consistent legal and social consequences.

NOTES

WHY CAN'T I SEE MY
SITUATION CLEARLY?

If you are being abused, you may feel ashamed because you believe the abuse is your fault. You may want to hide what is really going on from friends and family. You may have lied to your doctor about where your injuries came from or reassured a police officer and sent him away in the middle of the night.

"For many months I repeated to myself,
'This is not happening.'"

Denial, rationalization (making excuses for your abuser or blaming yourself) and minimization (pretending that the abuse is not as bad as it really is) are coping skills developed in order to survive a confusing and painful experience. They are also the result of a society that is denying the severity of abuse and reinforcing your self-blame. Years of abuse distort your reality. When you are constantly concerned with how to survive, you do not have time or space to feel your feelings and the fear and pain in your life. You may use things to "stuff" your feelings, like alcohol, drugs, or food. Your body may actually become numb in order to survive the beatings.

Your abuser may be denying his actions by blaming you, saying the next day that the abuse never happened, or that it was "only a shove." He may also say it was something you did or said that "caused" him to beat you; that if you did just what he wanted you to do, he wouldn't abuse you. You may hold onto the hope that something you can do will make the battering stop, which can give you a feeling of control over the situation. Most battered women, however, have discovered that changing their behavior does not change his abuse because it does not cause his abuse.

Another confusing thing that leads to denial is the period of calm and remorse that many abusers display after an incident of violence. There are promises like, "It'll never happen again: "I'll make it up to you, just give me another chance."; "You know how much I love you, I only did it because I was drunk": "I'll go to church with you, I promise"; "I know I'm really crazy but I want to change and I need your help to get turned around; please don't leave me." These promises are very hard to reject because it seems as though you are now being offered what you have wanted all along --- someone who is loving and considerate of your feelings. The man you fell in love with seems to reappear. In fact, the "hearts and flowers" stage, though perhaps satisfying at the time, is in the end another tactic that keeps you controlled and distorts your reality.

Unfortunately, his promises do not usually bring long-lasting change. His remorse is short-lived and he soon needs to feel powerful and in control. The abusive behaviors hat keep you walking on eggshells begin and continue until the violence erupts again. As much as you may want to believe he has really changed this time, it is important to remember that he has assaulted you, and the memory and fear of that happening again continues to control you. If you still find yourself adjusting your behavior to smooth the way for your partner, then his violence is still controlling you, even if it is not presently occurring.

The "hearts and flowers" stage, after a point, ceases to work as a tactic. You begin to see that he does not follow through with his promises. As abusive relationships continue, the contrite, loving period may get shorter and shorter and even disappear altogether. For some women, these promises become a test by which real change can be measured.

The atmosphere of denial within your self, your partner and the world around you can make you feel crazy and isolated, even though in the short run it may make life more bearable. Coming to grips with the reality of your situation may happen over time. Maybe it will be the day your friend notices your black eye and ask about it, or you realize that even though you made his favorite meal he still criticizes and belittles you or you hear "I'll never do it again" one too many times. Breaking through your own denial and identifying yourself as a battered woman is a difficult step. Once you have faced your situation you can begin to make changes in your life. Once you can listen to and feel your feelings, can you begin to take action.

WHAT IS THIS DOING
TO MY CHILDREN?

Violence is a learned behavior. The cultural beliefs that support the abuse of women are passed on in large part through families. If your children are surrounded by violence, they, too, are being abused. Although some battered women tell us "He would never hurt the children," the children are in fear and pain if they live with someone who is threatening and controlling.

Children who live in families where there is abuse struggle to survive and find safety. They often feel (or are told by the abuser) that they are responsible for the abuse. Children are very often used by the abuser to "get at" his partner. He may threaten to take them, use them physically as weapons, try to turn them against her and pump them for information about where she's been. Children end up walking a tightrope between wanting to please the abuser and wanting to hang onto their mother because she is the safer parent for them.

"Johnny acts just like his father, like he hates me, too.
I don't understand."

Children know who to be afraid of in the home, and they feel they must stay on that person's good side in order to stay safe. They may act like the abuser or act as though they like him better than you. It is important to remember that they are afraid. If they know you will not leave them, then they may be more apt to act out their scared and angry feelings towards you because you are safe. If they are afraid of their father, they will try to please him.

If children are preoccupied with fear about what happens at home, they may have a difficult time being at school or paying attention. They may feel they should be home protecting you. They may run away for fear of coming home at all.

Growing up with denial of the abuse distorts their reality, as it does yours. If you and the neighbors and relatives all pretend that nothing terrible is happening, your children will learn to doubt the tight feeling in their stomachs, which says that something is wrong. "Staying for the children" may mean continuing to keep your children in fear.

Once into their teens, your children may look for things like alcohol, drugs, and food to numb their feelings. Their feelings of powerlessness may be expressed as anger toward you for not being able to protect them. Their beliefs will be influenced by our culture's tendency to blame the victim. They may start acting violently toward you, others, and/or themselves.

If you are feeling battered now, the best thing you can do for your children is to be honest about the abuse in your lives. Next, begin to think about yourself so you can be a role model for how a person loves and takes care of herself. Once you are feeling your own feelings, you become a safe person with whom they can express their feelings. Seek help so you can free yourself and your children from abuse.

SHOULD I STAY OR LEAVE

There are some common stages in an abused woman's journey to freedom: denial, ambivalence, seeking help, and living without violence. Most of us do not jump from denial straight to living without violence. Each stage may be long and difficult.

Perhaps you have thought about or tried leaving the violent relationship. Most women who eventually free themselves have left and returned five to seven times. You may go back and forth between wanting to leave and struggling with some of these reasons for staying or returning.

THE UNKNOWN IS WORSE THAN THE KNOWN

At least you know what you've got here. The house and daily routine are familiar, If you leave, you'll be walking into the unknown and that is frightening.

I CAN'T MAKE IT ON MY OWN FINANCIALLY

Perhaps you've never had a job, or haven't worked outside the home for many years, or you live in an area with few job possibilities. Getting state aid may be familiar to you or totally new. Either way, it does not feel like enough money to maintain a household. If you get a job, you may have to pay for child care, an expensive double bind. Losing a standard of living you are accustomed to may be difficult.

HE MAY COME AFTER ME

You may feel safer knowing where your abuser is at all times than moving away and never knowing when he will appear to assault or harass you.

I STILL LOVE HIM AND HE ISN'T VIOLENT ALL THE TIME

Your relationship with him has been important to you, holding many dreams of happiness. There have been some good times, tender moments, plans made together. He is the father of your children. You are committed to your marriage vow. Is there still a chance the violence will stop?

I'M AFRAID OF BEING ALONE

You may never have been on your own before. Women are not taught to be independent or in charge of their lives, emotionally or practically, and you may feel you don't have the skills to pull it off. Raising children by yourself may also feel like an overwhelming task.

All of these reasons and many more are valid considerations as you move through your decision making process. Staying with your abuser does not mean you accept the violence, but rather that there are many obstacles to changing the situation. Everyday you are undoubtedly in either trying to stop the violence or deciding to leave.

You may have tried to stop the violence by changing yourself or your behavior. Slowly you come to realize that no matter what you do, he continues to abuse you. You cannot control his violence because it is not your fault or responsibility; the violence is his choice.

If you have never tried leaving, consider what a powerful step it is. You are no longer there to participate in his denial of the abuse. You are safe to think your own thoughts and make plans free of the constant fear of violence and the pressure to keep him happy. Being away from the violence and the relationship for awhile can allow you to see more clearly.

If you have left but are thinking of returning to give the relationship another try, look carefully at what has really changed. He may be promising to stop drinking, see a counselor, and never hit you again. He may say he cannot live without you. But the longer you are out of his control, the more his promises of love and changing may turn to threats. This is a sign that one of his main goals is to get you back under his control. If you return home with promises only, expect that eventually the violence will continue. Unless he is held accountable for his violence, there is little motivation for him to deal with his belief that he has a right to control you. It is perfectly reasonable for you to expect to see changed behavior on his part for a long period of time (maybe six months or more) before you attempt a reunion.

If you have attempted a reconciliation that has been unsuccessful, do not despair! This is part of your learning process. Each effort you make gives you new insight and strength to move forward.

Here are some tools you might find helpful in trying to make your decision.
CREATE YOUR OWN "BOTTOM LINES"

If you begin to think about what you will put up with and what you won't, you start building your limits and, therefore, your self respect. Your limits may change over time. Sometimes it is helpful to write them down and see where you stand.
KEEP A JOURNAL

Writing down what is happening to you is a good release of feelings, a way to stay aware of your own denial, and a way to watch your progress.
DEVELOP AN ACTION PLAN

Make a list of important phone numbers of friends, social services, police, shelters, etc. List your options and imagine what you will say and do when you feel ready to reach out for help. When you are faced with a crisis, this planning will be invaluable.

We hope your safety and freedom win out as primary goals. With help, you can move through the fears and hardships, one by one, to begin a life without violence.

USE AND CARE OF YOUR SAFETY PLAN

- Keep it in a safe place (at work, a friend's, etc.).
- Read the brochure carefully, then call the domestic violence hotline (1-800-500-1119), and ask a counselor to help you make a plan. Everyone is different, and your plan should cover your personal situation.
- Put your important phone numbers together so that they will be handy if you leave.
- Check-off items which will apply to your situation. See what will help you the most and concentrate on those items.
- Up-date your safety plan often, Review it with a supporter or hotline counselor.
- Share your plan only with those who will absolutely support you. Do not share it with anyone, including family members, who may tell or "let it slip" to the abuser or his supporters.

If You Are Living With or Dating Someone Who is Violent

Because danger can occur at any time, will you consider the following:

- Practice an escape plan for emergencies..................... _Yes _No
- Go over it with a counselor or advocate.........................._Yes _No
- Teach children emergency and escape action
  and phone use... . . . ._Yes _No
- Keep pay phone change in a safe place for
  self/children..._Yes _No
- Use portable or cellular phone if possible...................... . ._Yes _No
- Use noise-makers (whistle, personal alarm, etc.
  to get help.._Yes _No
- If you have neighbors, ask them to listen, watch
  and call police about suspicious
  people or activities.. .. .. .. ._Yes _No
- Let someone know if you feel violence
  is about to happen.._Yes _No

When violence does seem close, avoid the kitchen, bathroom and rooms without doors to the outside. Begin action on a safety plan at any sign of trouble.

If You Plan to Leave A Violent Relationship: What is Needed?

- It is always best to plan for emergencies before there is one.
- Plan how you will get away from the abuser pr get help to come to you.
  - o Emergency number to be called:_____
  - o Transportation will be:_____
  - o Helpers or supporters:_____
- Plan where you will go, if you choose to or are forced to leave.
- Plan what you will take with you if you leave.
- Plan for children.
- Plan for pets and animals.
- Plan for other responsibilities and needs.

Be Prepared to Get Away
Try to bring the following if possible:
- o ID for yourself
- o Car title, registration
- o Driver's license
- o Welfare ID
- o Birth certificates and Baptism certificates for you and your children
- o Lease, rental agreement or house deed
- o Passport
- o Green card
- o Insurance papers
- o Checkbook, ATM card
- o Medications, medical cards/records
- o Food, Food Stamps
- o Social Security cards
- o Marriage license
- o School records
- o Pictures (including one of the abuser)
- o Credit cards
- o Savings passbook
- o Set of house/car keys
- o Diapers and formula
- o Jewelry
- o Clothing
- o Any cash available
- o Address book
- o Favorite toys
- o Small salable objects
- o Personal hygiene products (tampons, toothbrush, deodorant, etc.)

o   Copies of bills you owe with your partner
o   Divorce papers or court orders, including Domestic Violence Injunction (if you have one)
o   Proof of income for partner (check stub)
o   Prepaid long distance / home calling card (calls can be traced).
o   If you have a joint bank account you might want to take out some or all of the money as it is not uncommon for the abuser to clean out joint accounts after learning a partner is leaving.
o   You may want to take joint bills and leases out of your name to protect your credit (Your abuser may use them as a way of trying to control you.)
o   Get new credit cards in your name only if possible.
o   If possible seek legal advice in advance to know rights and laws in your state of residence.
o   Date book or calendar showing current appointments.

Some Important Safety Tips

o   Remember: the danger often gets worse during an escape or after leaving a violent relationship.
o   Have a safety plan for as long as there is communication with/from the abuser and longer. Review it with a counselor often.
o   If you move, put rent, phone, and utilities in someone else's name.
o   Make sure all locks (doors and windows) and lights (inside and out) work properly.
o   Install alarms on doors and windows. Install smoke alarms, metal doors, or other safety items.
o   Get an unlisted phone number. (Change old number if necessary)
o   Get an Injunction for Protection. (Call 1-800-500-1119 for information)
o   Keep copies of injunction orders at home, work, and in your purse and in the car.
o   Have another person to deliver and pick up children if a judge orders visitation.
o   Use a post office box instead of a street address. Check it during busy hours.
o   Report suspicious things to the police; file violations of the injunction whenever they occur.
o   Keep a copy of divorce, custody orders, etc. at school.
o   Make special arrangements to pick up children from school.
o   Ask school to call about any unusual contact by the abuser.
o   Make the same arrangements with child care/babysitters as above.
o   Have mail sent to the domestic violence center to be forwarded to you or to another safe place. Do not file change of address card with post office (it is not private).

Safety Planning at Work

It is important for survivors of domestic violence to be alert and prepared for possible contacts by the abuser during a work day. A safety plan for work may help you if the abuser calls or shows up.

Which of these can you use?

                                                                          Yes No

- o   Tell co-workers boss about situation........................
- o   Ask the person(s) to call police in an emergency...........
- o   Have a back-up person if the first one is not at work or nearby...
- o   Ask someone to screen your calls...........................
- o   Ask someone to watch out for you. ....
- o   Plan your entry and exit each day...........................
- o   Keep a copy of your injunction at work.....................
- o   Let others know about the injunction........................
- o   Request office or desk be placed in a safe location.........
- o   Request help from employee assistance program...........
- o   Plan an escape route..
- o   Have a signal for help (whistle/alarm).......................
- o   Drive a different way to and from work each day...........
- o   Find a safe room to use in an emergency....................
- o   Be sure the safe room locks, has a telephone and a window or a second door.
- o   Locate a parking space close to the door and in a well lighted place, and have someone walk you to your car. ....
- o   If possible, get dropped off and picked up, trade cars with someone or carpool.

If You Live in a Rural Area
                                                            Yes   No

- o   See if is safe to stay with friends /family local or out of town.. . ..
- o   Make a special escape plan because it takes police too long to get there...
- o   Make a special escape plan because of problems with transportation or timing.....................................
- o   See if family car/truck can be taken without being seen or stopped...
- o   Get a ride from a trusted friend or family member.......
- o   Get transportation from the county or health department...
- o   Keep an escape bag at church, the health department, with

a friend, or some other safe place.
o   See if leaving and getting away safely can be done   YES NO
    without someone alerting the abuser..............................

KEEPING RECORDS

The following is a discussion of ways to document domestic violence, and is not meant as legal advice.

Documenting the Abuse

o   Photos are valuable evidence. Injuries should be photographed and dated by a trained police officer, doctor, or advocate. If this is not possible have someone else take them for you and date them preferably including a newspaper showing the date in the photo. Your photos may not be admissible in court, but they could be very useful anyway.
o   Take follow up photos if applicable.
o   Document the size of an injury by taking a photo with a ruler. Also show where on the body the injury is.
o   Do not rely on police reports but always obtain a copy of any taken.
o   Ask for a copy of any medical report.
o   Document where you were if you are not at home. For example, a motel receipt.
o   Be sure to get the name of the office, date, and case number if police are called. Also get a copy of the police report.
o   Get an ambulance record if applicable.
o   Keep your clothing if any is damaged in the exchange and date it. Get his clothes too, if possible.
o   Gather and photograph anything that was damaged or broken in the exchange.
o   It the person has any weapons, document make and model and take photos if possible.
o   Obtain a document of your work record if you missed any time and keep track of any out of pocket expenses.
o   If you made a 911 call ask the supervisor for a copy. They sometimes only keep them 30 days and you may need a subpoena to get it.
o   Save and make copies of any voluntary messages left on your answering machine. They are admissible in court.
o   Keep any correspondence you may receive and date it.
o   Make a diagram of the location where the incident occurred.
o   Take family photos when he is not present in the home to back up the fact that he is not living with you.

Documenting the Abuse-continued

- o Record dates and times of any incidents that occur (record of events).
- o Have a copy of all these documents in a safe place, like a safety deposit box or in the possession of an attorney, close trusted friend, relative.

NOTES

HOW DO I GO ABOUT LEAVING?

If you made the decision to leave, it is best to get out as safely as possible. If you have time to pack and plan, great; if not just get yourself and your children out. It may be possible to return to the house later with a police officer to collect your belongings. You may also be able to get legal possession of your residence (see chapter on Legal System)

Try to bring as many of the following items as possible:

ID for yourself	marriage license	driver's license
Birth certificates	credit cards	car title
Insurance papers	savings pass book	check book
Precious belongings	set of house/car keys	food
Medications	any cash available	food stamps
Medical cards/records	favorite toys	
Social Security cards	divorce papers or court orders	

If you have a joint bank account, you might want to take out some or all of the money, as it is not uncommon for abusers to clear out joint accounts after learning of the partner's leaving. You may want to take joint bills, and leases out of your name to protect your credit. Your abuser may use them as another way of trying to control you. Get new credit cards in your own name if possible.

If your children are not in physical danger and you are in extreme danger, you might have to consider leaving them. However, it can turn out to be more difficult legally to get them later, so if possible, bring them. (See chapter on Legal System-Custody).

If there has been a recent incident of abuse, seek medical treatment promptly, It is best to be honest about how your injuries were caused so your doctor can check you out for further problems, Ask the doctor to indicate in your medical records your statement about the cause of the injuries. These records could help you in a criminal prosecution.

Where to Go

Your first priority is to get yourself and your children to a safe, supportive place. You may have friends or family who will be supportive and willing to put you up. Consider these options carefully; if you think that you will be pressured in ways you don't want to be or that you or they will be put in danger (for instance, someone will tell your abuser where you are), consider other options.

If you have been abused by an intimate partner, remain in danger from the abuser, and have no safe alternative place to stay, you will want to consider contacting one of the local domestic violence shelters within the Holmes, Jackson, and Washington County area (See Resources), Besides emergency refuge, the Shelter can provide residents with emergency food and clothing, transportation, child care, case management and counseling. You and your children may remain at the shelter for up to eight weeks while you explore your housing options and make provisions for your immediate safety needs.

Finances and Housing

After you are out of the immediate physical danger, you will need to figure out how you will manage on your own. If you have a paying job, you may still suffer a loss of income and have to make decisions about housing, based on affordability and safety. If you have no other sources of income, you may have to rely on welfare, share housing, or make other adjustments in your lifestyle. It is often demoralizing and discouraging to have to be dependent on others, and dealing with state and local social services can be frustrating. Keep in mind, however, the hardships of living in an abusive relationship. As unfair as it is, you may lose some things in order to gain your emotional and physical safety. Most importantly, remember that your new situation does not have to be permanent. There is hope for finding better solutions once you are safe and have had a chance to get back on your feet.

Though a friend, relative, or shelter may help you through your immediate crisis, you will have to begin making more permanent living arrangements fairly quickly. Finding housing can be difficult. You may want to consider trying to share housing with other women. You can start by checking local newspapers and bulletin boards, or walking around neighborhoods looking for "For Rent" signs in buildings. Calling realtors can also be productive.

When meeting with a landlord, be assertive about your desirability as a tenant; be clear about your ability to pay, reliability, etc. It is against the law to be denied housing on the basis of race, color, sex, physical or mental handicap, religion, ancestry or national origin, or because an individual is a welfare recipient.

Think carefully about whether or not to tell the landlord about the abuse. On the one hand, he/she may be reluctant to rent to you and possibly be exposed to the violence. On the other hand, he/she maybe sympathetic and be able to help you with security plans. Remember that safety in your new home is a priority; you need secure doors, locks and a phone if possible, Getting to know your neighbors and alerting them about your situation can also be a good way to help insure your safety.

Sometimes all I needed to take that
next step was a little help from someone.
And then I felt stronger.

WELFARE AND PUBLIC ASSISTANCE

Temporary Assistance to Needy Families (TANF) is a form of assistance often available to women who are on their own. If you have at least one child in your custody and one parent who can't or won't support the child, you should be eligible for TANF if your income falls within the guidelines. You can apply for this assistance at the State of Florida Department of Children and Families

(DCF) office nearest you. If you apply for TANF, you will be asked the name and address of the children's father(s) so he/they can be contacted by the department to pay child support. However, this requirement can be waived in cases of domestic assault. If you feel that you will be put in more danger if DCF contacts him, explain this to your worker. You may be asked for some kind of "proof:" police or court record, a letter from a shelter worker, or a letter from a friend or relative who knows about the violence.

There are other forms of assistance you may be eligible for through DCF. If you are getting TANF, you will receive Medicaid health benefits and food stamps, but you may qualify for these benefits even if you are not on welfare if your income is low. There may be employment and training programs through DCF.

You may also be eligible for Supplemental Security Income (SSI) if you are 65 or older, disabled or blind, have limited resources and income and meet certain other requirements. Disabled or blind children as well as adults may be eligible, SSI recipients are also eligible for Medicaid. You apply for SSI through your local Social Security Administration Office.

When applying for various forms of public assistance, you may be required to bring birth certificates for yourself and your children, social security cards or numbers, receipts for rent and bills, proof of residence, etc. It is best to call ahead and find out exactly what you will need. If it is impossible for you to furnish the necessary papers, find out what the agency will accept instead, or where you can go to obtain these documents. Also, when you go to apply for assistance, try to arrive a little bit early, and be prepared to have a long wait. Most offices are crowded and take people on a first-come-first-serve basis. Don't be afraid to ask what you are entitled to, how decisions are made and how "need" is computed, why you're being denied if you are, and for what other forms of aid you might be eligible. The more you know about your rights before you walk in, the better off you are.

JOBS

If you are not presently employed, you may need or want a job. Many women have had educational and job experiences that were perhaps interrupted by the battering. Living without the violence may free you to continue your career. For women who have never worked or who have been out of the job market a long time, looking for work can be a difficult step, Think carefully about the things you have done and the skills and qualities that you already have; many of them may be marketable even if you have not been paid for them in the past. Past jobs, volunteer experiences, and life experiences can be useful credentials. You may want to think of self-employment schemes such as housecleaning services, yard work, or child care. Knitting, sewing or doing piecework at home may bring some extra money. You may want to consider entering a non-traditional trade (electrician, plumbing), sales job or a factory. You may also want to try to get more training or education to develop your skills.

There are a variety of places to go to find a job or training opportunities, The classified ads in local newspapers are a place to start. You can also check the telephone directory for offices of the Job Services of Florida and local temporary employment agencies. The Holmes/Washington Technical Center in Chipley, Florida offers adult education and GED (high school equivalency) courses, and many welfare offices also have job training and education programs. Many colleges and universities have part time as well as full time programs, and many have their own financial aid programs. The options discussed in this chapter often require time and energy, and it is easy to get discouraged along the way. It is our hope that you will be able to find the support you need as you make your choices and take each step toward freedom.

HOW DO I USE THE LEGAL SYSTEM?

Violence at the hands of a loved one is frightening, degrading, and confusing. It is also against the law. Despite your conflicting emotions, and despite the fact that police and judges are not always sympathetic to abused women, using the legal system may be one of the most effective ways to protect yourself and your children.

Here are some considerations for turning
to the criminal justice system
(police and courts) for help.

o   If a man is abusive and there are no serious consequences for his use of violence, his violent behavior is reinforced.
o   Most men who batter choose not to exercise self-control, so controls must be placed on them, at least initially.
o   The courts can place controls on batterers that friends and family cannot; they can order an abuser into counseling; they can also use jail sentences, protection orders, and bail restrictions to provide ongoing protection for those victimized by his violence.
o   Domestic violence is a crime. If you were physically attacked by a stranger on the street, you would expect an arrest.
o   Beating another person is a crime against the state and is prosecuted as such. This means that the State of Florida is pressing charges against the batterer, and the responsibility for stopping the abuse is not all on you.
o   If battering is to stop, the community must be aware that battering is wrong and will result in serious consequences.

ARREST
You should call the police when someone has threatened or battered you, even if it took place in your home.

Under Florida law, the police may arrest a person without a warrant if they have probable cause to believe the person has committed an act of domestic violence or has acted in violation of an injunction for protection.

Studies have shown that once abuse starts it nearly always continues and gets more serious. Arrest is a powerful deterrent to further violence and in Holmes, Jackson, and Washington Counties, police and sheriff's officers are directed to make an arrest if probable cause exists. Arrest imposes a penalty for crimes of abuse.

CRIMINAL CHARGES
The main reason women seek help through the courts is to end the abuse. When the abuser is someone to whom you have an emotional attachment, the issue of your right to safety in your home gets mixed up with dealings of guilt, love and/or fear. The pressure placed on you through

coercion, promises, and emotional ties may discourage you from involving the criminal justice system. Because domestic violence is a crime against the state and you become the witness, the criminal justice system can help remove you from the difficult position of initiating the court proceedings. This means that THE BURDEN OF RESPONSIBILITY IS NOT ON YOU TO PRESS CHARGES OR TO DROP THEM, BUT RATHER ON THE STATE.

Normally, charges are filed soon after a crime is committed. The incident is fresh in your memory and your resolve to end the violence is high.

When your partner finds out that he is
facing charges, he usually responds in the
following ways:

o   He will promise that it will never happen again, that he will seek help for his violence and/or drinking; he will plead/coax you into dropping charges.

o   He will intimidate and pressure you and may become violent again.

o   Both (if the first method doesn't work, he may resort to the second).

Remember he will try to use what has been successful in the past.

As time passes, physical pain and the memory of it begin to fade. You may experience persistent pressure from your partner, family, or friends to drop charges. Memories of the good times return and you begin to doubt that the abuse was really that bad. These feelings of self-doubt may make you reluctant to go through with the prosecution. It might be helpful for you to talk with a worker at the domestic violence shelter, or with a Victim-Witness Counselor at the State Attorney's office, Both can support you through the process and answer your questions.

THE PROCESS

1.   When police are called to a domestic violence incident, they are required to provide you with written notice of your legal rights and remedies including contact information for your local domestic violence shelter. Whether or not an arrest is made, police are required to take a report describing the incident. Be sure to obtain the number of the police report. When responding to a call, police can help you obtain medical treatment or locate safe, temporary housing if needed.

2.   When called to the scene, the police may make an arrest based on probable cause. A person arrested for domestic violence must be held in jail until first appearance, which is generally held within 24 hours of the arrest. At the hearing the judge will establish the conditions of the

defendant's release from jail. The judge may set a bond, release the defendant to Pre-Trial Services, and/or impose any other restrictions appropriate to ensuring victim safety. You have the right to attend this hearing if you wish to share information with the court that might influence the conditions of the defendant's release. (See Resources for the telephone number for case information)

3. If the police do not make an arrest, you can go to the State Attorney's Office and file a complaint yourself. An investigation will be opened and, if appropriate, the prosecutor (State Attorney) will sign the formal complaint against your partner. REMEMBER, IT IS THE STATE, NOT YOU, WHO IS PRESSING CHARGES. You are a witness of the state. Should anyone try to persuade you to drop the charges, you can safely say you have no power to do so. If someone threatens you to drop charges, this is an additional crime called "witness tampering" which should be reported immediately to the police and the prosecuting attorney.

4. If the State Attorney has sufficient evidence to file criminal charges, the defendant will be served with a summons ordering him to appear in court, or a warrant is issued and he is arrested and brought to court.

5. On the specified court date, the defendant appears before the judge for arraignment, at which time he is told what he is accused of and what his rights are. You may receive a subpoena to appear at the arraignment in order to make your opinion known to the prosecutor. There are several outcomes of the arraignment:

   a. Diversion: At arraignment, defendants with no prior history of domestic violence may be offered diversion with a nolle prosequi (i.e. prosecution is dropped) after successful completion of a batterer treatment program. Diversion may be offered only if both the state and the victim have no objection.

   b. Guilty Plea: If the defendant does have a history of domestic violence, he may wish to plead guilty or no contest, in which case the defendant may be sentenced to a batterer treatment program. Substance abuse treatment may also be ordered as a condition of probation or diversion.

   c. Not Guilty: Defendants who are not eligible for diversion and do not wish to plead guilty will be set for trial.

6. The case, if it goes to trial, will be tried by a judge or jury. (The choice is up to the defendant) You will be notified by service of subpoena if you are being asked to testify. This requires you to go to court and so again protects you from outside pressures not to appear. Failure to comply can bring contempt of court charges against you, which may result in a fine or other consequences. If you do not appear in court, you may find further dealings with the police and courts more difficult, since they may mistrust your credibility. The abuser has the right to a trial and does not have to plead guilty. If he does not, the trial is held to determine his guilt or innocence.

7. If he is found guilty, a pre-sentence investigation may be conducted. You may wish to be involved in this process with the probation officer. The probation officer talks to him, the officer checks his past record and makes a recommendation to the judge concerning a sentence. This is your chance to tell the court what you think the sentence should be. You may ask that the sentence include:

    a. Drug and alcohol education or treatment
    b. No possession or use of a gun
    c. No possession or use of alcohol
    d. Batterers education program
    e. Serving time in jail
    f. No contact with you or the children/supervised visitation
    g. A fine
    h. Restitution (payment of medical bills, money for lost wages, payment for damages to property, etc.
    i. A combination of these things.

    When the judge makes the final decision she/he will consider your wishes, You may speak to the judge at the time of sentencing, or you may submit a written statement which will be read to the judge in open court by the prosecutor,

8. The judge imposes a sentence on the defendant to punish him for committing the crime

INJUNCTIONS FOR PROTECTION AGAINST DOMESTIC VIOLENCE

An injunction for protection, sometimes referred to as a "restraining order," is a means of getting legal protection, whether or not you have ever called the police or pressed charges. It is an emergency order and you (the "petitioner") have to prove only that you have reason to fear your partner (the "respondent") and that fear is based on some serious threat or past violence. If he violates the order, he can be arrested. You do not need to have a lawyer to obtain an injunction for protection.

WHAT DOES THE INJUNCTION DO?

Some things the judge may order in an injunction are:

o   That the abuser not commit any acts of violence against you, your children, or others living with you.
o   That the abuser be barred from further contact with you.
o   That the abuser immediately leave the home you share.
o   That the abuser stay away from your home; workplace or other specified place.
o   That you have temporary custody of any children you and the abuser have together.

o   That the abuser go to counseling.

The judge can order other help, depending upon the circumstances.
This is why the contents of the petition and your attendance at all hearings is
so important. When you attend those hearings, you need to be assertive in letting
the judge know what you need and why you need it.

WHO CAN GET AN ORDER FOR PROTECTION?

You may be entitled to obtain an injunction under Florida Law if you fit
into one of the following categories:

Florida Statute 741.30 (Domestic violence)
Your relationship with the person whom the injunction is being filed against
must be that of.
(1) A spouse or ex-spouse
(2) A person related to you by blood or marriage
(3) Anyone who lives or has lived with you in the same dwelling as if
     family, or
(4) Anyone with whom you have had a child, with or without having lived
     together.
To be eligible to file for an injunction for Protection under F.S. 741.30, the
alleged perpetrator ("Respondent") must have committed an act of domestic
violence upon you (the "Petitioner"), or you must have reasonable cause to
believe that you are in imminent danger of becoming a victim of domestic
violence by this person. According to Florida Statute, "domestic violence"
includes an act of assault, aggravated assault, battery, aggravated battery, sexual
assault, sexual battery, stalking, aggravated stalking, kidnapping, false
imprisonment or any other criminal offense which results in physical injury to
you.
Domestic violence must at least involve an assault. An assault does not have
to be physical violence. An assault can occur if someone intentionally threatens
to cause you physical violence, even if they do not touch you. This threat must
be by word or act. The person threatening you must have done something to
make you believe that he has the ability to cause you physical violence, and you
must believe that this violence is about to happen. An act of domestic violence
becomes a battery when someone intentionally touches you without your
permission.
Florida Statute 748.046 (Repeat violence)
Anyone can file for an injunction if two incidents of violence have
occurred, but one of the incidents must have occurred within the last six
months. The "violence" must be an assault, a battery, or stalking.

HOW TO OBTAIN AN ORDER FOR PROTECTION

Where to file:

- o   Holmes County Courthouse..............................850-547-1100
    Clerk of Courts
    201 North Oklahoma St.
    Bonifay, FL 32425
- o   Jackson County Courthouse.............................850-482-9552
    Clerk of Courts
    4445 Lafayette St.
    Marianna, FL 32447
- o   Washington County Courthouse........................ 850-638-6285
    Clerk of Courts
    1293 Jackson Ave.
    Chipley, FL 32428

Applications for Injunctions for Protection are available at the Clerk of Courts office in Holmes, Jackson, and Washington County courthouses. It is suggested that anyone seeking an injunction for protection contact a Victim's Advocate (see Resources). Note that EMERGENCY INJUNCTIONS ARE ALSO AVAILABLE AFTER HOURS AND WEEKENDS.

To file for an injunction, you will be asked to complete an information packet given to you by the Clerk of Court. After you have filled out the paperwork, the staff will explain the injunction process to you and assist you in completing the petition.

If a judge decides you meet the statutory requirements for the injunction, he/she will issue a Temporary Injunction before you leave. A hearing will be set within 15 days, and at that hearing, the judge will decide whether to grant a Permanent Injunction. A police officer will try to serve the Respondent with a copy of the Temporary Injunction and an Order to Appear for the Permanent Injunction hearing. If a permanent injunction is granted at that hearing, it will remain in effect until modified or dissolved by the court.

If a judge decides you do not meet the statutory requirements for the Temporary Injunction, you may still request a hearing for a permanent injunction where you and the Respondent will appear before the judge. A police officer will try to serve the Respondent with a copy of the notice of hearing date. However, you will not have the protection of an injunction during the time prior to the hearing.

There is no fee for filing the injunction.

The Order for Protection is not in effect until the abuser has been served with the injunction. That is not to say that if he attacks you again, he cannot be arrested; assault and other crimes continue to be crimes. However, provisions such as removal from the house or visitation schedules do not go into effect until the Order has been served. It is a good idea to call the Civil Division of the Sheriff's office to check on service about 24 hours after the order is issued. If the abuser has not been located, you may be able to offer other locations to check. Your persistence with the police may also encourage a faster service of the Order. Injunctions are valid in other states. Be certain to register in the county you will be residing in.

Keep your copy of the Order with you at all times and be prepared to call the police for any and all violations. If you have custody of the children, you may want to notify the schools so that officials there know to contact you and the police should your abuser try to take the children. Police are mandated by law to arrest the abuser for certain violations of this Order. If the Order states that the abuser is prohibited from coming to your residence, then it is very important that you don't fall into the trap of thinking that "nice" violations are O.K. (such as his coming to the door with flowers or wanting to go someplace special and talk). The longer you maintain no-contact provisions, the greater chance there is of his "owning his problem." You are no longer there to blame for all of his problems and to be responsible for solving them.

DIVORCE

If you are legally married and decide you want to get a divorce, you may do so without a lawyer through a "pro se" divorce procedure. For uncontested cases, only, involving no minor children and you are not pregnant, you may qualify for a simplified divorce. You and your spouse may file at the Holmes, Jackson, and Washington County Clerk of Courts office. The filing fee ranges from $128 to $138.

Whether the divorce is contested or uncontested, you may obtain a "self-help divorce kit" at the Clerk's office. The price ranges from $20 to $25. The kit is also available at some office supply stores.

If you need to get a lawyer, you may want to shop around until you find one with whom you are comfortable. Some lawyers offer free first-time consultations, which give you an opportunity to meet them without paying or making a commitment. Sometimes the legal system and language can be intimidating and overwhelming. Remember that you pay lawyers for a service and they are working for you. You deserve to get someone who is respectful, understanding, and willing to work for your needs. You will need to be clear and persistent about your expectations with your lawyer throughout your case. LEGAL AID (see Resources) may be able to represent you in your divorce if your income does not exceed 125% of federal poverty guidelines, you have physical custody of your children at this time, and you have been living apart from your husband for a minimum of six weeks.

CUSTODY

If you are separating from your abuser, the legal custody of your children will be of great concern for you. If there are no court orders, and if the abuser is the natural or adoptive father of your children or shares legal guardianship in some way, then you both have equal rights to custody of the children, which in the worst case may mean he can leave with them at any time. An Injunction for

Protection may give you custody of the children for the duration of the Order. If either parent files in court for divorce, a hearing may be held preceding the divorce hearing to establish temporary custody arrangements.

If you are not married, either parent can file in court for custody and the judge will decide.

The judge will award custody on the basis of what is in the best interest of the child. The court may appoint a Guardian Ad Litem or may order a Home Study from the Administrative Office of the Courts' Child Custody Investigation Unit to investigate and make recommendations regarding child custody and visitation.

Joint custody (technically called "shared parental rights and responsibilities") is an arrangement that gives separated parents equal rights to the caretaking of children and determines living arrangements, visitation, holidays, etc. on an equal basis. This means that parents must consult each other regarding decisions related to the care of the children. Sole custody (or sole parental responsibility), on the other hand, gives all the decision-making power to one parent. Joint custody could mean contact with your abuser each time decisions are made about the children.

A parent who is not granted custody is almost always given "reasonable rights" of visitation. Generally, the court allows the parents to work out the visitation schedule between them; however, be aware that you can ask the court to specify particular days and times. If abuse of children has been shown, visitation may be denied or supervised visitation may be ordered, which raises the difficult issue of finding an appropriate person to be the supervisor. Under Florida law, domestic violence must be taken into account when parental rights and responsibilities are being decided (FS 61.13(2)b(2)).

Under a court order granting custody or visitation rights is changed, that order is in force. If you have custody, and the other parent is threatening to take the children, you may seek help from the police or sheriff's office in enforcing the court order. You may also go into court for an order holding the offending parent in contempt, or ordering your children returned if they have been taken from you.

If there are important changes in circumstances, a court order on custody may be changed by a later court order. If you feel that the circumstances have changed to a large degree since the original custody order was made, you may ask the court to change its order. You will have to prove that it is in the best interest of the child to make this change. You will not be allowed to fight the original order, but will have to show that the situation has changed.

Abusers often use the children as a way to control you while you are together and even after you have separated. Threats such as "I'll make sure you never see those kids again," and "Wait till we get to court and I tell them what a lousy mother you are," or, "You're the one in counseling! They won't give our kids to a woman who's nuts," are common tactics. These tactics have a big impact on you, since you have experienced that your abuser gets what he wants in your home. But the reality is that the judge's responsibility is to look out for the children's best interest. The judge will be looking for the present primary caretaker of the children and may be able to recognize your partner's abuse.

You may want to be very specific about visitation when you're filling out your petition for an Injunction of Protection or working with your lawyer for a custody or divorce arrangement, rather than just use the words" reasonable visitation." Determining in the order that you only want him to see the kids on Tuesday and Thursday nights, for example, will free you from continuous dialogue with your abuser about scheduling what he thinks is reasonable visitation that might turn out to be every day. His apparent love and devotion to the children may also be an excuse to continue to harass you.

Your abuser may push for joint custody so that he can continue to control you. Get as much information from your lawyer as you can regarding future involvement with your abuser so that you know how to protect yourself and your children.

If there is disagreement about child custody, visitation, and support during a divorce proceeding, Florida law requires the parties to participate in mediation. Court-appointed mediators meet with the parties together or individually to help work out disagreements. This may be productive under normal circumstances. However, the key elements that make mediation successful elsewhere (voluntary participation, a balance of bargaining power, and the goodwill and fairness of the participants) are usually absent in an abusive relationship, and it may become another arena for your abuser to attempt to control and intimidate you. It is unlikely, given the history of threats and violence, that you will be safe to ask for what you need. Fortunately, Florida law recognizes this by providing an exception to the requirement of mediation in abuse cases. The statute provides that "upon motion or request of a party, a court shall not refer any case to mediation if it finds there has been a history of domestic abuse that would compromise the mediation process." (FS 44.102 (2) (b).

Attempts to control you through the children may go on after your separation from the abuser. He may push visitation limits, take you back to court again and again over custody issues, and pump the children for information about you. All of these are a frustrating reality of sharing children. You will need to get yourself a strong support system to help you cope and stand strong.

NOTES

WHEN WILL I FEEL BETTER?

Recovering from an abusive relationship may be a long, difficult process. Whether you decide to end the relationship or stay and try to work things out, it is important for you to establish a system of support for yourself. You may have been isolated and lost the self-confidence to be with other people. As you slowly take back control of your life, you will want and need support, and you deserve it.

It is wonderful if you have friends or family who are supportive in your efforts to make changes in your life. However, your abuser may have alienated these people by his behavior, or your friends or family may even side with him. Perhaps they may try to step in and attempt to overprotect or control you. You will need to assess what kind of help to expect from whom. Trust your feelings. You can choose not to see people who make you feel bad about yourself.

Reaching out to old or new ties may be exhausting with everything else that is going on, yet breaking the isolation is an essential part of healing. Many women find support groups to be tremendously helpful resources for meeting other women who have shared their experiences, learning more about their options and the dynamics of domestic abuse, and gaining a clearer perspective on their situations. Life Management Center and the Salvation Army offer weekly based educational support groups in Holmes, Jackson, and Washington Counties. The groups are for any woman who is currently or has in the past been involved in an abusive and controlling relationship. The groups are confidential, open-ended, and free of charge. (See Resources for contact information on the group times and locations nearest you.)

You may choose to see a counselor to work on letting go of the relationship with the abuser, or to take a look at the history of abuse in your life and its effect on you. Marriage or couples' counseling while you're still in the relationship most likely will be ineffective and possibly unsafe for you if your partner continues to abuse and control you. To be effective, counseling requires trust and the freedom to express yourself without the fear that what you say may be used against you by the abuser. He must take full responsibility for his violence, and it must stop before progress can be made in the relationship. Choose a counselor who supports you and does not place blame on you for the abuse. You were not abused because there is something is wrong with you. You were abused because of choices your abuser made.

Over time, the strength that comes with being in charge of yourself and your life will help you develop good feelings and new confidence. It does not happen overnight and will require you to learn some new self-care skills. But remember: you deserve to be happy; you deserve a life free from abuse.

NOTES

SHELTER

We are here to LISTEN
    Not to work miracles.

We are here to HELP a woman DISCOVER
    What she is feeling
    Not to make feelings go away.

We are here to HELP a woman IDENTIFY her OPTIONS
    Not to decide for her
    What she should do.

We are here to DISCUSS STEPS with a woman
    Not to take steps for her.

We are here to HELP a woman DISCOVER her own
STRENGTH
    Not to rescue her and leave her
    Still vulnerable.

We are here to HELP a woman DISCOVER SHE CAN
HELP HERSELF
    Not to take responsibility
    For her.

We are here to HELP a woman LEARN TO CHOOSE
    Not make it unnecessary for
    Her to make difficult choices.

WE ARE HERE TO PROVIDE SUPPORT FOR CHANGE.

NOTES

RESOURCES

HOTLINES (24-hour information and phone counseling)
Florida Domestic Violence Hotline   1-800-500-1119
Salvation Army Domestic Violence Rape Crisis 1-800-252-2597
Hotline
Alabama House of Ruth   1-800-650-6522
  In Alabama   1-334-793-2232

BATTERED WOMEN'S SHELTERS
(Emergency shelter for battered women and their children)
Salvation Army, Panama City, FL   1-800-252-2597
House of Ruth, Dothan, AL   1-800-650-6522

CRIMINAL PROSECUTION
(For walk-in criminal complaints)
State Attorney's Office
Holmes County   850-547-2262
Jackson County   850-482-9555
Washington County   850-638-6150
State Attorney's Office Victims Advocate   1-800-842-9867
Holmes/Washington County   850-638-6150
Jackson County   850-482-9555
            1-800-344-7532

LEGAL ASSISTANCE
Legal Aid (for divorce, child custody, support)
Holmes/Washington County   850-769-3581
Jackson County   850-875-9881

**FLORIDA COALITION AGAINST DOM. VIOLENCE
LEGAL HOTLINE**   1-800-500-1119
          EXT. #3

FLORIDA BAR ATTORNEY REFRRAL   1-800-342-8060

**INJUNCTIONS FOR PROTECTION,
Clerk of Courts Office**
Holmes County   850-547-1100
Jackson County   850-482-9552
Washington County   850-638-6285
Salvation Army Rural Advocate   850-547-1399
Holmes County, Sheriff's Office Advocate   850-547-0394
Jackson County. Sheriff's Office Advocate   850-482-9624
Washington County Sheriff's Advocate   850-638-6111

Rural Organizer Women of Color   850-482-9624

COUNSELING

Life Management Center, Inc.   850-547-2472
Salvation Army Rural Organizer   850-547-1399
FCADV Rural Organizer Women of Color   850-482-9624
Anchorage Children's Home   850-763-7102
Salvation Army Counseling for Children   850-769-7989
Chemical Addictions Recovery Effort   850-526-3133

FINANCIAL
Victims Compensation   1-800-226-6667
                    850-414-3300
Child Support Enforcement   1-800-622-5437
One Stop Career Center
    Jackson County   850-718-0326
    Holmes/Washington County   850-638-6089

MISCELLANEOUS
Social Security   1-800-772-1213
Florida Abuse Hotline   1-800-962-2873
Florida Bureau of Victim Compensation   1-800-226-6667
Florida Department of Children and Families
    Holmes County   850-547-4631
    Jackson County   850-482-9568
    Washington County   850-638-6160

24 Hour computerized case information for
victims of crime   1-800-398-2808
Victim Information and Notification
Everyday Line   1-877-846-3435

DOMESTIC VIOLENCE BIBLIOGRAPHY

1. *The Battered Woman.*, Lenore Walker (1979) New York: Harper and Row.
2. *Battered Women as Survivors: An Alternative to Treating Learned Helplessness:* (1990) Lanham, MD: Lexington Books.
3. *Battering and Family Therapy: A Feminist Perspective.* Marsala Hansen and Michele Harway eds. (1993) Thousand Oaks, CA: Sage.
4. *Empowering and Healing the Battered Woman.* Mary Ann Dutton (1992), Springer.
5. *Feminist Perspectives on Wife Abuse,* Kersti Yllo and Michelle Bograd, eds. 1988. Thousand Oaks, CA: Sage.
6. *Getting Free: A Handbook For Women in Abusive Relationships,* Ginny McCarthy (1982). San Francisco: Seal.
7. *It Could Happen to Anyone,* Olga W. Barnett, Alyce D. LaViolette (1993) Thousand Oaks, CA: Sage.
8. *Keeping the Faith* Marie Fortune (1989) New York: Harper and Row.
9. *Leaving Abusive Partners,* Catherine Kirkwood (1993) Thousand Oaks, CA: Sage.
10. *Man Against Woman: What Every Woman Should Know About Violent Men.* Edward W. Gondolf (1989) Tab Books.
11. *Naming the Violence: Speaking Out About Lesbian Battering.* Kerry Lobel (1986) Boston: Beacon.
12. *Next Time She'll Be Dead: Battering and How to Stop It.* Ann Jones (1993) Boston: Beacon.
13. *The Ones Who Got Away: Women Who Left Abusive Partners.* Ginny McCarthy (1987). San Francisco: Seal.
14. *Verbal Abuse: Survivors Speak Out.* Patricia Evans (1993) Bob Adams, Inc.
15. *When Love Goes Wrong: What to Do When You Can't Do Anything Right.* Ann Jones, Susan Schechter (1992) New York: Harper Collins.
16. *Women and Male Violence: The Visions and Struggles of the Battered Women's Movement.* Susan Schechter (1982) Cambridge, MA: South End.

RESOURCES

Ammerman, Robert T. and Michel Hersen (eds.) *Case Studies in Family Violence.* (2nd ed.) New York: Kluwer Academic/Plenum Publishers, 2000.

Florida Coalition Against Domestic Violence. *Domestic Violence in Rural America: A Resource Guide for Service Providers.* Tallahassee, FL: FCADV, 1998.

_____. *Domestic Violence in Rural Underserved Areas: A Guide to Working within Diverse Communities.* Tallahassee, FL: FCADV, 1999.

Florida Department of Children and Families. *Domestic Violence Digest.* Tallahassee, FL: Florida Department of Children and Families, 2002

Goetting, Ann. *Getting Out: Life Stories of Women Who Left Abusive Men.* New York: Columbia University, 1999.

Gondolf, Edward W.. *Men Against Women: What Every Woman Should Know About Violent Men.* Blue Ridge Summit, PA: TAB Books, 1989.

Henderson, Helene. *Domestic Violence and Child Abuse Sourcebook.* Detroit: Omnigraphics, 2000.

Hoyle, Carolyn H. *Negotiating Domestic Violence: Police, Criminal Justice, and Victims.* New York: Oxford University Press, 1998.

Jones, Ann. *Next Time She'll Be Dead.* Boston: Beacon Press, 1994.

Klein, Ethel, et al. *Ending Domestic Violence: Changing Public Perceptions/Halting the Epidemic.* Thousand Oaks, CA: Sage Publications, 1997

Knudsen, Dean D. and JoAnn L. Miller. *Abused and Battered: Social and Legal Responses to Family Violence.* New York: A. deGruyter, 1991.

Lawless, Elaine J. *Women Escaping Violence: Empowerment Through Narrative.* Columbia, MO: University of Missouri Press, 2001.

Martin, Del. *Battered Wives.* Volcano, CA: Volcano Press, 1976, 1981.

Nelson, Noelle. *Dangerous Relationships: How to Stop Domestic Violence Before It Stops You.* New York: Perseus Publishing, 1997.

Profitt, Norma Jean. *Women Survivors, Psychological Trauma, and the Politics of Resistance.* New York: Haworth Press, 2000.

RESOURCES

Raphael, Jody. *Saving Bernice: Battered Women, Welfare, and Poverty.* Boston: Northeastern University Press, 2000.

Roberts, Albert R. *Handbook of Domestic Violence Intervention Strategies and Policies , Programs, and Legal Remedies.* New York: Oxford University Press, 2002.

Ross, Susan Deller, et al. *The Rights of Women: The Basic ACLU Guide to Women's Rights.* Carbondale: Southern Illinois University Press, 1983.

Russell, Diana E.H.. *The Secret Trauma: Incest in the Lives of Girls and Women.* New York: Basic Books, 1986.

Schechter, Susan. *Women and Violence: The Visions and Struggles of the Battered Women's Movement.* Cambridge, MA : South End Press, 1982.

Shepard, M, and Pence, E. *Coordinating Community Responses to Domestic Violence.* Thousand Oaks, CA: Sage Publications, 1999.

Sipe, Beth. *I Am Not Your Victim.* Thousand Oaks, CA: Sage Publications, 1996.

Stahl, Sandra K.D. "The Oral Personal Narrative in Its Generic Context." *Fabula* 18, 1977 pp. 18-39

_____. "The Personal Narrative as Folklore." *Journal of the Folklore Institute* 14, 1977 pp. 9-30.

Tiff, Larry L. *Battering of Women: The Failure of Intervention and the Case for Prevention.*   Boulder, CO: Westview Press, 1993.

Walker, Lenore. *The Battered Woman Syndrome.* (2nd ed.) New York: Springer Publishing Co., 2000.

Yllo, K. and M. Bograd (eds.). *Feminist Perspectives on Wife Abuse.* Newbury Park, CA: Sage Publications.

INDEX

About the Author

Jan Rosenberg is an independent folklorist, currently based in Tallahassee, Florida. She is founder and President of Heritage Education Resources, Inc, a non-profit organization devoted to providing and developing resource materials and services for the exploration of heritage and cultural diversity.

www.ingramcontent.com/pod-product-compliance
Lightning Source LLC
Chambersburg PA
CBHW020626110726
47899CB00002B/667